Pierrett

Pierrette's guide

WHAT DISH TO CHOOSE ?

942 photos 959 dishes explained

FRENCH CUISINE

Publisher Pierrette FELOUX

Preface

This guide is intended as an approach to our French cuisine, without guaranteeing that the dish served will be identical to the dish shown, since every chef adds a personal touch.

Each dish is described according to the traditional principles of our gastronomy and comes in two parts: the ingredients and a quick recipe.

Based on a menu in French, you can search as follows:

- In the alphabetical glossary of dishes in French, with numbers in ascending order (in red if there is a photo of the dish).
- In the Index of Dishes by category: starters – soups – salads – cooked meats and similar – fish and shellfish – poultry – game – meat – tripe and offal – regional dishes – vegetables - pasta– fruit – (cream) sweets – desserts – ice-cream – cakes and pastries – sauces - bread - cheeses.

A few dishes have been added that are not French as they may feature on certain menus.

Problems raised by the menus in gastronomic restaurants run by famous top chefs.

You will not find the dish but I suggest you look up the various names of the dish proposed in this guide.

Examples:

– Braised calf's sweetbreads with asparagus and mushrooms;
(In the guide look up: "sweetbreads" to see the photo, then "asparagus" and afterwards "mushroom")

– Calf's kidney with smoked bacon flavoured with ceps:
(In the guide look up: "calf's kidney" then "ceps").

How to use this guide in traditional restaurants ?

☞ *Look up by category (starter, fish, etc.) or by name (pot au feu, bœuf miroton, etc.).*

☞ *To understand how the dish is described in the guide:*

- *In the ingredients §: read the description of the recipe steps, e.g. "to cook", "for the presentation sauce".*
- *In the recipe §, these ingredients are only referred to with the phrases "for the presentation sauce" or "to cook".*

The photos were taken by the author after preparing the dish defined in this guide.

Typical French dishes are:
Stewed beef, steak and chips, calf's head, mussels in wine, herrings with potato salad, Burgundy snails, frogs legs.

The most refined dishes are:
Foie gras, scallops, caviar, wild salmon, Bresse capon.

The author welcomes your comments and suggestions
on her web site:

cuisine-francaise.org

Photos taken by the author and are her personal property.
Translation by SVP Traductions

Publisher Pierrette FELOUX
Domaine de Pierre Longue
65, boulevard Leader
06150 Cannes la Bocca
Tél. 00 33 (0)6 99 53 13 13
E-mail: guidepierrette@neuf.fr

ISBN : 978-2-9531516-2-6

GLOSSARY IN ALPHABETICAL ORDER

dishes with photos in red
the first numbers are those of the dishes

C

D

E

F

G

N

O

P

Q

R

S

T

V

Fromages

INDEX OF DISHES

POTAGES ET SOUPES
SOUPS

HORS-D'ŒUVRE
APPETISERS
ENTRÉES
STARTERS

SALADES
SALADS

ŒUFS
EGGS

ESCARGOTS - GRENOUILLES
SNAILS - FROGS LEGS
POISSONS - CRUSTACÉS
FISH - SHELLFISH

VOLAILLES ET GIBIERS
POULTRY AND GAME

VIANDES
MEAT

BŒUF
BEEF

TAUREAU - BULL

MOUTON – AGNEAU
MUTTON - LAMB

PORC
PORK

VEAU
VEAL

CHARCUTERIE
COOKED MEATS AND SIMILAR
TRIPES ET ABATS
TRIPE AND OFFAL

PLATS COMPLETS RÉGIONAUX
REGIONAL, ONE-DISH MEALS

PLATS DE PÂTES - RIZ
PASTA - RICE

LÉGUMES FRAIS
FRESH VEGETABLES
POMMES DE TERRE
POTATOES
CHAMPIGNONS
MUSHROOMS

FRUITS – DESSERTS - CRÊPES
FRUIT - DESSERTS - PANCAKES
GLACES - ENTREMETS
ICE CREAM – (CREAM) SWEETS

PÂTISSERIE - SOUFFLÉ
PASTRIES - SOUFFLES

SAUCES
SAUCES

PAINS
BREAD

FROMAGES
CHEESE

ABR

1 - ABRICOTS EN GRATIN * FRUITS

Photo Baked apricots.

BAKED APRICOTS * FRUIT
INGREDIENTS: halved apricots, ground almonds, butter, sugar, flour, egg yolk, rum, cream. For the syrup: sugar, water, lemon juice.
RECIPE: the apricots are poached in the "syrup". All the other ingredients are mixed and added to the apricots. The dish is then flashed for 3' under the grill. Served warm.

ACC

2 - ACCRAS DE MORUE * POISSON

Photo Spicy salt cod nuggets.

SPICY SALT COD NUGGETS * FISH
INGREDIENTS AND RECIPE: from the French West Indies. Dried salt cod mixture in a batter of 1/3 flour, 2/3 cod, milk, small chillies, eggs and curry, shaped into small balls and fried in oil. Served hot.

3 - ACCRAS DE LÉGUMES * LÉGUMES

Photo Spicy vegetable nuggets.

SPICY VEGETABLE NUGGETS
* VEGETABLES
Mixture with a batter of 1/3 flour, 2/3 vegetables, carrots or aubergines, milk, onions, garlic, eggs and chilli, shaped into balls and fried in oil. Served hot.

AIG

4 - AIGUILLETTES DE CANARD * VOLAILLE

Photo Slices of duck breast.

SLICES OF DUCK * POULTRY
INGREDIENTS: slices of duck breast, butter or duck fat. For the sauce: cooking juices.
RECIPE: the slices are browned, the sauce prepared separately and added. Served hot.

AIL

5 - AILE DE RAIE AU BEURRE NANTAIS * POISSON

Photo Skate wing with lemon butter sauce.

SKATE WING WITH LEMON BUTTER SAUCE * FISH

INGREDIENTS: skate wing. For the poaching liquid: onion, carrot, cider vinegar, bouquet garni. For the butter sauce: shallots, butter, lemon.

RECIPE: the skate is poached in the liquid then drained and the sauce ingredients are added. Served hot.

6 - AILE DE RAIE AUX CÂPRES * POISSON

Photo Skate wing with caper sauce.

SKATE WING WITH CAPER SAUCE * FISH

RECIPE: identical to the previous dish but with capers.

AIO

7 - AÏOLI * PLAT PROVENÇAL - PLAT COMPLET RÉGIONAL

Photo Salt cod and vegetables.

SALT COD AND VEGETABLES WITH GARLIC MAYONNAISE * PROVENÇAL ONE-DISH MEAL

INGREDIENTS: potato, carrot, boiled egg, French beans, cauliflower, salt cod, salt.

RECIPE: the salt cod and vegetables are cooked in hot stock then drained and served with garlic mayonnaise sauce N°8.

8 - AÏOLI * SAUCE

Photo Garlic mayonnaise – raw garlic, olive oil.

GARLIC MAYONNAISE * SAUCE

INGREDIENTS: garlic, egg yolk, olive oil.

RECIPE: the garlic is reduced to a puree, the egg yolks and oil added and mixed until the sauce forms an emulsion.

ALI

9 - ALIGOT DE LA RÉGION DE L'AVEYRON * LÉGUMES

Photo Creamed garlic potato forming a ribbon.

CREAMED GARLIC POTATO AND CHEESE * VEGETABLES
INGREDIENTS: potatoes, "Tomme de Laguiole" cheese, cream, garlic, butter.
RECIPE: the potatoes are boiled then mashed with all the other ingredients. Served hot.

ALL

10 - ALLUMETTES AUX ANCHOIS * ENTRÉE

Photo Cheese straws.

ANCHOVY STRAWS * STARTER
INGREDIENTS: flaky pastry (flour and butter mixed, rested and turned several times) - the anchovies or cheese are added before baking; cut into straws after baking.

ALO

11 - ALOUETTES SANS TÊTE * VIANDE ROUGE

Photo Stuffed beef rolls.

STUFFED BEEF ROLLS * RED MEAT
INGREDIENTS: finely sliced beef. For the stuffing: diced bacon, parsley, soft bread soaked in stock, chopped garlic, beaten egg. To cook: small chopped onions, flour, wine, mushrooms.
RECIPE: spread each slice of beef with the stuffing mixture, then roll and cook for 30' in oil, with all the cooking ingredients; served hot.

AMA

12 - AMANDES * MOLLUSQUES

Photo Small clams, buttered bread.

SMALL CLAMS * SHELLFISH
Eaten raw with bread and butter. Served cold.

AMU

13 - AMUSE-BOUCHES * ENTRÉE

Photo *Various canapés.*

APPETISERS * STARTER
INGREDIENTS: canapés with salmon roe, ham, cheese, vegetables on sliced bread.

ANA

14 - ANANAS ET MANGUE POÊLÉS * FRUITS

Photo *Slices of pineapple and mango with a scoop of vanilla ice cream.*

SAUTEED PINEAPPLE AND MANGO * FRUIT
INGREDIENTS: slices of mango, pineapple, butter and sugar.
RECIPE: the fruits are sautéed in butter and sugar and served warm.

ANC

15 - ANCHOIS * POISSON

Photo *Small fish on the left.*

ANCHOVIES * FISH
Served raw or marinated as an appetiser.

16 - ANCHOYADE OU ANCHOÏADE * POISSON

Photo *Anchovy spread.*

ANCHOVY SPREAD * FISH
RECIPE: anchovies pureed with garlic and whipped mustard plus olive oil to make a thick sauce.

AND

17 - ANDOUILLE DE VIRE * CHARCUTERIE DE NORMANDIE

Photo Vire chitterling sausage.

VIRE CHITTERLING SAUSAGE * COOKED MEATS AND SIMILAR FROM NORMANDY
INGREDIENTS AND RECIPE: andouille de Vire is a cooked pork chitterling sausage. It is served cold, cut into slices.

18 - ANDOUILLETTE SAUCE MOUTARDE * CHARCUTERIE

Photo Chitterling sausage, mustard sauce and sliced potato bake.

CHITTERLING SAUSAGE WITH MUSTARD SAUCE: COOKED MEATS AND SIMILAR
INGREDIENTS: pork innards, intestines and stomach, spices, herbs and condiments. Sauce: mustard, shallots, cream. RECIPE: the ingredients are cooked in a seasoned court bouillon for 5 hrs. The sausage is then baked in the oven with the sauce. Served hot.

ANE

19 - ANETH * AROMATE

Photo Dill.

DILL * HERB
Herb of Italian origin.

ANG

20 - ANGUILLE DE MER AU BLEU * POISSON

Photo Conger eel cooked in stock.

CONGER EEL COOKED IN STOCK * FISH
INGREDIENTS: snake-shaped fish with extremely tasty flesh.
RECIPE: cooked whole in stock with onion, wine, cut into pieces after cooking, served hot with lemon, potatoes and caper sauce.

21 - ANGUILLE EN MATELOTE * POISSON

Photo Stewed eels.

STEWED EEL * FISH
INGREDIENTS: eel cut in pieces, butter, diced smoked bacon, chopped onion and garlic, sliced carrot, bouquet garni, red wine, brandy, sliced cultivated mushrooms, flour.
RECIPE: all the ingredients are cooked then flamed with the brandy and cooked for 30' after adding the red wine; served hot.

22 - ANGUILLE AU VERT - RECETTE DE LA RÉGION DE FLANDRE * POISSON

Photo Eels with green vegetables.

EELS WITH GREEN VEGETABLES, A DISH FROM FLANDERS * FISH
INGREDIENTS: eel cut into large slices, butter, flour, parsley, tarragon, sage, chervil, wine. Sauce: cream, egg yolks, eel cooking juice. To garnish: sorrel, spinach.
RECIPE: after cooking the ingredients in butter with the wine the eels are coated with sauce and the cooked spinach and sorrel added.

ARA

23 - ARAIGNÉE DE MER * CRUSTACÉS

Photo Cooked spider crab.

SPIDER CRAB * SHELLFISH
RECIPE: cooked by immersing in hot stock with carrots and onions then served cold with herb or lemon mayonnaise.

24 - ARAIGNÉE FARCIE À LA QUIBERONNAISE * CRUSTACÉS

Photo Cooked spider crab.

STUFFED SPIDER CRAB QUIBERON STYLE * SHELLFISH
INGREDIENTS: spider crabs. To cook: butter, cream, shallots, thyme, bay leaf, parsley, port and brandy.
RECIPE: the spider crabs are plunged into boiling water, drained, the flesh mixed with the ingredients and cooked in butter, flamed in brandy, the port is added and then the cream; flashed under the grill to brown before serving hot.

ARD

25 - ARDÉCHOIS * PÂTISSERIE DE LA RÉGION DE L'ARDÈCHE

Photo Chestnut cream dessert.

CHESTNUT CREAM DESSERT FROM THE ARDÈCHE REGION
INGREDIENTS: chestnuts, butter, sugar, eggs, almonds, cocoa and chocolate butter cream.

ART

26 - ARTICHAUTS À LA BARIGOULE * LÉGUMES SPÉCIALITÉ PROVENÇALE

Photo Garnished artichoke.

GARNISHED ARTICHOKES WITH SAUCE PROVENÇAL SPECIALITY * VEGETABLES
INGREDIENTS AND RECIPE: only the bases of the artichoke are used, cooked with ham, shallots and chopped cultivated mushrooms, sprinkled with flour and then the wine, tomato, onions and stock are added. Served when cooked with a rich butter sauce.

27 - ARTICHAUTS CUITS SERVIS AVEC DE L'HUILE D'OLIVE * LÉGUMES

Photo Artichoke with olive oil.

COOKED ARTICHOKE SERVED WITH OLIVE OIL * VEGETABLES

28 - ARTICHAUTS À LA BRETONNE * LÉGUMES

Photo Artichoke with butter and cider.

ARTICHOKE WITH BUTTER AND CIDER * VEGETABLES
INGREDIENTS: artichokes with the leaves cut in 4, chopped onions, butter, cider.
RECIPE: all the ingredients are cooked in the butter and cider for 30'. Served hot.

29 - ARTICHAUT À LA CRÈME D'AUBERGINE * LÉGUMES

Photo Artichoke with aubergine cream.

ARTICHOKE WITH AUBERGINE CREAM * VEGETABLES
INGREDIENTS: artichokes. For the aubergine cream: aubergines cut into pieces, chopped garlic, anchovy fillets, oil. To garnish: pureed tomatoes.
RECIPE: all the ingredients for the cream are cooked in oil for 30' then blended into a puree. The artichokes are cooked and allowed to cool; the aubergine cream is spread in the hollow of the artichokes with the pureed tomato. Served cold.

ASP

30 - ASPERGES * ENTRÉE

Photo Green asparagus with cheese sauce.

ASPARAGUS * STARTER
INGREDIENTS: two varieties: green and white.
RECIPE: the asparagus is boiled in salted water and drained. Served warm with a cheese (see n° 793) or Béarnaise (see n° 783) butter sauce.

31 - ASPIC * ENTRÉE

Photo Egg in aspic jelly.

EGGS IN ASPIC JELLY * STARTER
INGREDIENTS: eggs, jelly, diced ham, sliced gherkin, tarragon, parsley.
RECIPE: the eggs are cooked and the tarragon scalded. The tarragon, diced ham, cooked egg, gherkin and parsley is laid in a mould. Covered in liquid jelly and put to cool. Served cold.

ASS

32 - ASSIETTE DE CHARCUTERIE * CHARCUTERIE

Photo Ham, sausage, country paté.

PLATE OF COOKED MEATS AND SAUSAGE * COOKED MEATS AND SIMILAR
INGREDIENTS: consists of ham, dry sausage and country pate.

33 - ASSIETTE DE FRUITS DE MER * CRUSTACÉS

Photo Oysters, crayfish, prawns, winkles, crab claws and lemon.

SEAFOOD PLATTER * SHELLFISH
INGREDIENTS: consists of cupped and/or flat oysters, small and large clams, whelks, winkles, brown shrimp, prawns, firm-flesh clams.

AUB

34 - AUBERGINE À LA BORDELAISE * LÉGUMES

Photo Aubergines with minced garnish.

AUBERGINES WITH MINCED GARNISH * VEGETABLES
INGREDIENTS: sliced aubergines. For the minced garnish: oil, flour, shallots, garlic, parsley, breadcrumbs.
RECIPE: the minced garnish is prepared and cooked separately from the aubergines. Served hot separately.

35 - AUBERGINES FARCIES * LÉGUMES

Photo Stuffed aubergines.

STUFFED AUBERGINES * VEGETABLES
INGREDIENTS: aubergines halved lengthwise, onion, olive oil. For the stuffing: shoulder of veal, breadcrumbs soaked in milk, garlic, basil, black olives, cream, chilli.
RECIPE: the flesh of the aubergines is mixed with the stuffing to garnish the aubergines and cooked for 25'. Served hot.

36 - AUBERGINE À LA LYONNAISE * LÉGUMES

Photo Aubergines with onion garnish.

AUBERGINES WITH ONION GARNISH * VEGETABLES
RECIPE: the aubergines are cooked, part of the inside removed and stuffed with onions, garlic, olive oil, butter, mustard and covered with breadcrumbs.

37 - AUBERGINE GRILLÉE À L'HUILE D'OLIVE * LÉGUMES

Photo Slice of aubergine grilled with olive oil.

AUBERGINES GRILLED WITH OLIVE OIL * VEGETABLES

RECIPE: the aubergines are sliced then grilled with olive oil.

AVO

38 - AVOCAT AU CRABE * ENTRÉE

Photo Avocado mayonnaise with crab.

AVOCADO WITH CRAB * STARTER

RECIPE: the avocado flesh and crabmeat are mixed with mayonnaise, cream, herbs (chives, parsley), lemon juice: the avocado is served raw.

39 - AVOCAT VINAIGRETTE * CRUDITÉS

Photo Avocado vinaigrette.

AVOCADO WITH VINAIGRETTE DRESSING * SALAD VEGETABLE

RECIPE: the avocado is served with a vinaigrette sauce.

BAB

40 - BABA AU RHUM * PÂTISSERIE

Photo Rum baba with whipped cream.

RUM BABA * DESSERT

INGREDIENTS: for the dough: flour, eggs, butter, sugar, yeast. For the syrup: hot water, sugar, rum.

RECIPE: all the dough ingredients are mixed together and it is then poured into a "baba" mould to rest for 30' and rise before baking. The syrup is added to the hot baba. Served cold.

BAC

41- BACKEOFFE * PLAT COMPLET RÉGIONAL D'ALSACE

Photo Meat and potato bake.

MEAT AND POTATO BAKE * ONE-DISH MEAL FROM ALSACE

INGREDIENTS: various kinds of meat: pork knuckle or shoulder, boned shoulder of mutton and blade of beef.

RECIPE: the meat is cooked slowly for 2 hours with potatoes, onions, shallots, garlic, dry Alsatian wine (Riesling or Pinot), parsley, thyme, bay leaf, in a closed casserole dish after macerating for 24 hours. Served hot.

BAN

42 - BANANES FLAMBÉES * FRUITS

Photo Bananas flamed in rum.

FLAMED BANANAS * FRUIT

INGREDIENTS AND RECIPES: sauteed in butter in a pan with cane sugar, lemon and orange juice and flamed with rum and served immediately.

BAR

43 - BAR EN CROÛTE DE SEL * POISSON

Photo Sea bass in salt crust.

SEA BASS IN SALT CRUST * FISH

INGREDIENTS: a whole sea bass, coarse salt, beaten egg whites.

RECIPE: the sea bass is covered with salt mixed with beaten egg whites and cooked for 40' in a foil case. The salt crust is broken as it is served. Served hot.

44 - BAR AU VIN ET AROMATES * POISSON

Photo Sea bass with wine and herbs.

SEA BASS WITH WINE AND HERBS * FISH

INGREDIENTS AND RECIPE: whole sea bass baked in a dish with prawns, courgettes, tomatoes, shallots, garlic, oil, a little wine, lemon, parsley, basil and chives, served hot.

45 - BAR FARCI À LA BRETONNE * POISSON

Photo Stuffed sea bass Breton style.

STUFFED SEA BASS BRETON STYLE* FISH
INGREDIENTS: A whole sea bass. For the stuffing: butter, cultivated mushrooms, onions, parsley. To garnish: sliced tomatoes and carrots, Muscadet wine, cream, salted butter, parsley, thyme, bay leaf.
RECIPE: the sea bass is stuffed and cooked for 10' with the garnish. Served hot.

46 - BAR GRILLÉ AU FENOUIL * POISSON

Photo Sea bass grilled with fennel.

SEA BASS GRILLED WITH FENNEL * FISH
INGREDIENTS AND RECIPE: the fish is stuffed with stems of fennel herb then left in lemon juice and olive oil until grilled, served hot with melted butter and a little lemon juice.

47 - BAR POCHÉ * POISSON

Photo Poached sea bass.

POACHED SEA BASS * FISH
INGREDIENTS AND RECIPE: the sea bass is poached in fish stock made with carrots, leek, stick of celery, shallots and garlic, then baked with butter and a little dry white wine, shallots, garlic and cream. Served whole straight from the oven with a sauce or butter.

48 - BARON D'AGNEAU AU FOUR * VIANDE

BAKED BARON OF LAMB * MEAT
INGREDIENTS: baron of lamb (saddle plus two legs). To prepare the meat: garlic, chillies, sprigs of thyme. To cook: butter, sliced potato, wine, poultry stock.
RECIPE: the meat is prepared then baked with the cooking ingredients. 1hr30mins before the end of the cooking time, the baron is placed on a rack above the dish of potatoes, served hot.

49 - BAVAROIS AU CHOCOLAT * DESSERT FROID

CHOCOLATE BAVAROIS * COLD DESSERT
INGREDIENTS AND RECIPE: flour-free dessert, set with gelatine to which an egg yolk, sugar, dark chocolate, vanilla, cream and Benedictine liqueur has been added.

Photo Chocolate bavarois.

50 - BAVAROIS AUX FRAMBOISES * DESSERT FROID

RASPBERRY BAVAROIS * COLD DESSERT
INGREDIENTS AND RECIPE: see N° 49 - the chocolate is replaced with raspberries.

Photo Raspberry bavarois.

51 - BAVETTE À L'ÉCHALOTE * VIANDE JUTEUSE ET D'UNE GRANDE SAVEUR

FLANK STEAK WITH SHALLOTS * JUICY, FLAVOURSOME BEEF
INGREDIENTS AND RECIPE: the shallots are cooked with wine vinegar, butter, flour and stock. The meat is grilled separately. Served hot.

Photo Flank steak with shallots.

52 - BAVETTE GRILLÉE * VIANDE DE BŒUF

GRILLED FLANK STEAK * BEEF
RECIPE: the meat is grilled and served with lemon and parsley butter: butter with a little chopped parsley and lemon worked into it; the steak is garnished with a slice of the lemon butter, served hot.

Photo Grilled flank steak with chips.

53 - BAVETTE D'ALOYAU * VIANDE

Photo Skirt steak.

SKIRT STEAK * BEEF
INGREDIENTS AND RECIPE: the meat is grilled and then served hot.

BEI

54 - BEIGNET À L'ANANAS * PÂTISSERIE

Photo Pineapple fritter.

PINEAPPLE FRITTER * CAKE
INGREDIENTS AND RECIPE: sliced pineapple, batter: flour, baking powder, egg and milk mixed. To cook: the fruit is dipped into the batter to coat and then plunged into the fat. Sprinkled with sugar and served hot.

55 - BEIGNETS DE CALMARS * MOLLUSQUES

Photo Squid fritters.

SQUID FRITTERS * SHELLFISH
INGREDIENTS AND RECIPE: for the batter: flour, baking powder, egg and milk mixed. To cook: the piece of squid is dipped into the batter to coat and then plunged into the fat. Served hot.

56 - BEIGNETS DE FLEURS DE COURGETTES * LÉGUMES

Photo Courgette flower fritters.

COURGETTE FLOWER FRITTERS
* VEGETABLES
INGREDIENTS AND RECIPE: for the batter: flour, baking powder, egg and milk mixed to coat the courgette flowers before plunging into the fat. Served hot.

57 - BEIGNETS AUX POMMES * PÂTISSERIE

Photo Apple doughnuts.

APPLE DOUGHNUTS * CAKE
INGREDIENTS: peeled apples, sugar, Grand Marnier liqueur. For the batter: flour, egg, beer, milk.
RECIPE: the slices of apple are dipped into the Grand Marnier liqueur, then into the batter made with all the ingredients and cooked in oil for 2'. Served hot sprinkled with sugar.

58 - BEIGNETS DE SCAMPIS * CRUSTACÉS

Photo Scampi fritters.

SCAMPI FRITTERS * SHELLFISH
INGREDIENTS: for the batter: flour, egg, beer, milk.
RECIPE: the scampi are dipped into the batter and then fried in oil. Served hot.

59 - BEIGNETS DE CERVELLE * ABATS

Photo Brain fritters.

BRAIN FRITTERS * OFFAL
INGREDIENTS: for the batter: flour, egg, beer, milk.
RECIPE: the brains are dipped into the batter and then fried in oil. Served hot.

BET

60 - BETTES À LA CRÈME * LÉGUMES

Photo Creamed Swiss chard.

CREAMED SWISS CHARD * VEGETABLES
INGREDIENTS AND RECIPE: green part of the Swiss chard chopped and cooked in vegetable stock. Served hot with cream.

61 - BETTERAVES ROUGES * CRUDITÉS

Photo Beetroot in salad.

BEETROOT * SALAD VEGETABLES
INGREDIENTS AND RECIPE: the beetroot is cooked, peeled, diced and served with a vinaigrette dressing. Served cold.

BIF

62 - BIFTECK HACHÉ * VIANDE

Photo Beefburger.

BEEFBURGER * BEEF
INGREDIENTS AND RECIPE: the beefburger is grilled. Served hot.

62-1 - BIFTECK AVEC ŒUF À CHEVAL * VIANDE

Photo Beefburger topped with an egg.

BEEFBURGER TOPPED WITH AN EGG * MEAT
INGREDIENTS AND RECIPE: the beefburger is grilled. Served hot, topped with an egg.

63 - BIFTECK POITEVIN - RECETTE DU POITOU * VIANDE

Photo Beefburger with beef marrow.

BEEFBURGER POITOU STYLE * MEAT
INGREDIENTS: lean minced beef, beef marrow, dry bread soaked in milk, onions cooked in butter, eggs, chopped parsley, cream, mustard.
RECIPE: all the ingredients are mixed and then cooked in a pan with cream. Served hot with onions.

64 - BIFTECK FRITES * VIANDE

Photo Minute steak and chips.

MINUTE STEAK AND CHIPS * MEAT
INGREDIENTS: grilled minute steak (beef) served well done, rare or medium to choice.

BIS

65 - BISCUITS À LA NOIX DE COCO OU CONGOLAIS * PÂTISSERIE

Photo Coconut macaroons.

COCONUT MACAROONS * BISCUITS
INGREDIENTS AND RECIPE: biscuits prepared with a mixture of desiccated coconut, flour, honey and eggs and baked in the oven. Served cold.

66 - BISCUIT ROULÉ À LA FRAISE * PÂTISSERIE

Photo Strawberry Swiss roll.

STRAWBERRY SWISS ROLL * CAKE
INGREDIENTS: for the dough: eggs, sugar, flour, milk, butter.
RECIPE: the dough is cooked on a tray and filled with the desired preparation (chocolate or jam) when still warm before rolling up. Served cold.

67 - BISQUE D'ÉCREVISSES * CRUSTACÉS

Photo Crayfish soup with croutons and grated gruyere cheese.

CRAYFISH SOUP * SHELLFISH
INGREDIENTS: crayfish. To cook: butter, onions, carrots, celery, tomatoes, garlic, bay leaf, brandy and wine.
RECIPE: the crayfish are plunged into boiling water, the shell is broken then browned in butter with the cooking ingredients, poultry stock added and then cooked for 65'. The mixture is sieved and the coral of the crayfish added with the yolk of an egg. Served hot.

68 - BISQUE DE HOMARD * CRUSTACÉS

Photo Lobster soup.

LOBSTER SOUP * SHELLFISH
INGREDIENTS AND RECIPE: the lobster replaces the crayfish in Recipe 67.

69 - BISQUE DE LANGOUSTINES * CRUSTACÉS

Photo Langoustine soup.

LANGOUSTINE SOUP * SHELLFISH
INGREDIENTS AND RECIPE: the langoustines (Dublin Bay prawns) replace the crayfish in recipe 67.

BLA

70 - BLANC DE TURBOT À LA JULIENNE DE LÉGUMES * POISSON

Photo Fillet of turbot with finely-sliced vegetables.

FILLET OF TURBOT WITH FINELY-SLICED VEGETABLES * FISH
INGREDIENTS: fillet of turbot. Vegetables: courgettes, baby leeks, carrots, fresh peas. To cook: poultry stock, butter, wine, lemon juice, fish stock. For the sauce to garnish: egg yolk, cream.
RECIPE: the vegetables are cooked for 5' in the poultry stock. The turbot and its ingredients are cooked in butter and are accompanied by the sauce when served hot.

71 - BLANC DE TURBOT SUR LIT D'ÉPINARDS * POISSON

Photo Fillet of turbot on a bed of spinach.

FILLET OF TURBOT ON A BED OF SPINACH * FISH
INGREDIENTS: fillet of turbot, onions, butter, oil, cream, fish stock, precooked spinach.
RECIPE: for the garnish: the onions are sautéed in butter then mixed with the cream and fish stock. The turbot is cooked in oil and then served with the garnish.

72 - BLANQUETTE DE VEAU * VIANDE

Photo Blanket of veal.

BLANKET OF VEAL * MEAT
INGREDIENTS: veal cut into pieces. To cook: butter, onions, carrots, shallots, wine, clove, bouquet garni. To garnish: cultivated mushrooms, for the sauce: cream, flour, butter, egg, lemon.
RECIPE: the meat is simmered for 1 hr with the cooking ingredients, the mushrooms are added at the end of cooking. Served hot with the sauce ingredients.

BLI

73 - BLINIS * GALETTE D'ORIGINE NORDIQUE

Photo Blini pancakes.

BLINI PANCAKES * FROM THE FAR NORTH
INGREDIENTS AND RECIPE: small, 15-cm pancakes made with wheat and buckwheat flour, eggs, cream and milk. Served hot.

BOE

74 - BŒUF AUX OIGNONS DE LÉZIGNAN * VIANDE

Photo Beef with Lézignan onions.

BEEF WITH LEZIGNAN ONIONS * MEAT
INGREDIENTS: stewing beef cut into pieces. To cook: Lézignan onions, olive oil, clove, coriander seeds, bouquet garni, garlic, parsley.
RECIPE: the meat is browned in oil, all the other ingredients are then added and cooked for 3 hours; served hot with chopped garlic and parsley.

75 - BŒUF BOURGUIGNON - RECETTE DE LA RÉGION DE BOURGOGNE * VIANDE

Photo Burgundy beef.

BURGUNDY BEEF, A BURGUNDY REGIONAL DISH * MEAT
INGREDIENTS: beef rump or similar cut into pieces. To cook: carrots, tomato, onion, garlic, oil, flour, red Burgundy wine, stock, bouquet garni. To garnish: diced pork belly or bacon, small onions, mushrooms, butter, chopped parsley.
RECIPE: the meat and bacon are browned in lard before cooking for 2 hours 30 mins. The garnish is cooked in butter, served hot.

76 - BŒUF EN DAUBE * VIANDE

Photo Beef stewed in wine.

BEEF STEWED IN WINE * MEAT
INGREDIENTS AND RECIPE: (blade of beef or topside). The day before the meat is marinated in a cool place with red wine, shallots, onions, clove, orange zest, oil, garlic and carrots. The next day, the meat is drained and browned with diced bacon, tomatoes, shallots and onions. The dish is then cooked for 4 to 5 hours after adding the filtered marinade. Served hot with fresh pasta.

77 - BŒUF À LA FICELLE * VIANDE

Photo Beef on a string.

BEEF ON A STRING * MEAT
INGREDIENTS AND RECIPE: piece of fillet or sirloin attached by a string in the stock without the meat touching the bottom and cooked for 40'; served hot with a little stock.

78 - BŒUF À LA MODE OU BŒUF MODE OU BŒUF BRAISÉ AUX CAROTTES * VIANDE

Photo Braised beef with carrots.

BRAISED BEEF WITH CARROTS * MEAT
INGREDIENTS: braising beef, calf's foot, bard, lard (pork fat). To cook: sliced carrot and onions, wine, bouquet garni, sage and basil leaves, rosemary, garlic.
RECIPE: the meat cooks for 2 hours, then for 1 hour 30 minutes after adding the other ingredients. Served hot.

79 - BŒUF EN GELÉE * VIANDE

Photo Beef in jelly.

BEEF IN JELLY * MEAT
INGREDIENTS AND RECIPE: see N°77
When cooked, the meat and carrots are removed, the cooking juices filtered and then poured over the meat to cool and form a jelly. Served cold.

80 - BŒUF MIROTON - RECETTE DE LA RÉGION D'ILE-DE-FRANCE * VIANDE

Photo Sliced stewed beef.

SLICED STEWED BEEF, AN ILE DE FRANCE DISH * MEAT
INGREDIENTS: thinly-sliced beef, chopped onions, flour, stock, tomato puree, butter, bouquet garni. To garnish when cooked: chopped parsley, vinegar, breadcrumbs, butter.
RECIPE: all the ingredients are cooked for 20'; the meat and other ingredients are layered, the sauce poured over, sprinkled with breadcrumbs and melted butter and browned in the oven; served immediately.

81 - BŒUF RÔTI À LA BROCHE * VIANDE

Photo Spit-roasted beef.

SPIT-ROASTED BEEF * MEAT
INGREDIENTS AND RECIPE: the joint is covered with bacon, secured with string and spit roast for 15'. Served hot.

82 - BŒUF STROGONOF * VIANDE

Photo Beef Stroganoff.

BEEF STROGANOFF * MEAT
INGREDIENTS: sirloin cut in strips. To garnish: diced bacon, mushrooms, butter, tomatoes, onions, tomato puree, paprika, cream.
RECIPE: the meat is cooked for 10' with all the other ingredients. Served hot with cream.

BOL

83 - BOLETS OU CÈPES * CHAMPIGNONS FERMES AU PARFUM DÉLICAT

Photo Boletus or ceps.

BOLETUS OR CEPS
Firm mushrooms with a delicate fragrance.

84 - BOMBINE ARDÉCHOISE - RECETTE DE LA RÉGION DU LANGUEDOC * VIANDE

Photo Pork and potato casserole.

PORK AND POTATO CASSEROLE
A LANGUEDOC REGION DISH * MEAT
INGREDIENTS: pork belly. To cook: sliced potatoes, chopped onions, garlic, bouquet garni.
RECIPE: the meat is boiled for 20' then cut in pieces to cook with the other ingredients, served hot. This speciality may be served with sausages or saveloys.

85 - BOUCHÉES À LA REINE À L'ANCIENNE * VIANDE

Photo Chicken and veal vol-au-vent.

CHICKEN AND VEAL VOL-AU-VENT
* MEAT
INGREDIENTS: flaky pastry vol-au-vent. To garnish: cooked chicken, diced veal, onion, bouquet garni, leek, carrots, celery stalk, wine, lemon. Sauce base: butter, flour, stock, mushrooms, egg yolk, whipped cream.
RECIPE: A boiled chicken (see recipe) is mixed with the pieces of veal. The sauce base is prepared. Before serving, the hot vol-au-vents are filled with all the ingredients.

86 - BOUCHÉE À LA REINE AU HOMARD ET LANGOUSTINES * CRUSTACÉS

Photo Seafood vol-au-vent.

LOBSTER AND LANGOUSTINE
VOL-AU-VENT * SHELLFISH
INGREDIENTS: same as the previous recipe but the meat is replaced with shellfish.

87 - BOUCHÉE À LA REINE AU RIS DE VEAU * ABATS

Photo Calf's sweetbread vol-au-vent.

CALF'S SWEETBREAD VOL-AU-VENT
* OFFAL
INGREDIENTS: calf's sweetbreads, stock, shallots, butter, cream.
RECIPE: the sweetbread (see Photo n° 730) is sauteed in butter before it is cooked with all the other ingredients; the vol-au-vents are reheated and filled with the sweetbreads and their sauce and served hot.

88 - BOUDIN NOIR AUX DEUX POMMES * ABATS

Photo Black pudding with apples and potatoes.

BLACK PUDDING WITH APPLES AND POTATOES * OFFAL

INGREDIENTS: the cooked pork blood pudding is browned in butter for 10', the apples and potatoes are cooked separately. Served hot together.

89 - BOUDIN À LA FLAMANDE - RECETTE DE VALENCIENNE * ABATS

Photo Flemish black pudding.

FLEMISH BLACK PUDDING * OFFAL

INGREDIENTS: black pudding with raisins. For the garnish: quartered eating apples, butter, sugar.

RECIPE: the black pudding is heated in the oven. The apples are cooked in butter. The dish is served hot.

90 - BOUDIN BLANC * CHARCUTERIE FINE

Photo White pudding.

WHITE PUDDING

INGREDIENTS: lean and fat pork, cream, egg, milk (sometimes truffles).

RECIPE: the white pudding is sauteed in butter and served hot.

91 - BOUILLABAISSE * POISSON

Photo Mediterranean fish stew.

MEDITERRANEAN FISH STEW * FISH

INGREDIENTS: fish stew: rockfish, gurnard, whiting, John Dory, monkfish, sea bass, conger eel and potatoes.

RECIPE: the fish is cooked in rock fish stock, cut in large pieces and served hot with the garlic saffron sauce, toasted bread and garlic to rub on the bread.

92 - BOUILLON DE BŒUF AUX QUENELLES * POTAGE

Photo Beef broth with dumplings.

BEEF BROTH WITH DUMPLINGS * SOUP
INGREDIENTS: to cook: beef broth. For the dumpling: flour, egg, garlic, chopped parsley, breadcrumbs, semolina.
RECIPE: the dumpling is prepared to cook and rise in the warm broth; served hot with parsley.

93 - BOUILLON DE LÉGUMES * POTAGE

Photo Vegetable broth.

VEGETABLE BROTH * SOUP
INGREDIENTS AND RECIPE: the vegetables: carrots, potatoes, turnips, leeks, onion, garlic, cloves are cooked in water for 1 hour; only the broth is served, with toast.

94 - BOUILLON DE VOLAILLE * POTAGE

Photo Chicken broth.

CHICKEN BROTH * SOUP
INGREDIENTS AND RECIPE: chicken wings and feet are cooked in the water for 1 hour 30 mins with the following vegetables: leeks, carrots, celery stalk, onions, garlic, clove, thyme, bay leaf. Only the broth is served hot, sometimes with ravioli.

95 - BOULETTES DE BŒUF * VIANDE

Photo Meatballs.

MEATBALLS * MEAT
INGREDIENTS: minced beef, shallots, garlic, sage, tomato puree, eggs. To cook: oil.
RECIPE: all the ingredients are mixed and shaped into balls, refrigerated and then rolled in breadcrumbs before frying. Served hot.

96 - BOURRIDE MARSEILLAISE DE LA RÉGION DE PROVENCE * POISSON

Photo Marseille fish stew.

MARSEILLE FISH STEW FROM THE PROVENCE REGION * FISH

INGREDIENTS: monkfish, sea bass, whiting cut into large pieces, Provence wine, white of leek, onion, olive oil, potatoes, shallots, garlic, garlic mayonnaise. RECIPE: the fish and onions are sautéed in the oil. The potatoes, shallots and garlic are cooked in the stock with the fish. A garlic mayonnaise (see n° 8) is prepared and stirred into the stock. Served hot with toasted bread rubbed with garlic.

97 - BOURRIDE DE LOTTE ET PÉTONCLES * POISSON ET MOLLUSQUES

Photo Monkfish and queen scallop stew.

MONKFISH AND QUEEN SCALLOP STEW * FISH AND SHELLFISH

INGREDIENTS AND RECIPE: identical to the previous one but only monkfish, mussels and queen scallops are used as fish.

98 - BOUQUET GARNI * AROMATES

Photo Bouquet garni.

BOUQUET GARNI

INGREDIENTS : thyme and bay leaves.

BRA

99 - BRANDADE DE MORUE DE NÎMES DE LA RÉGION DU LANGUEDOC * POISSON

Photo Creamed salt cod with potatoes.

CREAMED SALT COD – A LANGUEDOC REGION DISH * FISH

INGREDIENTS AND RECIPE: the salt cod is soaked for 12 hours, then boiled, shredded and mashed with garlic, lemon juice, milk and oil until a creamy puree is obtained. Served hot with croutons. Variation: with the potatoes and cod left in pieces.

BRI

100 - BRIOCHE * PÂTISSERIE

Photo Brioche bun.

BRIOCHE BUN * CAKE
INGREDIENTS AND RECIPE: dough consisting of flour, yeast, sugar, warm milk, a lot of butter and eggs, cooked for 15' after kneading and allowing to rest.

101 - BRIOCHE VENDÉENNE DE LA RÉGION DE VENDÉE * PÂTISSERIE

Photo Vendée brioche bun.

VENDEE REGION BRIOCHE BUN * CAKE
INGREDIENTS: flour, eggs, sugar, warm butter, cream, warm water and milk, yeast, milk, fruit brandy, orange flower water.
RECIPE: the yeast is dissolved in warm milk, all the other ingredients are mixed and allowed to prove in a cool place for 3 hours. The dough is divided into a long sausage shape and left for 1 hour, the surface is brushed with egg, it is baked for 25', marked with a knife and cooked for another 20'. Served cold.

BRO

102 - BROCHET DU CHER À L'OSEILLE * POISSON

Photo River Cher pike with sorrel.

RIVER CHER PIKE WITH SORREL * FISH
INGREDIENTS: for the stuffing: breadcrumbs, milk, sorrel, garlic, shallots, parsley, egg. To cook: shallots, wine, fish stock. For the sauce: cream, butter, sorrel, lemon.
RECIPE: the stuffing ingredients are mixed and the fish stuffed before cooking. Served hot with the sauce.

103 - BROCHETTE D'AGNEAU * VIANDE

Photo Lamb kebabs.

LAMB KEBABS * MEAT
INGREDIENTS AND RECIPE: pieces of lean lamb, onion, pepper and tomato cubed and cooked on a grill.

104 - BROCHETTES DE POISSONS * POISSON

Photo Fish kebab.

FISH KEBAB * FISH
INGREDIENTS AND RECIPE: pieces of fish grilled and served hot.

105 - BROUILLADE D'ŒUFS OU ŒUFS BROUILLÉS * ŒUFS

Photo Scrambled eggs.

SCRAMBLED EGGS * EGGS
INGREDIENTS: butter and beaten eggs.
RECIPE: the ingredients are cooked in a bain marie on the heat over a saucepan of water. Refined dish, served hot.

106 - BROUILLADE AUX TRUFFES DE LA RÉGION DE GASCOGNE * ŒUFS

Photo Truffled scrambled eggs.

TRUFFLED SCRAMBLED EGGS
A GASCONY REGION DISH * EGGS
INGREDIENTS: eggs, butter, freshly sliced truffle, Madeira wine.
RECIPE: the truffle is cooked with the Madeira for 15'. The eggs are cooked in the bain marie over a source of heat and water, stirred, then adding: the truffle, its cooking juice and butter. Served hot.

BUC

107 - BÛCHE DE NOËL * PÂTISSERIE TRADITIONNELLE DE DÉCEMBRE

Photo Chocolate and vanilla logs.

CHRISTMAS LOG * TRADITIONAL DECEMBER CAKE
INGREDIENTS: for the sponge: flour, sugar, vanilla sugar, eggs. For the custard cream: hot milk, sugar, egg yolks, flour. For the topping: butter, sugar, chocolate or flavouring chosen.
RECIPE: the sponge ingredients are mixed the previous day. The egg yolks and sugars are beaten until frothy and mixed with the whites before the 1-cm sponge is baked for 8'. The sponge is cooled on a damp cloth, rolled with another cloth and rested. It is filled with cooked custard cream before rolling and covering with butter cream.

BUG

108 - BUGNES - RECETTE DE LA RÉGION LYONNAISE * PÂTISSERIE TRADITIONNELLE DE FÉVRIER

Photo Lyon Carnival specialities.

LYON CARNIVAL SPECIALITIES
* A TRADITIONAL FEBRUARY CAKE
INGREDIENTS: for the dough: flour, sugar, butter, eggs, baking powder, rum, lemon. To cook: cooking oil.
RECIPE: the dough is prepared 1 hour previously. Strips are drawn out, fried in oil and sprinkled with icing sugar; served hot.

BUL

109 - BULOTS À LA MAYONNAISE * MOLLUSQUES

Photo Whelks with garlic mayonnaise.

WHELKS WITH MAYONNAISE * SHELLFISH
INGREDIENTS AND RECIPE: cooked in a court bouillon stock, served cold with garlic or plain mayonnaise. The whelk is extracted with the special "prong" provided.

CAB

110 - CABILLAUD EN PAPILLOTE * POISSON

Photo Cod in a foil case.

COD IN A FOIL CASE * FISH
INGREDIENTS: cod. To cook: green pepper, red pepper, tomatoes, lemons, thyme, olive oil.
RECIPE: the cod steaks are put with all the other ingredients into a foil case which is closed and then baked for 20' in the oven. Served hot.

111 - CABILLAUD OU DOS DE CABILLAUD POÊLÉ * POISSON

Photo Cod with butter and lemon.

FRIED COD FILLET OR BACK * FISH
INGREDIENTS AND RECIPE: the cod is sautéed in butter and served hot with a butter sauce and lemon.

CAF

112 - CAFÉ LIÉGEOIS * DESSERT GLACÉ

Photo Coffee ice cream sundae.

COFFEE ICE CREAM SUNDAE * ICE DESSERT
INGREDIENTS AND RECIPE: coffee ice cream decorated with whipped cream. Served iced.

CAG

113 - CAGOUILLES SAUTÉES DE LA RÉGION DE SAINTONGE

Photo Sauteed Saintonge snails.

SAUTEED SAINTONGE SNAILS
INGREDIENTS: snails. For the stock: carrot, onion, shallots, dry white wine, water, butter, parsley, chopped chives and tarragon. For the garnish: pork belly, chopped shallots and cut bread.
RECIPE: all the stock ingredients and the snails are cooked for 3 hours. The garnish ingredients are cooked for 5'. Served hot.

CAI

114 - CAILLE AUX RAISINS * VOLAILLE

Photo Quail with grapes.

QUAIL WITH GRAPES * POULTRY
INGREDIENTS: quail. For the sauce: wine, cream. To garnish: grapes browned in butter.
RECIPE: the quail are cooked for 15', the sauce is cooked and they are served together hot.

115 - CAILLES FARCIES AU FOIE GRAS * VOLAILLE

Photo Quail stuffed with foie gras.

QUAIL STUFFED WITH FOIE GRAS * POULTRY
INGREDIENTS AND RECIPE: the goose liver is browned in butter with Madeira wine, chopped truffles are added, the quail cavities filled with the mixture and cooked in the oven for 20'. Served hot.

CAK

116 - CAKE AUX FRUITS CONFITS * PÂTISSERIE D'ORIGINE ANGLAISE

Photo Fruit cake with pear.

ENGLISH FRUIT CAKE
INGREDIENTS AND RECIPE: a mixture is prepared consisting of butter and sugar, egg yolks, vanilla, rum, candied orange and lemon, flour and raisins are then added. The whites are beaten stiff and the mixture cooked for 1 hour. Served cold.

117 - CAKE AUX PETITS LÉGUMES * LÉGUMES

Photo Savoury vegetable cake.

SAVOURY VEGETABLE CAKE
* VEGETABLES
INGREDIENTS AND RECIPE: a mixture is prepared with butter to which egg yolks, precooked vegetables (courgettes, olives, tomatoes, etc.) and then flour are added. The whites are beaten stiff and the mixture cooked for 1 hour. Served hot or cold.

CAL

118 - CALMARS À L'AMÉRICAINE * MOLLUSQUES

Photo Squid in tomato brandy sauce with rice.

SQUID IN TOMATO BRANDY SAUCE * FISH
INGREDIENTS AND RECIPE: the squid is cut into pieces, browned in butter, tomatoes added and then cooked for 20'; wine, brandy, bouquet garni and garlic are added and cooked for a further 45'; served hot.

119 - CALMARS FARCIS * MOLLUSQUES

Photo Stuffed squid.

STUFFED SQUID * FISH
INGREDIENTS: squid. For the stuffing: onions, garlic, parsley, mushrooms, minced meat, egg. For the sauce: poultry stock, dry white wine, flour.
RECIPE: the stuffing is prepared to fill the squid before they are sautéed in oil. The sauce is cooked. Served together hot.

120 - CANAPÉS * ENTRÉE

Photo Canapés.

CANAPÉS * STARTER

121 - CANAPÉS AU JAMBON DE PARME * ENTRÉE

Photo Parma ham canapés.

PARMA HAM CANAPÉS * STARTER
INGREDIENTS: sliced bread, butter, raw Parma ham. Served cold.

122 - CANAPÉS AU SAUMON * ENTRÉE

Photo Smoked salmon canapés.

SALMON CANAPÉS * STARTER
INGREDIENTS: sliced bread, cream, smoked salmon. Served cold.

123 - CANARD EN COCOTTE AUX CÈPES - RECETTE DE LA RÉGION DE GASCOGNE * VOLAILLE

Photo Duck with ceps.

CASSEROLED DUCK WITH CEPS
A GASCONY REGION DISH * POULTRY
INGREDIENTS: barbary duck. To cook: oil. For the sauce: Muscat wine, poultry stock, garlic. For the garnish: cep mushrooms, goose fat, chopped parsley.
RECIPE: the duck is browned in the oil then cooked for 40'. The other ingredients are cooked and served hot all together.

124 - CANARD AUX GRIOTTES * VOLAILLE

Photo Duck with cherry sauce.

DUCK WITH CHERRY SAUCE * POULTRY
INGREDIENTS: duck, butter. For the sauce: chopped, shallots, clove, red wine, port, poultry stock, cream, cherry jam.
RECIPE: the duck is cooked in the oven, the sauce precooked and then added when the duck comes out of the oven, served hot.

125 - CANARD AUX NAVETS * VOLAILLE

Photo Duck with turnips.

DUCK WITH TURNIPS * POULTRY
INGREDIENTS: a whole duck, oil, onions, garlic, Alsatian wine, lemon, juniper berries, clove, thyme, bay leaf, turnip.
RECIPE: the duck and all the ingredients are cooked in the oven for 45'. Served hot.

126 - CANARD SAUVAGE AUX OLIVES * VOLAILLE

Photo Duck with olives.

WILD DUCK WITH OLIVES * POULTRY
INGREDIENTS: a whole duck, oil, onions, garlic, Alsatian wine, lemon, olives, clove, thyme, bay leaf.
RECIPE: the duck is cooked in the oven with all the ingredients for 45'. Served hot.

127 - CANARD À L'ORANGE * VOLAILLE

Photo Duck with orange sauce.

DUCK WITH ORANGE SAUCE * POULTRY
INGREDIENTS: duck. To cook: carrots, onions, poultry stock. For the orange sauce: sugar, orange zest, lemon and orange juice, Cointreau liqueur, vinegar, flour, orange marmalade.
RECIPE: the duck is cooked in the oven for 55' with all the cooking ingredients added. The orange sauce is prepared with a little of the duck cooking juices, served immediately.

128 - CANARD AUX PÊCHES * VOLAILLE

Photo Duck with peach sauce.

DUCK WITH PEACH SAUCE * POULTRY

INGREDIENTS AND RECIPE: same recipe as for duck with cherry (n° 124) sauce but the cherries are replaced with peaches. Served hot.

129 - CANARD AUX PRUNEAUX D'AGEN * VOLAILLE

Photo Duck with prunes.

DUCK WITH AGEN PRUNES * POULTRY

INGREDIENTS: whole duck. For the garnish: stoned prunes, chopped carrots and onions, butter, olive oil, wine, bouquet garni.

RECIPE: the garnish ingredients are cooked separately; the duck is cooked in the oven for 1 hour before finishing cooking above the other ingredients. Served hot.

130 - CANETON AU CAVIAR D'AUBERGINES * VOLAILLE

Photo Duckling with pureed aubergine.

DUCKLING WITH PUREED AUBERGINE * POULTRY

INGREDIENTS: duckling, olive oil for the aubergine puree (see recipe n° 149).

RECIPE: the duck is cooked for 50', basting with the cooking juices. Served hot, with the aubergine puree in another dish.

131 - CANNELÉS GIRONDINS - RECETTE DE LA RÉGION DE LA GIRONDE * PÂTISSERIE

Photo Gironde fluted cakes.

GIRONDE FLUTED CAKES * PASTRY

INGREDIENTS: milk, egg yolks, flour, cream, sugar, butter, vanilla, rum, fluted moulds.

RECIPE: all the ingredients are mixed together and then baked for 1 hour in the moulds. Served warm or cold.

132 - CANNELLONIS À LA VIANDE * PLAT COMPLET D'ORIGINE ITALIENNE

Photo Meat cannelloni.

MEAT CANNELLONI * A ONE-DISH ITALIAN PASTA MEAL

INGREDIENTS: cannelloni (hollow tubes of pasta). For the stuffing: sausage meat or cooked minced beef, onion, garlic, tomato, cream, oregano, sage. For the white sauce (see n° 784). For the topping: grated Parmesan cheese.

RECIPE: the stuffing ingredients are sauteed in the oil then blended; the cannelloni are filled, coated with white sauce and grated cheese and flashed under the grill to brown; served hot.

133 - CANNELLONIS D'AUBERGINES - RECETTE DE LA RÉGION DE PROVENCE * LÉGUMES

Photo Aubergine cannelloni.

AUBERGINE CANNELLONI - A PROVENÇAL DISH * VEGETABLES

INGREDIENTS: peeled aubergines cut lengthways into thin slices. For the sauce: chopped tomatoes, onion, garlic. For the stuffing: roast pork or ham, soft bread, milk, egg, shallots, garlic, Parmesan cheese, for the topping: grated cheese.

RECIPE: the sauce ingredients are cooked and pureed. The aubergines are cooked, the stuffing mixed and placed on the aubergine before rolling and flashing under the grill to brown with the tomato sauce, served hot.

CAR

134 - CARBONNADE * VIANDE

Photo Beef stewed in beer.

BEEF STEWED IN BEER * MEAT

INGREDIENTS: finely sliced stewing beef. To cook: lard, onions, flour, vinegar, bouquet garni, beef stock, lager beer.

RECIPE: the meat is browned in the lard then simmered for 3 hours with the cooking ingredients. Served hot with boiled potatoes.

135 - CARDES AU GRATIN * LÉGUMES

Photo Baked swiss chard.

BAKED SWISS CHARD * VEGETABLES
INGREDIENTS: green vegetable with a thick edge. For the white sauce: shallots, flour, egg yolks. For the topping: grated cheese.
RECIPE: the chard is cooked in boiling water and then in vegetable stock. The sauce ingredients are mixed and cooked. The mixture is placed in a dish, covered with grated cheese and browned in the oven for 20'. Served hot.

136 - CARDONS AU JUS * LÉGUMES

Photo Cardoons with meat juices.

CARDOONS WITH MEAT JUICES * VEGETABLES
INGREDIENTS AND RECIPE: the cardoons are cooked as in the above recipe then served hot with the meat cooking juices and no white sauce.

137 - CARPACCIO DE BŒUF * VIANDE

Photo Beef carpaccio.

BEEF CARPACCIO * MEAT
INGREDIENTS AND RECIPE: wafer-thin slices of beef refrigerated for 2 hours and drizzled with olive oil. Leave at room temperature for 10 mins. Served cold with slivers of Parmesan cheese.

138 - CARPACCIO DE SAUMON * POISSON

Photo Salmon carpaccio with chives.

SALMON CARPACCIO * FISH
INGREDIENTS AND RECIPE: the salmon is cut into wafer-thin slices, lemon, olive oil and chives. Served cold.

139 - CARPACCIO DE LANGUE DE VEAU * ABATS

CALF'S TONGUE CARPACCIO * OFFAL
INGREDIENTS AND RECIPE: after cooking in a court bouillon stock with celery, carrots, leek, clove and bouquet garni, the tongue is refrigerated and then cut into thin slices. Served cold with green salad (rocket, mesclun), lemon, olive oil.

140 - CARRÉ D'AGNEAU * VIANDE

Photo Loin of lamb.

LOIN OF LAMB * MEAT
INGREDIENTS AND RECIPE: the lamb is rubbed with thyme, bay leaf and oil, studded with garlic and then cooked with wine for 30', served hot.

141 - CARRÉ D'AGNEAU AUX POMMES BRESSANES * VIANDE

Photo Loin of lamb with Bresse potatoes.

LOIN OF LAMB WITH BRESSE POTATOES * MEAT
INGREDIENTS AND RECIPE: see Recipe N°140 which is identical. Bresse potatoes are cooked separately with butter and salt. Served hot.

142 - CARRÉ DE CÔTES DE PORC RÔTI * VIANDE

Photo Loin of pork with sauté potatoes.

ROAST LOIN OF PORK * MEAT
INGREDIENTS: loin of pork, sage, oil,
RECIPE: the oil is heated and the loin browned before cooking for 45' in a closed casserole dish. Served hot.

143 - CARRÉ DE PORC * VIANDE

Photo Loin of pork.

LOIN OF PORK * MEAT
Served hot or cold.

144 - CARRÉ DE PRÉ SALÉ BONNE FEMME - RECETTE DE LA RÉGION DE BRETAGNE * VIANDE

Photo Loin of salt-meadow lamb.

LOIN OF SALT-MEADOW LAMB, A DISH FROM BRITTANY * MEAT
INGREDIENTS: loin of lamb with 8 chops, bones stripped back, butter, oil. For the garnish: small potatoes and onions, diced bacon. To serve: butter, bunch of watercress. RECIPE: the potatoes are boiled; the diced bacon and onions are cooked separately; the loin is then coated in butter and roast in the oven for 20'; the garnish ingredients are added at the end of cooking; served hot.

145 - CAROTTES CUITES « VICHY » * LÉGUMES

Photo Vichy carrots.

VICHY CARROTS * VEGETABLES
RECIPE: the carrots are thinly sliced, browned in butter and cooked for 30' after adding some Marsala wine. Served immediately with parsley.

146 - CAROTTES GLACÉES À LA CRÈME * LÉGUMES

Photo Glazed carrots.

GLAZED CARROTS WITH CREAM * VEGETABLES
INGREDIENTS AND RECIPE: the carrots are diced then sautéed in maple syrup and oil, vegetable stock is then added and they are cooked for 20'; the cream is added to thicken when cooked. Served hot.

147 - CASSOLETTE D'ESCARGOTS FARCIS

Photo Dish of stuffed snails.

DISH OF STUFFED SNAILS
INGREDIENTS AND RECIPE: the precooked snails are put into their shells with butter, garlic and parsley, heated in the oven and served hot.

148 - CASSOULET * PLAT COMPLET DE LA RÉGION DE TOULOUSE

Photo Meat, poultry and bean bake.

MEAT * POULTRY AND BEAN BAKE
A ONE-DISH MEAL FROM THE TOULOUSE REGION
INGREDIENTS: boned mutton, pork, lean bacon, Toulouse sausages, garlic sausage, preserved goose, dried white beans, garlic, tomatoes, onions, oil, breadcrumbs, goose fat, bouquet garni (preserved goose or duck can also be added)
RECIPE: the meat and dried beans are cooked separately, then simmered together with stock and tomato, garlic and onions for 3 hours before browning under the grill. Hot dish.

149 - CAVIAR D'AUBERGINES - RECETTE DE LA RÉGION DE PROVENCE * LÉGUMES

Photo Aubergine puree.

AUBERGINE PUREE - PROVENÇAL DISH * VEGETABLES
INGREDIENTS: aubergines, garlic, lemon juice, olive oil, stoned black olives, basil leaves.
RECIPE: the aubergines are halved lengthwise and cooked on an oiled tray for 45'; the aubergine flesh is blended with all the other ingredients, served hot.

CEL

150 - CÉLERI REMOULADE * ENTRÉE

Photo Celery with mayonnaise-type sauce on the left with grated carrot.

CELERY WITH MAYONNAISE - TYPE SAUCE * STARTER

INGREDIENTS AND RECIPE: the celery is finely sliced and mixed with a mayonnaise type sauce, served cold.

CEP

151 - CÈPES * LÉGUMES

Photo Sliced ceps with garlic and parsley.

CEPS * VEGETABLES

INGREDIENTS AND RECIPE: firm flesh mushrooms in season in autumn. Served hot.

152 - CÈPES À LA BORDELAISE * LÉGUMES

Photo Ceps in garlic butter.

CEPS IN GARLIC BUTTER * VEGETABLES

INGREDIENTS AND RECIPE: the ceps are sliced and cooked in butter for 15' with lemon juice, then browned in oil with garlic and parsley. Served hot.

153 - CÈPES À LA PROVENÇALE * LÉGUMES

Photo Ceps Provençal style.

CEPS PROVENÇAL STYLE * VEGETABLES

INGREDIENTS AND RECIPE: the cep caps are cooked with shallots and garlic, the stalks chopped and mixed with mashed boiled egg and breadcrumbs and then browned in oil for 10'; the mushroom caps are placed in a dish on top of the chopped mixture and cooked in the oven for 20'; served hot.

154 - CERVELLE D'AGNEAU AU CITRON * ABATS

Photo Brains cut up, with butter and parsley.

LAMB BRAINS WITH LEMON * OFFAL
INGREDIENTS AND RECIPE: the brains are poached in boiling water with vinegar added then drained and browned in hot butter with capers. Served hot whole or cut up with chopped parsley and lemon.

155 - CERVELLE DE CANUT * ENTRÉE FROMAGE

Photo Cheese dip.

CHEESE DIP * STARTER
INGREDIENTS: cheese, cream, olive oil, wine vinegar, chopped shallots, chives, parsley, tarragon, chervil and garlic.
RECIPE: the ingredients are blended and refrigerated. Served cold with toast.

156 - CHAMPIGNONS DE PARIS, CRUS * LÉGUMES

Photo Raw cultivated mushrooms.

RAW CULTIVATED MUSHROOMS * VEGETABLES
Served cold.

157 - CHAMPIGNONS DE PARIS À LA CRÈME ET À LA CIBOULETTE * LÉGUMES

Photo Cultivated mushrooms with cream and chives.

CULTIVATED MUSHROOMS WITH CREAM AND CHIVES * VEGETABLES
Served cold.

158 - CHAMPIGNONS À LA GRECQUE * ENTRÉE

Photo Greek-style mushrooms.

GREEK-STYLE MUSHROOMS * STARTER
INGREDIENTS AND RECIPE: the cultivated mushrooms are halved and garlic, coriander seeds and tomato added to shallots to cook in oil for 5'; dry white wine, basil, lemon juice and tomato puree are added at the end of cooking. Served cold.

159 - CHAPON DE BRESSE AU GROS SEL - RECETTE DE LA RÉGION DE BOURGOGNE * VOLAILLE

Photo Bresse capon with cooked chestnuts.

BRESSE CAPON IN A SALT CRUST - A BURGUNDY REGION DISH * POULTRY
INGREDIENTS: Bresse capon, truffle, coarse salt, butter.
RECIPE: butter and slivers of truffle are slid under the capon skin; it is then covered in salt in a casserole and cooked in the oven for 1 hr 45 mins. The salt crust is removed and it is served hot.

160 - CHARLOTTE AUX FRAMBOISES * PÂTISSERIE - FRUITS

Photo Charlotte with red fruit.

RASPBERRY CHARLOTTE * CAKE - FRUIT
INGREDIENTS: sponge fingers, gelatine, raspberries, milk, vanilla sugar. For the cream: egg yolks, cream.
RECIPE: the softened gelatine is cooked with the vanilla-flavoured milk and egg yolks, the sides of the mould lined with the sponge fingers and the cream, raspberries and remaining biscuits added; it is refrigerated for 12 hours. Served cold.

160-1 - CHATEAUBRIAND * VIANDE

Photo Chateaubriand fillet steak.

CHATEAUBRIAND FILLET STEAK * MEAT
INGREDIENTS AND RECIPE: 5cm-thick steak, grilled quickly with butter. Served hot.

161 - CHAUD FROID DE VOLAILLE * VOLAILLE

Photo Chicken with chaud froid sauce.

CHICKEN WITH CHAUD FROID SAUCE * POULTRY
INGREDIENTS: Bresse fatted chicken, calf's foot. To cook: carrots, leek, stick of celery, onion. For the sauce: cooking stock, butter, flour, cream, egg yolks and lemon juice.
RECIPE: the meat and cooking ingredients are cooked in a large pot for 1 hour 30 mins. The chicken is coated with the sauce and served cold with chopped aspic jelly.

162 - CHAUSSON AUX POMMES * PÂTISSERIE - FRUITS

Photo Apple turnover.

APPLE TURNOVER * FRUIT PASTRY
INGREDIENTS: flaky pastry. To garnish: apple puree, sugar.
RECIPE: apple puree is spread in the centre of the squares of flaky pastry which are folded over and then baked in the oven. Served cold or warm.

CHE

163 - CHÈVRES CHAUDS SUR LIT DE SALADE * ENTRÉE - FROMAGE

Photo Hot goat's cheese on a bed of lamb's lettuce.

HOT GOAT'S CHEESE ON A BED OF GREEN SALAD * STARTER - CHEESE
INGREDIENTS: goat's cheese, butter, bread croutons, green salad.
RECIPE: the goat's cheeses are sauteed in butter, placed on bread croutons and seasoned salad. Served hot and cold.

164 - CHÈVRES FRAIS EN SALADE OU SALADE DE CHÈVRES FRAIS * SALADE - FROMAGE

Photo Goat's cheeses on a bed of endive.

GOAT'S CHEESE ON A BED OF GREEN SALAD * SALAD, CHEESE
INGREDIENTS: goat's cheese, green salad.
RECIPE: small, whole goat's cheeses are served on a bed of salad dressed with vinaigrette. Served cold.

165 - CHICORÉE FRISÉE AUX LARDONS * SALADE

Photo Endive with bacon pieces and poached eggs.

ENDIVE WITH DICED BACON * SALAD
INGREDIENTS: endive. Vinaigrette sauce: vinegar, mustard, oil. To garnish: fried garlic bread, whole poached eggs.
RECIPE: the diced bacon is pan-fried and poured over the salad with the cooking oil, the other ingredients are added. Served hot and cold.

166 - CHIFFONADE DE LAITUE AUX PETITS POIS * LÉGUMES

Photo Finely-sliced lettuce with peas.

FINELY-SLICED LETTUCE WITH PEAS * VEGETABLES
INGREDIENTS AND RECIPE: the lettuce leaves are sliced finely in strips and the peas cooked in boiling water. Served hot with mayonnaise or cooked in butter.

167 - CHIPIRONS À L'ESCABÈCHE DE SAINT-JEAN-DE-LUZ RECETTE DE LA RÉGION DU BÉARN * POISSON

Photo Tiny squid, a dish from Béarn.

TINY SQUID, A DISH FROM BÉARN * FISH
INGREDIENTS: squid, onions, oil. For the sauce: tomatoes, garlic, chopped parsley, brandy, paprika.
RECIPE: the squid are cut into thin strips and the ink retained. The fish is browned and cooked in the oil. The onions are put in, the preparation flamed in brandy and the wine, herbs, spice and tomatoes added. Served hot.

168 - CHIPOLATAS * CHARCUTERIE

Photo Chipolata sausages with lentils.

CHIPOLATA SAUSAGES * COOKED MEATS AND SIMILAR
INGREDIENTS AND RECIPE: long, thin pork sausages pan-fried in fat. Served hot.

169 - CHIPS * LÉGUMES

Photo Crisps.

CRISPS * VEGETABLES
INGREDIENTS: potato cut into slices.
RECIPE: they are fried in hot oil. Salted and served warm.

170 - CHOCOLAT VIENNOIS * DESSERT GLACÉ

Photo Chocolate ice cream sundae.

CHOCOLATE ICE CREAM SUNDAE * ICE DESSERT
INGREDIENTS AND RECIPE: chocolate ice cream, whipped cream, served cold.

171 - CHOUCROUTE GARNIE À LA STRASBOURGEOISE OU CHOUCROUTE ALSACIENNE * PLAT COMPLET RÉGIONAL

Photo Sauerkraut meal.

STRASBOURG OR ALSATIAN SAUERKRAUT * ONE-DISH MEAL FROM ALSACE
INGREDIENTS: sauerkraut. To garnish: bard, pork loin, smoked blade of pork, lean, smoked bacon, salted pork belly, Strasbourg sausages. To garnish: smoked sausages, onion, carrots, potatoes, dry white wine, juniper berries.
RECIPE: the sauerkraut is cooked in lard, poultry stock and Alsatian wine with juniper berries, cumin, thyme and bay leaf for 1 hour 30 mins. Add the cooked meats and sausages and garnish at the end of cooking. Served hot.

172 - CHOUCROUTE DE LA MER - PLAT COMPLET RÉGIONAL * POISSON

Photo Fish sauerkraut.

SAUERKRAUT WITH FISH - ONE-DISH REGIONAL MEAL * FISH

INGREDIENTS: uncooked sauerkraut, mussels, smoked haddock, sea bream, monkfish tail, langoustines, to cook, lard, dry white wine, milk, court bouillon stock, onions, juniper berries. For the sauce: butter, shallots, wine, cider vinegar, lemon.

RECIPE: the sauerkraut is cooked for 1 hour. The fished is cooked in a court bouillon and served hot with the sauerkraut and cooked sauce.

173 - CHOU À LA CRÈME CHANTILLY * PÂTISSERIE

Photo Cream puff.

CREAM PUFF * CAKE

INGREDIENTS: choux pastry (flour, sugar, eggs and water). For the cream filling: sweetened whipped cream.

RECIPE: the choux pastry is mixed and divided into tiny puffs, baked in the oven and filled with whipped cream when cool. Served cold.

173-1 - CHOUX DE BRUXELLES * LÉGUMES

Photo Brussels sprouts.

BRUSSELS SPROUTS * VEGETABLES

Served hot.

174 - CHOU FARCI - PLAT COMPLET RÉGIONAL D'AUVERGNE * LÉGUMES

Photo Stuffed cabbage.

STUFFED CABBAGE * ONE-DISH MEAL FROM AUVERGNE * VEGETABLES

INGREDIENTS: a Savoy cabbage. For the stuffing: sausage meat, onions, nutmeg, soft bread, milk.

RECIPE: the stuffing is prepared, the cabbage boiled and drained; the leaves are stuffed and the whole cooked in court bouillon stock for 1 hour 30 mins; served hot.

CIB

174-1 - CIBOULETTE * AROMATE

Photo Chives.

CHIVES * HERB
A flavoursome herb.

CIT

175 - CITRON CONFIT * FRUITS

Photo Preserved lemons.

PRESERVED LEMONS * FRUIT
INGREDIENTS AND RECIPE: the lemons are cut in quarters without separating them at the centre, salt is inserted and they are kept in a jar for 3 weeks until preserved. Used for cooking or dipped in sugar for desserts.

175-1 - CITRON GIVRÉ * FRUITS

Photo Lemon sorbet.

SORBET SERVED IN A LEMON * FRUIT
INGREDIENTS AND RECIPE: the wine, sugar and lemon pulp are mixed and put to freeze for 4 hours. Egg white is firmly beaten and mixed with the Cointreau liqueur and lemon zest. A lemon is filled with the preparation and put into the freezer. Served iced.

CIV

176 - CIVET DE LAPIN

Photo Jugged rabbit.

RABBIT CASSEROLE
INGREDIENTS AND RECIPE: the rabbit and onions are cut in pieces and browned in the butter, the bacon is grilled and put at the bottom of a casserole dish to cook with the oil, red wine, bay leaf, thyme and crushed garlic for 30'; flour and butter are added to thicken the sauce and the dish cooked for another 30'. Served hot.

177 - CIVET DE LIÈVRE À L'ALSACIENNE - RECETTE DE LA RÉGION D'ALSACE * GIBIER

Photo Jugged hare.

JUGGED HARE - A REGIONAL DISH FROM ALSACE * GAME

INGREDIENTS: hare cut into pieces, onion, butter, flour, wine, bouquet garni, garlic. For the marinade: red wine, brandy, oil, onions, garlic, clove. To garnish: mushrooms, smoked bacon pieces, butter, lemon.

RECIPE: the hare is marinated for 12 hours. The garnish is cooked with the liver then mixed with the reserved blood of the hare and added to the sauce. Everything is served hot.

178 - CIVET DE CHEVREUIL * GIBIER

Photo Casseroled venison.

CASSEROLED VENISON * GAME

INGREDIENTS: cubed venison. For the marinade: cocoa, onion. To cook: meat stock, red wine, water, orange juice, oil, butter, flour, juniper berries, pepper, cinnamon.

RECIPE: the meat and onion are cooked separately in butter and the meat covered with cocoa to marinate. The next day, the cooking ingredients are added and the dish cooked for 5 hours. Served hot.

CLA

179 - CLAFOUTIS AUX CERISES * PÂTISSERIE AUX FRUITS

Photo Cherry batter pudding.

CHERRY BATTER PUDDING * CAKE WITH FRUIT

INGREDIENTS AND RECIPE: a batter is prepared with flour, egg, milk and butter; cherries are added and the mixture cooked for 40'. Served warm.

180 - CLAFOUTIS AUX PÊCHES * PÂTISSERIE AUX FRUITS

Photo Peach batter pudding.

PEACH BATTER PUDDING * CAKE WITH FRUIT

INGREDIENTS AND RECIPE: see 179, the cherries are replaced with peaches.

CLU

181 - CLUB SANDWICH * ENTRÉE

Photo Chicken and salmon club sandwich, crips.

CLUB SANDWICH * STARTER
INGREDIENTS AND RECIPE: triangles of sliced bread with pieces of meat (chicken, turkey, fish - salmon or tuna), green salad, tomato, mayonnaise and ketchup in between, stacked with another slice of bread plus meat, fish, salad, etc. Served cold, often with crisps or chips.

COE

182 - CŒUR DE SUCRINE * LÉGUMES

Photo Little gem lettuce heart.

LITTLE GEM LETTUCE HEART
* VEGETABLES
Variety of lettuce.

183 - CŒUR DE VEAU EN TRANCHE * ABATS

Photo Calf's heart with spring vegetables.

SLICED CALF'S HEART * OFFAL
INGREDIENTS: slice of heart
RECIPE: sautéed 3' in butter with onions, then cooked in the oven for 2'. Served hot.

184 - CŒUR DE VEAU ENTIER * ABATS

Photo Whole calf's heart with braised carrots and onions.

WHOLE CALF'S HEART * OFFAL
INGREDIENTS: a heart cut in 2. To cook: carrots, tomatoes, leeks, celery. For the sauce: cooking juices, tomato puree, flour, cream.
RECIPE: the heart is cooked in stock for 1 hour 30 mins and the vegetables then added. The sauce is prepared and served separately, served hot.

COL

185 - COLIN AU CIDRE * POISSON

Photo Hake in cider.

HAKE IN CIDER * FISH
INGREDIENTS AND RECIPE: onion, parsley and garlic are cooked with the hake; the fish is removed and the sauce prepared with cider and flour; cream is added and it is served hot.

186 - COLIN PANÉ * POISSON

Photo Breaded hake with tomato pasta.

BREADED HAKE * FISH
INGREDIENTS AND RECIPE: the fish is dipped in beaten, egg and breadcrumbs and then cooked. Served hot.

187 - COLOMBO DE POULET OU DE PORC - ORIGINE DES ANTILLES SPÉCIALITÉ ANTILLAISE * VOLAILLE

Photo Spicy chicken.

SPICY CHICKEN OR PORK - A WEST INDIAN SPECIALITY * POULTRY
INGREDIENTS AND RECIPE: the meat is cooked with a West Indian curry spice mix called "colombo", made with: coriander, mustard seeds, chilli, turmeric and saffron, etc.). Served hot.

COM

188 - COMPOTE DE PÊCHES * DESSERT - FRUITS

Photo Peach compote.

PEACH COMPOTE * FRUIT DESSERT
INGREDIENTS AND RECIPE: made with white wine, water, sugar, cinnamon and lemon zest brought to the boil and the peaches added. Served cold.

189 - COMPOTE DE POMMES * DESSERT - FRUITS

Photo Apple compote.

APPLE COMPOTE * FRUIT DESSERT
INGREDIENTS: the apples are cooked for 15' with a little water, sugar, vanilla and lemon zest and then blended. Served cold.

190 - COMPOTE DE RHUBARBE * DESSERT - FRUITS

Photo Rhubarb compote.

RHUBARB COMPOTE * FRUIT DESSERT
INGREDIENTS: sliced rhubarb, wine, sugar, lemon zest, lemon juice and cinnamon.
RECIPE: the preparation is boiled for 10' and the raspberry syrup added. Served cold.

191 - COMPOTÉE DE LAPEREAU * VOLAILLE

Photo Rabbit terrine.

RABBIT TERRINE * GAME
INGREDIENTS: rabbit. To cook: calf's foot, carrots, onions, bouquet garni, wine, water. For the terrine: foie gras, rabbit cooking liquid.
RECIPE: the ingredients are cooked for 1 hour before adding the rabbit and cooking extended for another hour. The ingredients for the terrine are laid in layers with the pieces of rabbit. Served cold.

192 - COMPOTÉE D'ABRICOTS * DESSERT - FRUITS

Photo Apricot compote.

APRICOT COMPOTE * FRUIT DESSERT
INGREDIENTS: apricots, water, verbena, lemon juice.
RECIPE: the apricots are poached in the verbena syrup for 3'. Served cold with the juice.

193 - COMPOTÉE DE PÊCHES * DESSERT - FRUITS

Photo Peach compote.

PEACH COMPOTE * FRUIT DESSERT
INGREDIENTS: peaches, sugar, water, lemon.
RECIPE: the peaches are poached in the water with sugar and lemon for 4'. Served cold with the juice.

194 - COMPOTÉE DE PRUNES ROUGES * DESSERT - FRUITS

Photo Red plum compote.

RED PLUM COMPOTE * FRUIT DESSERT
INGREDIENTS: plums, sugar.
RECIPE: the ingredients are cooked. Served cold.

195 - COMPOTÉE DE REINES-CLAUDES * DESSERT - FRUITS

Photo Greengage plum compote.

GREENGAGE PLUM COMPOTE * FRUIT DESSERT
INGREDIENTS: greengages, water, sugar.
RECIPE: the ingredients are cooked. Served cold.

196 - COMPOTÉE DE PRUNEAUX * DESSERT - FRUITS

Photo Prune compote.

PRUNE COMPOTE * FRUIT DESSERT
INGREDIENTS: prunes, sugar, Ceylon tea.
RECIPE: sugar is added to Ceylon tea and the prunes poached for 4'. Served cold with the juice.

197 - CONCOMBRES À LA CRÈME * LÉGUMES

Photo Cucumber in cream.

CUCUMBER IN CREAM * VEGETABLES
INGREDIENTS: raw cucumber.
RECIPE: sliced and served as a starter with a cream-based sauce. Served cold as a starter.

198 - CONFIT D'ÉCHINE DE PORC * VIANDE

Photo Conserved pork chine.

CONSERVED PORK CHINE * MEAT
INGREDIENTS: pork chine, mustard seeds. To cook: lard.
RECIPE: the chine is covered with the mixed ingredients, left for 6 hours and then cooked in lard for 3 hours. Served hot.

198-1 - CONSOMMÉ DE VOLAILLE * POTAGE

Photo Poultry consommé.

CHICKEN CONSOMMÉ * SOUP
INGREDIENTS AND RECIPE: a chicken is cooked with onion, carrot, celery, bouquet garni and at the end of cooking, the consommé is filtered and served hot with or without vermicelli pasta.

199 - COQ À LA BIÈRE - RECETTE DE LA RÉGION DE PICARDIE * VOLAILLE

Photo Chicken in beer, a Picardy dish.

CHICKEN IN BEER, A PICARDY DISH
* POULTRY
INGREDIENTS: small chicken. For the preparation: lard, chopped carrots and shallots, juniper liqueur. For the sauce: beer, cream. For the garnish: mushrooms, lemon, butter.
RECIPE: the chicken is cooked, then flamed and the sauce added. Served hot with the cooked garnish, coated with sauce.

200 - COQ AU VIN - PLAT TRADITIONNEL FRANÇAIS * VOLAILLE

Photo Chicken in wine.

CHICKEN IN WINE, A TRADITIONAL FRENCH DISH * POULTRY
INGREDIENTS: chicken cut into pieces, for the sauce: red wine, chicken stock, butter, flour. For the garnish: garlic, carrots, diced bacon, onions, thyme, bay leaf, butter, lemon. To finish: cultivated mushrooms, brandy to flame.
RECIPE: the chicken is browned with the garnish ingredients then cooked for 40'. Served hot.

201 - COQ AU RIESLING (VIN D'ALSACE) * VOLAILLE SPÉCIALITÉ D'ALSACE

Photo Chicken in riesling.

CHICKEN IN RIESLING WINE, A SPECIALITY OF ALSACE * POULTRY
INGREDIENTS: chicken cut into pieces. For the stock: wings, neck. To cook: shallots, wine, garlic, tarragon. For the sauce: cultivated mushrooms, cream.
RECIPE: the stock is prepared and the pieces of chicken cooked with the cooking ingredients for 25'; served hot with the sauce.

202 - COQUELET GRILLÉ * VOLAILLE

Photo Grilled baby chicken, crips.

GRILLED BABY CHICKEN * POULTRY
RECIPE: the chicken is browned in butter for 20' then grilled in the oven. Served hot.

203 - COQUES ET MOULES EN CASSOLETTE * MOLLUSQUES

Photo dish of cockles and mussels.

DISH OF COCKLES AND MUSSELS * SHELLFISH
RECIPE: the shallots are cooked in butter, the wine incorporated to cook the cockles and mussels. The cooking juices are kept and combined with cream and parsley. Served hot.

204 - (NOIX DE) COQUILLES * OU COQUILLES SAINT-JACQUES AUX ENDIVES * MOLLUSQUES

Photo Scallops with braised chicory.

SCALLOPS WITH CHICORY * SHELLFISH
INGREDIENTS: butter, scallops, sherry, lemon juice and chicory cooked separately.
RECIPE: the scallops are browned for 2'. The wine and lemon juice are added. Served hot.

205 - COQUILLES SAINT-JACQUES GRATINÉES * MOLLUSQUES

Photo Baked scallops.

BAKED SCALLOPS * SHELLFISH
INGREDIENTS: scallops, butter, shallots, spinach, cream, cultivated mushrooms, dry white wine, breadcrumbs, Emmenthal cheese.
RECIPE: each ingredient is cooked quickly in butter and the cream incorporated with a little dry white wine. The scallops are put back in their shells with the breadcrumbs and Emmenthal and baked for 10' in the oven. Served immediately.

206 - COQUILLE SAINT-JACQUES NANTAISE DE LA RÉGION DE BRETAGNE * MOLLUSQUES

Photo Scallops nantes style, a regional dish from brittany.

SCALLOPS NANTES STYLE, A REGIONAL DISH FROM BRITTANY * SHELLFISH
INGREDIENTS: scallops, butter. For the garnish: mussels, shallots, lemon, butter. For the sauce: glass of wine, fish stock. At the end of cooking: cream, butter, cultivated mushrooms.
RECIPE: the scallops are cooked with the sauce and the mussels added. The other ingredients are added at the end of cooking, the dish is flashed under the grill in a shell and served hot.

207 - (NOIX DE) COQUILLE SAINT-JACQUES À LA PROVENÇALE * MOLLUSQUES

Photo Scallops provençal style.

SCALLOPS PROVENÇAL STYLE * SHELLFISH
INGREDIENTS: scallops, garlic, chopped parsley, chervil, chives and tarragon, lemon juice, butter.
RECIPE: the scallops are browned with all the ingredients, served hot.

208 - COQUILLETTES AU BEURRE * PÂTES

Photo Pasta shells with butter.

PASTA SHELLS WITH BUTTER * PASTA
INGREDIENTS AND RECIPE: the pasta is cooked in stock, drained and served with a knob of butter.

COR

209 - CORNET DE MURAT * PÂTISSERIE D'AUVERGNE

Photo Cream horns.

CREAM HORNS, AN AUVERGNE SPECIALITY * CAKE
INGREDIENTS: eggs, sugar, flour, butter.
RECIPE: the eggs and sugar are beaten and the flour added. 15-cm circles of pastry are baked for 6' and then rolled into a horn shape. Served cold filled with whipped cream or ice cream.

210 - CORNICHONS * LÉGUMES PETITS CONCOMBRES

Photo Gherkins.

GHERKINS * TINY CUCUMBERS VEGETABLES
INGREDIENTS: gherkins, vinegar, pepper, marinade spices, dill, tarragon, garlic.
RECIPE: the gherkins are cleaned, covered with salt for 24 hours, rinsed and put into a glass jar with vinegar for 20 days before use. Served cold.

211 - CÔTE DE BŒUF AU THYM * VIANDE

Photo Grilled rib of beef with whole roast potatoes.

RIB OF BEEF WITH THYME * MEAT
INGREDIENTS AND RECIPE: rib of beef, 8 to 10 cm thick. The meat is rubbed with olive oil and thyme before cooking under the grill as desired (rare, medium or well done). Served hot.

212 - CÔTE DE PORC BOULANGÈRE * VIANDE

Photo Pork chop with sliced potato bake.

PORK CHOP WITH SLICED POTATO BAKE * MEAT
INGREDIENTS: pork chop, thinly-sliced potatoes, chopped onions.
RECIPE: the potatoes are layered with the onions and cooked in lard and beef stock for 45 mins; the pork chops are cooked separately in lard and then the ingredients are all baked in the oven and served hot.

213 - CÔTE DE PORC À LA NORMANDE OU À LA CRÈME * VIANDE

Photo Normandy pork chop.

NORMANDY PORK CHOP OR PORK CHOP IN CREAM * MEAT
INGREDIENTS: pork chop, sliced apples and onions, Calvados applejack brandy, cream
RECIPE: the onions and apples are softened in lard, the Calvados and cream added to the pork chop cooked separately. Served hot.

214 - CÔTE DE PORC À LA PROVENÇALE * VIANDE

Photo Pork chop.

PROVENÇAL PORK CHOP * MEAT
INGREDIENTS: pork chops, olive oil, parsley, garlic, rosemary, thyme, breadcrumbs for a brown crust before serving.
RECIPE: the ingredients are mixed and rubbed into the meat before cooking. The breadcrumbs are added to form a brown crust before serving hot.

215 - CÔTE DE VEAU À LA NORMANDE * VIANDE

Photo Normandy veal chop.

NORMANDY VEAL CHOP * MEAT
RECIPE: the chop is cooked in butter and the mushrooms cooked in cream. Served hot.

216 - CÔTE DE VEAU SPAGHETTIS DE COURGETTE * VIANDE

Photo Veal chop with courgette spaghetti.

VEAL CHOP WITH COURGETTE SPAGHETTI * MEAT
INGREDIENTS: veal chop, garlic, onion, tomatoes, olives, chopped parsley, olive oil.
RECIPE: the veal chop and other ingredients are cooked separately and then served hot.

216-1 - CÔTELETTES D'AGNEAU GRILLÉES * VIANDE

Photo Grilled cutlets.

GRILLED LAMB CUTLETS * MEAT
INGREDIENTS: grilled cutlets. Served hot.

217 - COTRIADE DE LA RÉGION DE BRETAGNE * POISSON

Photo Fish stew.

FISH STEW * A REGIONAL DISH FROM BRITTANY * FISH
INGREDIENTS: conger eel, gurnet, John Dory or turbot, onion, potatoes, lard or butter, bouquet garni, fish stock.
RECIPE: the fish is cut into large pieces and then cooked in lard with the potatoes. The broth is poured into a soup bowl and served hot separately with croutons.

218 - COU D'OIE FARCI * ABATS

Photo Stuffed goose neck.

STUFFED GOOSE NECK * OFFAL
INGREDIENTS: the fatty skin of a goose neck, poultry flesh, sausage meat, truffle shavings, Marc spirit or Armagnac brandy, egg, fresh foie gras, goose fat.
RECIPE: the ingredients are cooked in stock then allowed to cool before serving cold.

219 - COULIS DE FRUITS JAUNES * DESSERT

Photo Yellow fruit puree.

YELLOW FRUIT PUREE * DESSERT
INGREDIENTS: pears, peaches, apricots. To cook: water, caster sugar.
RECIPE: the fruit is cooked for 10', blended and sieved to obtain a smooth consistency. Served cold.

220 - COULIS DE FRUITS ROUGES * DESSERT

Photo Red fruit puree.

RED FRUIT PUREE * DESSERT
INGREDIENTS: strawberries, cherries, raspberries, water, sugar.
RECIPE: the fruit is blended, reduced to a puree, the juice obtained then sieved and sugar and lemon juice added. Served cold.

221 - COULIS DE TOMATES * LÉGUMES

Photo Tomato puree.

TOMATO PUREE * VEGETABLES
INGREDIENTS: cooked tomatoes, garlic, onions, oil.
RECIPE: garlic and onions are sautéed in oil for 5', the tomatoes are cooked for 35'; the preparation is blended then sieved.

222 - COUPE DE FRUITS EXOTIQUES * DESSERT - FRUITS

Photo Pineapple, mango, kiwi.

EXOTIC FRUIT SALAD * FRUIT DESSERT
INGREDIENTS AND RECIPE: pineapple, melon, mango and kiwi mixed with grenadine syrup, Cointreau liqueur, lemon juice, vanilla and cream or sugar and water simply sprinkled on the fruit. Served cold.

223 - COUPE DE FRUITS ROUGES * DESSERT - FRUITS

Photo Blackberries, raspberries, cherries, blueberries, redcurrants, almonds.

RED FRUIT SALAD * FRUIT DESSERT
INGREDIENTS AND RECIPE: they may include: blackberries, strawberries, blueberries, raspberries, blackcurrants, redcurrants, a little champagne or only sugar and water or with a fruit puree. Served cold.

224 - COUPE DE PRUNES AU VIN ROUGE * DESSERT - FRUITS

Photo Bowl of plums in red wine.

PLUMS IN RED WINE * FRUIT DESSERT
INGREDIENTS: plums, red wine, cinnamon, clove.
RECIPE: the plums are cooked with all the ingredients. Served cold.

225 - COUPE DE GRIOTTES * DESSERT - FRUITS

Photo Griotte cherries with a scoop of vanilla ice cream.

CHERRIES IN WINE * FRUIT DESSERT
INGREDIENTS AND RECIPE: griotte cherries cooked in wine are served sprinkled with Kirsch cherry-based spirit. Served cold.

226 - COUPE DE PÊCHES AU VIN ROSÉ * DESSERT - FRUITS

Photo Peaches in rosé wine.

PEACHES IN ROSÉ WINE
* FRUIT DESSERT
INGREDIENTS: peaches, wine, lemon, ginger, sugar, cinnamon.
RECIPE: the peaches are cooked with all the ingredients. Served cold.

227 - COURGETTES EN GRATIN * LÉGUMES

Photo Courgette cheese bake.

COURGETTE CHEESE BAKE * VEGETABLES
INGREDIENTS: courgettes, olive oil, peppers, tomatoes, garlic, basil. White sauce: flour, butter, milk. To brown: grated Emmenthal cheese.
RECIPE: The courgettes are boiled and the other ingredients added. Flashed under the grill topped with white sauce and cheese.

228 - COUSCOUS - SPÉCIALITÉ D'ORIGINE MAROCAINE, TUNISIENNE, ALGÉRIENNE * PLAT COMPLET

Photo Couscous.

COUSCOUS - AN ALGERIAN, MOROCCAN AND TUNISIAN SPECIALITY
* A ONE-DISH MEAL
INGREDIENTS: cooked semolina granules plus, depending on the origin - raisins, almonds, chick peas, mint - with meat: lamb, beef, spicy sausages, chicken. Vegetables: carrots, courgettes, tomatoes, spices, onions, harissa hot sauce, coriander, saffron.
RECIPE: the meat is browned in fat and then put into a couscous cooking pot with the vegetables, spices and stock (traditional dish). The semolina is rolled in butter and put into the top of the pot. The sauce is prepared with a little stock and the harissa when served hot.

229 - CRABES À LA BRETONNE * CRUSTACÉS

Photo Crab Breton-style.

CRAB - BRETON STYLE * SHELLFISH
INGREDIENTS: crabs. For the stock: bouquet garni, chopped carrots, onions, vinegar.
RECIPE: the crabs are plunged live into the very hot court bouillon then served cold with mayonnaise.

230 - CRABES FARCIS * CRUSTACÉS

Photo Stuffed crabs.

STUFFED CRABS * SHELLFISH
INGREDIENTS: crab. For the stuffing: lean bacon, bread soaked in milk, lemon, shallots, garlic, butter, curry, chilli powder.
RECIPE: the crab is cooked in court bouillon stock, the flesh mixed with the stuffing ingredients, put back into the shell and sprinkled with breadcrumbs to be browned under the grill. Served hot.

231 - CRÈME D'ASPERGES * POTAGE

Photo Cream of asparagus soup.

CREAM OF ASPARAGUS * SOUP
INGREDIENTS: asparagus tips, chicken stock, milk or water, butter, flour, nutmeg.
RECIPE: the asparagus are cooked for 12' in the stock, the flour added with the milk and then the cream. Served hot.

232 - CRÈME AUX CÈPES * POTAGE

Photo Cream of cep mushroom soup.

CREAM OF CEP MUSHROOM * SOUP
INGREDIENTS: ceps, butter, cream, poultry stock.
See Recipe 231, the asparagus is replaced with cep mushrooms.

233 - CRÈME ANGLAISE * DESSERT

Photo Floating islands with custard sauce.

CUSTARD SAUCE * DESSERT
INGREDIENTS: eggs, sugar, milk, vanilla pod.
RECIPE: the ingredients are cooked. Served cold.

234 - CRÈME BRÛLÉE * DESSERT

Photo Crème brûlée.

CRÈME BRÛLÉE * DESSERT
INGREDIENTS: egg yolks, caster sugar and icing sugar, milk, single cream, vanilla pod.
RECIPE: the yolks are beaten with the vanilla seeds, the milk is added followed by the cream. It is cooked in a bain marie in the oven in small dishes. When cold, the top is sprinkled with sugar and browned under the grill. Served cold.

235 - CRÈME CARAMEL * DESSERT

Photo Caramel cream.

CARAMEL CREAM * DESSERT
INGREDIENTS: made with whole eggs, extra yolks, sugar and milk.
RECIPE: the ingredients are mixed and cooked, caramel poured into the bottom of the pot before the hot preparation is poured in and then allowed to cool. Served cold.

236 - CRÈME DE CAROTTES * POTAGE

Photo Cream of carrot soup.

CREAM OF CARROT * SOUP
INGREDIENTS: carrots, onions, garlic, egg yolk, butter, single cream, poultry stock, flour, curry powder, ginger, chives
RECIPE: the ingredients are browned then blended and cooked in the poultry stock. A cream and egg yolk mixture is added at the last minute. Served hot.

237 - CRÈME DE CÉLERI * POTAGE

Photo *Cream of celery soup.*

CREAM OF CELERY * SOUP
INGREDIENTS: celeriac, chopped walnuts possible, butter, milk, single cream, lemon, flour.
RECIPE: the celery is cooked separately and pureed, the other ingredients are mixed and cooked, the cream is whipped and added to the bowl when served. Served hot.

238 - CRÈME DE CHAMPIGNONS * POTAGE

Photo *Cream of mushroom soup.*

CREAM OF MUSHROOM * SOUP
INGREDIENTS: for the preparation: cultivated mushrooms, onion, butter. For the sauce: cream, poultry stock, flour, parsley.
RECIPE: The preparation ingredients are cooked separately from the sauce. The two preparations are added to the cream. Served hot.

239 - CRÈME CHANTILLY * DESSERT

Photo *Whipped cream.*

WHIPPED CREAM * DESSERT
INGREDIENTS: cream, sugar and vanilla sugar.
RECIPE: all the ingredients are whipped with a whisk until a frothy, firm preparation is obtained. To decorate cakes, cream desserts, ice cream, fruit salad. Was on the table of King Louis XIV. Served cold.

240 - CRÈME CHIBOUTZ * PÂTISSERIE

Photo *Chiboutz custard cream.*

CHIBOUTZ CUSTARD CREAM * CAKE
INGREDIENTS: milk, sugar, eggs, flour, vanilla pod and sheet of gelatine. Custard cream (see n° 243).
RECIPE: the pastry cream is cooked with the gelatine, the sugar and water are cooked, the egg whites whipped stiffly and the cooked sugar incorporated. This meringue preparation is added to the cold pastry cream.

241 - CRÈME DE MOULES * MOLLUSQUES - POTAGE RECETTE BRETONNE

Photo Mussel cream soup.

MUSSEL CREAM SOUP * A BRETON DISH
INGREDIENTS: basic preparation: small mussels, butter, chopped shallots, wine, onions, fish stock, cream, flour. For the garnish: dry bread, a little lemon juice, chives.
RECIPE: the basic ingredients are cooked and mixed. Served hot with diced toasted bread; the mussels are served separately with croutons.

242 - CRÈME CATALANE * DESSERT

Photo Catalan cream.

CATALAN CREAM * DESSERT
INGREDIENTS: for the basic preparation: milk, cinnamon, orange and lemon zest, vanilla pod. For the mixture: egg, caster sugar, egg yolk, flour.
RECIPE: the basic preparation is cooked and added to the other mixture which is then cooked and put into small dishes. Served cold.

243 - CRÈME PÂTISSIÈRE * DESSERT

Photo Custard cream.

CUSTARD CREAM * DESSERT
INGREDIENTS: basic preparation: sugar, egg yolks. For the mixture: milk, flour.
RECIPE: the preparation ingredients are mixed, added to the mixture and cooked until thick. Used for éclairs and choux pastries, etc.

244 - CRÈME RENVERSÉE * DESSERT

Photo Cooked cream.

COOKED CREAM * DESSERT
INGREDIENTS: ingredients: for the preparation: milk, sugar. For the mixture: eggs, egg yolk.
RECIPE: the preparation ingredients are heated, then mixed with the mixture ingredients and baked in a bain marie for 45'. Served cold.

245 - CRÊPES AU JAMBON * ENTRÉE

Photo Ham pancakes.

HAM PANCAKES * STARTER
INGREDIENTS: for the batter: flour, eggs, milk. To garnish: ham, Bechamel sauce and mushrooms.
RECIPE: all the ingredients are mixed. The batter is left to rest and small amounts used to cook pancakes in the pan which are then filled with ham or mushrooms. Served hot.

246 - CRÊPES SUCRÉES * DESSERT

Photo Sweet pancakes.

SWEET PANCAKES * DESSERT
INGREDIENTS AND RECIPE: flour, eggs, mixed milk. A ladle of batter is cooked in the pan and the pancake sprinkled with sugar. Served hot.

247 - CRÊPES AU CHOCOLAT * DESSERT

Photo Chocolate pancakes.

CHOCOLATE PANCAKES * DESSERT
See above recipe. The panpastrys are filled with melted chocolate. Served hot.

248 - CRÊPES FLAMBÉES AU CALVADOS * DESSERT

Photo Pancakes flamed in Calvados.

PANCAKES FLAMED IN CALVADOS
* DESSERT
INGREDIENTS: see ingredients for "sweet pancakes".
RECIPE: the pancakes are cooked over a high heat, then filled with apples cooked with cinnamon, butter and a little Calvados applejack brandy and next flamed in Calvados. Served hot.

249 - CRÊPE DE POMMES DE TERRE * LÉGUMES

Photo Potato pancakes.

POTATO PANCAKES * VEGETABLES
INGREDIENTS: potatoes, onions, flour, eggs.
RECIPE: the potatoes are grated and mixed with the flour, eggs and onions then cooked in a pan and served hot.

250 - CRÊPES SUZETTE * DESSERT

Photo Flamed pancakes.

FLAMED PANCAKES * DESSERT
INGREDIENTS: hot pancakes. To garnish: juice: orange and lemon, zest of orange, sugar, butter, Grand Marnier liqueur.
RECIPE: the butter and sugar is caramelised, the juice and pancakes are added and flamed in Grand Marnier. Served hot.

251 - CRÉPINETTES AU VIN * CHARCUTERIE

Photo Faggots cooked in wine.

FAGGOTS COOKED IN WINE * COOKED MEATS AND SIMILAR
INGREDIENTS: sausage meat. For the preparation: shallots. For the stuffing: wine, foie gras, calf's caul.
RECIPE: the preparation ingredients are cooked, mixed with the other ingredients and formed into small cakes that are wrapped in the caul and cooked in a pan for 6'. Served hot.

252 - CRESSON * LÉGUMES

Photo Watercress.

WATERCRESS * VEGETABLES

253 - CREVETTES MAYONNAISE * CRUSTACÉS

Photo Prawns with mayonnaise.

PRAWNS WITH MAYONNAISE * SHELLFISH
INGREDIENTS AND RECIPE: cooked prawns served with mayonnaise. Served cold.

CRI

254 - CRIQUE DE POMMES DE TERRE * LÉGUMES

Photo Large potato cake.

LARGE POTATO CAKE * VEGETABLES
INGREDIENTS: eggs, potatoes, butter, milk.
RECIPE: the potatoes are peeled, grated and mixed with beaten egg and milk. Cooked in butter. Served hot.

CRO

255 - CROISSANT AU JAMBON * ENTRÉE

Photo Ham croissant.

HAM CROISSANT * STARTER
INGREDIENTS: for the flaky pastry: flour, butter, water; rolled and folded several times. For the filling: white sauce, ham, grated Gruyere cheese.
RECIPE: the filling is inserted before baking. Served hot.

256 - CROISSANT * PÂTISSERIE

Photo Croissant.

CROISSANT * PASTRY
INGREDIENTS AND RECIPE: see N° 255 for the pastry. Served cold.

257 - CROQUE-MONSIEUR * ENTRÉE

Photo Ham and cheese on toast.

HAM AND CHEESE ON TOAST * STARTER
INGREDIENTS: sliced bread, ham, grated cheese, white sauce.
RECIPE: ham and cheese between two slices of bread, topped with white sauce and cheese and then browned. Served hot.

258 - CROQUE-MADAME * ENTRÉE

Photo Ham and cheese on toast with an egg.

HAM AND CHEESE ON TOAST WITH AN EGG * STARTER
INGREDIENTS AND RECIPE: see N° 257, a fried egg is added. Served hot.

259 - CROQUETTES DE MAÏS * LÉGUMES

Photo Sweetcorn croquettes.

SWEETCORN CROQUETTES * VEGETABLES
INGREDIENTS: potatoes, eggs, oil, sweetcorn, breadcrumbs.
RECIPE: the potatoes are cooked and mashed. The egg and sweetcorn are added and formed into squares that are dipped into egg yolk and breadcrumbs and cooked in hot oil. Served hot.

260 - CROQUETTES DE POMMES DE TERRE * LÉGUMES

Photo Potato croquette.

POTATO CROQUETTE * VEGETABLES
INGREDIENTS AND RECIPE: see N° 259 without the sweetcorn. Served hot.

261 - CROUSTADE DE FRUITS DE MER * POISSON

Photo Seafood in pastry.

SEAFOOD IN PASTRY * FISH
INGREDIENTS: for the flaky pastry: flour, water, butter. To garnish: salmon, peeled shrimps or prawns, cultivated mushrooms, shallots, butter, egg, cream, fish stock.
RECIPE: the ingredients are browned in butter and cooked in the oven in the pastry. Served hot.

262 - CROÛTES AU FROMAGE OU PAYSANNE * ENTRÉE

Photo Goat's cheese and figs on French stick.

HOT CHEESE FRENCH STICK SNACKS * STARTER
INGREDIENTS: buttered French stick.
RECIPE: the filling (meat, etc.) is baked in the oven for 5' on the baguette and the cheese added for a further 3'. Served hot.

263 - CROÛTONS ET SA ROUILLE * SAUCE

Photo Croutons and garlic saffron sauce.

CROUTONS AND GARLIC SAFFRON * SAUCE
See n° 800. Served cold.

CRU

264 - CRUMBLE * DESSERT ANGLAIS - FRUITS

Photo Apple crumble.

CRUMBLE * AN ENGLISH FRUIT DESSERT
INGREDIENTS: apples or red fruit. For the topping: butter, sugar, flour, water and cinnamon.
RECIPE: the topping is mixed roughly with a fork, spread over the fruit and then baked. Served hot or warm.

265 - CUISSE DE CANARD CONFITE * VOLAILLE

Photo Leg of duck.

PRESERVED LEG OF DUCK * POULTRY
INGREDIENTS: the duck is cooked in pork lard for 2 hours.
RECIPE: each piece covered with fat is reheated. Served hot.

266 - CUISSES DE GRENOUILLES À LA PROVENÇALE

Photo Provençal frog's legs.

PROVENÇAL FROG'S LEGS
INGREDIENTS: frog's legs, butter, garlic, parsley.
RECIPE: the frog's legs are rolled in flour and sautéed in oil with garlic and parsley. Served hot.

CUL

267 - CUL DE VEAU À LA CASSEROLE * VIANDE - SPÉCIALITÉ D'ANJOU

CASSEROLED THICK END OF VEAL LOIN
AN ANJOU MEAT SPECIALITY
INGREDIENTS: boned thick end of veal loin, butter, carrot, onion. For the sauce: veal stock, cream. For the garnish: small onions, butter, lemon. To cook: carrots, mushrooms, cream.
RECIPE: the meat is cooked in the oven. The garnish ingredients are cooked separately, the dish put together and served hot.

CUR

268 - CURRY D'AGNEAU * VIANDE

Photo Lamb curry.

LAMB CURRY * MEAT
INGREDIENTS: shoulder of lamb, tomatoes, onions, garlic, ginger, turmeric, cumin, coriander, ground cinnamon, cardamom.
RECIPE: the spices are heated in hot oil, followed by the meat and cooked for 1 hour. Served hot.

269 - DARIOLES DE CAROTTES * LÉGUMES

Photo Potted carrots.

POTTED CARROTS * VEGETABLES
INGREDIENTS: carrots, eggs, butter, cream, veal stock, nutmeg.
RECIPE: the carrots are cooked in butter with the stock, sugar and nutmeg. The preparation is blended with eggs and cream and then put into ramekins and cooked for 25'. Served hot.

270 - DARIOLES DE BROCOLIS * LÉGUMES

Photo Potted broccoli.

POTTED BROCCOLI * VEGETABLES
INGREDIENTS AND RECIPE: see N° 269, the carrots are replaced with broccoli. Served hot.

271 - DARNE DE SAUMON GRILLÉE * POISSON

Photo Salmon steak with spinach.

GRILLED SALMON STEAK * FISH
INGREDIENTS: salmon steak with bone
RECIPE: the steak is brushed with oil and grilled. Served hot.

272 - DAUBE DE BŒUF PROVENÇALE * VIANDE SPÉCIALITÉ DE PROVENCE

Photo Provençal stewed beef.

PROVENÇAL STEWED BEEF - A SPECIALITY FROM PROVENCE * MEAT
INGREDIENTS: pieces of beef, a calf's foot, bard, chopped carrots, onions and tomatoes, olives, sliced orange, oil, garlic, bouquet garni, red wine.
RECIPE: the meat is browned and the wine added with all the vegetables and herbs and cooked for 4 hours. Served hot.

273 - DAUBE BÉARNAISE * VIANDE - SPÉCIALITÉ DU BÉARN

Photo Béarn stewed beef.

BEARN STEWED BEEF - A BÉARN SPECIALITY * MEAT
INGREDIENTS: pieces of stewing beef (rump or boned blade), small onions, carrots, lard, bard. For the marinade: shallots, garlic, bouquet garni, red wine, for the garnish: Bayonne raw ham.
RECIPE: the meat is marinated for 12 hours with the ingredients; the garnish is added and the stew cooked for 4 hours in a special dish called a "daubière" or stewpot. Served hot.

DEM

274 - DEMOISELLES DE CHERBOURG * CRUSTACÉS SPÉCIALITÉ DE NORMANDIE

NORMANDY LOBSTERS * SHELLFISH
INGREDIENTS: small lobsters weighing 500 gr each. For the coral butter: butter, cream, shallots, tomatoes, tarragon.
RECIPE: the coral is blended with the butter. The other ingredients are added and the lobsters grilled. Served hot with the sauce handed separately.

DOR

275 - DORADE ROYALE AU FOUR * POISSON

Photo Baked gilthead sea bream.

BAKED GILTHEAD SEA BREAM * FISH
INGREDIENTS AND RECIPE: the fish is brushed with olive oil and grilled for 10'. Served hot.

276 - DORADE EN PAPILLOTE * POISSON

Photo Sea bream baked in a foil case.

SEA BREAM IN A FOIL CASE * FISH
INGREDIENTS: fillet of sea bream, onions, leeks, garlic, olive oil.
RECIPE: the fillet is cooked for 15' in a closed foil case with all the ingredients. Served hot.

DOS

276-1 - DOS DE CABILLAUD * POISSON

Photo Cod back.

COD BACK * FISH
INGREDIENTS AND RECIPE: the cod back is cooked in the butter. Served hot.

DUX

277 - DUXELLE DE CHAMPIGNONS * LÉGUMES

Photo Chopped mushroom and onion mixture.

CHOPPED MUSHROOM AND ONION MIXTURE * VEGETABLES
INGREDIENTS: chopped mushrooms, lemon, chopped shallots and onions, oil, butter. For the presentation: cream
RECIPE: the shallots and mushrooms are cooked in the butter and cream added. Served hot.

ECH

278 - ÉCHINE DE PORC CONFITE * VIANDE

Photo Braised pork chine.

BRAISED PORK CHINE * MEAT
INGREDIENTS AND RECIPE: the chine is cooked in the oven for 1 hour with oil and onions. Served hot or cold.

279 - ÉCHALOTE, OIGNON, AROMATES

Photo Shallots, onions, herbs and spices.

SHALLOTS – ONIONS

ECL

280 - ÉCLAIRS * PÂTISSERIE

Photo Coffee and chocolate éclairs.

ÉCLAIRS * CAKES
INGREDIENTS: choux pastry (flour, butter and sugar are added to boiling milk, quickly mixed and egg yolks added)
RECIPE: this cake is baked then filled with custard cream flavoured to choice. The top is iced (icing sugar and water) with the same flavour as the inside of the éclair. Served cold.

ECR

281 - ÉCREVISSES À L'ANETH * CRUSTACÉS

Photo Crayfish with toast.

CRAYFISH WITH DILL * SHELLFISH
INGREDIENTS AND RECIPE: the live crayfish are cooked until red in salted boiling water with dill seed and allowed to marinate in the cooking juices for 12 hours. Served cold with dill.

282 - ÉCREVISSES À LA BORDELAISE * CRUSTACÉS

Photo Crayfish Bordeaux style.

CRAYFISH BORDEAUX STYLE * SHELLFISH
INGREDIENTS: crayfish. For the preparation: ham, onions, carrots, butter, flour, dry white wine, a little spirit liqueur, bouquet garni.
RECIPE: the preparation ingredients are cooked together. The crayfish are cooked until they turn red then served hot, covered with the cooking juices.

EGL

283 - ÉGLEFIN EN FILET * POISSON

Photo Pan-fried fillet of haddock.

FILLET OF HADDOCK * FISH
INGREDIENTS: to cook: haddock, lemon, lean bacon, wine, butter. For the sauce: cream, parsley, chives, onion.
RECIPE: the haddock fillets are cooked with the ingredients. Served hot with the sauce added as they are served.

284 - ÉGLEFIN AU FOUR * POISSON

Photo Baked haddock.

BAKED HADDOCK * FISH
INGREDIENTS AND RECIPE: a tail of haddock, lemon juice, sprig of dill, bacon, paprika, wine baked for 45'. Tomatoes are added. Served hot.

EMI

285 - ÉMINCÉ D'AGNEAU AU RIZ PILAF * VIANDE

Photo Slivers of lamb.

SLIVERS OF LAMB WITH PILAFF RICE * MEAT
INGREDIENTS: slivers of lamb. To cook: chopped tomatoes, onions and garlic, olive oil, full-bodied red wine, meat stock, paprika, nutmeg.
RECIPE: the meat is sautéed in the oil with the cooking ingredients. Served hot.

286 - ÉMINCÉ DE DINDE AU CURRY * VIANDE

Photo Turkey slivers in curry sauce.

TURKEY SLIVERS IN CURRY SAUCE * POULTRY
INGREDIENTS: fillet of turkey cut into slivers, onion, flour, cocoa butter, bunch of herbs. For the sauce: veal stock (chervil, tarragon, parsley), capers, curry, cream.
RECIPE: the strips are rolled in flour and then cooked with the onion. The prepared sauce is added. Served hot.

287 - ÉMINCÉ DE VOLAILLE DE BRESSE * VOLAILLE

Photo Chicken slivers with mushrooms.

CHICKEN SLIVERS WITH WILD MUSHROOMS * POULTRY
INGREDIENTS: chicken cut into slivers. For the sauce: onion, flour, cream, wine, meat stock, parsley, mushrooms.
RECIPE: the ingredients are cooked together to coat the chicken cooked separately. Served hot.

ENC

288 - ENCHAUD * VIANDE - SPÉCIALITÉ DE RÔTI DE PORC DU PÉRIGORD

Photo Preserved pork.

PRESERVED PORK - A ROAST PORK SPECIALITY FROM PÉRIGORD * MEAT
INGREDIENTS: fillet of pork, pig's feet, pork fat, garlic, carrots, celeriac, bouquet garni, onions, stock, thyme, bay leaf, parsley.
RECIPE: the fillet is rubbed with salt, studded with garlic and left for 48 hours; it is then wiped, rolled, tied with string, cooked for 2 hours in lard and then refrigerated for 15 days. Served cold sliced.

288-1 - ENCORNETS FARCIS * MOLLUSQUES

Photo Stuffed squid.

STUFFED SQUID * FISH
See N°119. Served hot.

END

289 - ENDIVES BRAISÉES * LÉGUMES

Photo Braised chicory.

BRAISED CHICORY * VEGETABLES
INGREDIENTS: chicory. To cook: butter, oil.
RECIPE: the chicory is cooked. Served hot.

290 - ENDIVES AU JAMBON * LÉGUMES

Photo Baked chicory with ham.

CHICORY WITH HAM * VEGETABLES
INGREDIENTS: chicory, ham, butter, flour, milk.
RECIPE: the chicory is cooked then rolled in a slice of ham, coated with white sauce and topped with grated cheese to brown. Served hot.

291 - ENDIVES EN SALADE * ENTRÉE

Photo Chicory salad with hard-boiled eggs.

CHICORY SALAD * STARTER
Served cold.

ENT

292 - ENTRECÔTE BERCY * VIANDE

Photo Rib steak with shallot sauce.

RIB STEAK WITH SHALLOT SAUCE * MEAT
INGREDIENTS: rib steak, oil, for the Bercy. Butter sauce: wine, shallots, butter, parsley, bone marrow, lemon. Ingredients: bunch of watercress.
RECIPE: the bone marrow, meat and ingredients are cooked separately. Served hot.

293 - ENTRECÔTE À LA BORDELAISE OU MARCHAND DE VIN * VIANDE

Photo Rib steak with red wine sauce.

RIB STEAK WITH RED WINE SAUCE * MEAT
INGREDIENTS: rib steak. For the sauce: shallots, butter, flour, red wine, meat stock.
RECIPE: the steak is grilled, coated with the sauce and served hot.

294 - ENTRECÔTE MAÎTRE D'HÔTEL * VIANDE

Photo Rib steak with parsley butter.

RIB STEAK WITH PARSLEY BUTTER * MEAT
INGREDIENTS: rib steak, butter.
RECIPE: a mixture of butter and parsley is served on top of the hot steak.

295 - ÉPAULE D'AGNEAU ROULÉE * VIANDE

Photo Rolled shoulder of lamb.

ROLLED SHOULDER OF LAMB * MEAT
INGREDIENTS: boned shoulder of lamb. For the rub: garlic, olive oil, chopped marjory, oregano, thyme. For the sauce: white wine, meat stock, cream.
RECIPE: all the rub ingredients are mixed and worked into the meat before it is rolled and cooked in the oven. Served hot with the sauce.

296 - ÉPAULE D'AGNEAU RÔTIE * VIANDE

Photo Roast shoulder of lamb.

ROAST SHOULDER OF LAMB * MEAT
INGREDIENTS: shoulder, tomatoes, onion, garlic, rosemary, thyme.
RECIPE: the shoulder is studded with garlic and cooked in the oven with all the other ingredients. Served hot.

297 - ÉPAULE D'AGNEAU CONFITE OU AGNEAU DE 11 HEURES * VIANDE

Photo 11-hour lamb.

BRAISED SHOULDER OF LAMB
OR 11-HOUR LAMB * MEAT
INGREDIENTS: shoulder, oil, thyme.
RECIPE: the shoulder is brushed with oil and cooked very slowly in the oven. Served hot.

298 - ÉPERLANS FRITS * POISSON

Photo Fried smelts.

FRIED SMELTS * FISH
INGREDIENTS: smelts, flour.
RECIPE: the smelts are fried in oil and served hot.

EPI

299 - ÉPINARDS À LA CRÈME * LÉGUMES

Photo Creamed spinach.

CREAMED SPINACH * VEGETABLES
INGREDIENTS: spinach, cream.
RECIPE: the spinach is steamed and then reheated with the cream.

300 - ÉPINARDS AUX FOIES DE VOLAILLE * ABATS

Photo Poultry livers on a bed of salad.

SPINACH WITH POULTRY LIVERS * OFFAL
INGREDIENTS: spinach, poultry livers, bread, butter. For the sauce: olive oil, parsley.
RECIPE: the livers are browned in butter and served on spinach salad with the sauce. Served hot and cold.

ESC

301 - ESCALOPES DE FOIE GRAS POÊLÉ * ABATS

Photo Pan-fried foie gras with grapes.

PAN-FRIED FOIE GRAS ESCALOPES * OFFAL
INGREDIENTS: slices of foie gras, flour.
RECIPE: the floured escalopes are cooked quickly over a high heat and served immediately.

302 - ESCALOPES DE FOIE GRAS POÊLÉ AUX ABRICOTS ET PAIN D'ÉPICES * ABATS

Photo Pan-fried foie gras escalopes with apricots and gingerbread.

PAN-FRIED FOIE GRAS ESCALOPES WITH APRICOTS AND GINGERBREAD * OFFAL
Served hot and cold.

303 - ESCALOPE DE VEAU À LA CRÈME * VIANDE

Photo Veal escalope with cream and mushrooms.

VEAL ESCALOPE WITH CREAM SAUCE * MEAT

INGREDIENTS: escalopes, cultivated mushrooms. For the sauce: cream, butter, cooking juices.

RECIPE: the escalope and mushrooms are cooked separately, the sauce added and served hot.

304 - ESCALOPE VIENNOISE OU PANÉE * VIANDE

Photo Breaded veal escalope.

BREADED VEAL ESCALOPE * MEAT

INGREDIENTS: veal escalope, lemon, breadcrumbs, egg, butter, oil.

RECIPE: the escalope is dipped in beaten egg and breadcrumbs and then cooked. Served hot.

305 - ESCALOPE DE VEAU POÊLÉE * VIANDE

Photo Pan-fried veal escalope.

PAN-FRIED VEAL ESCALOPE * MEAT

INGREDIENTS: veal escalope, butter, oil.

RECIPE: the escalope is cooked in the fat. Served hot.

306 - ESCALOPE CORDON BLEU * VIANDE

Photo Stuffed breaded escalopes.

STUFFED BREADED ESCALOPES * MEAT

INGREDIENTS: veal escalopes, smoked bacon, Emmenthal cheese, eggs, breadcrumbs, parsley, paprika.

RECIPE: a slice of bacon, Emmenthal cheese and paprika are laid on the escalopes before folding over. The escalopes are dipped in beaten egg and breadcrumbs and then cooked. Served hot.

307 - ESCALOPE DE VEAU À LA COMTOISE * VIANDE

Photo Veal escalopes with cheese and brandy cream.

VEAL ESCALOPE WITH CHEESE AND BRANDY CREAM SAUCE * MEAT

INGREDIENTS: veal escalopes, butter, flour. For the garnish: mushrooms, Comté cheese, ham. For the sauce: cream, brandy, port.

RECIPE: the escalopes are dipped in flour, cooked with the mushrooms and flamed in brandy. Port and cream is added. They are then cooked in the oven with a slice of Comté and ham on the top. Served hot.

308 - ESCARGOTS À LA PÉRIGOURDINE

Photo Snails with Périgord stuffing.

SNAILS WITH PERIGORD STUFFING

INGREDIENTS: precooked Burgundy snails, raw ham, preserved goose or duck, walnuts, shallots, garlic, butter and parsley.

RECIPE: the ham, preserved goose or duck and walnuts are finely chopped and added to the butter, parsley, garlic and shallots. A snail is placed in each shell, stuffed with a little of the mixture and cooked for 10' in the oven. Served hot.

309 - ESCARGOTS DE BOURGOGNE - SPÉCIALITÉ FRANÇAISE

Photo Burgundy snails.

BURGUNDY SNAILS, A FRENCH SPECIALITY

INGREDIENTS: snails. For the stuffing: the butter, garlic and parsley is mashed together with a fork.

RECIPE: the snail is placed in a shell with the stuffing, refrigerated and then cooked in the oven and served hot.

310 - ESCARGOTS PETITS GRIS AU PERSIL ET À LA FONDUE DE TOMATE

Photo Brown snails with parsley and tomato.

BROWN SNAILS WITH PARSLEY AND TOMATO

INGREDIENTS: fresh snails, parsley, garlic, shallots, cream, butter, diced tomato.

RECIPE: for the parsley cream: the tomatoes are cooked and the blended cream and parsley added. The snails are cooked in the pan with the shallots and butter, then placed in small moulds with the parsley cream. Served hot.

EST

311 - ESTOUFFADE PROVENÇALE - RECETTE DE LA RÉGION DE PROVENCE * VIANDE

Photo Provençal beef and tomato stew.

PROVENCAL BEEF AND TOMATO STEW
* A PROVENÇAL MEAT DISH
INGREDIENTS: cubed beef, flour, oil, white wine. Vegetables: onions, carrots, garlic. For the garnish: fresh tomatoes, green olives, diced bacon, garlic, butter.
RECIPE: the ingredients are cooked for 2 hours 30 mins and the tomatoes cooked with garlic and olives added at the end of the cooking time. Served hot.

312 - ESTRAGON FRAIS * PLANTE AROMATIQUE

Photo Fresh tarragon.

FRESH TARRAGON * HERB

ETR

313 - ÉTRILLES * CRUSTACÉS

VELVET SWIMCRABS * SHELLFISH
Atlantic shore crab, 6 cm long.

EVE

314 - ÉVENTAIL

Photo Éventail.

ÉVENTAIL – FAN
Food presented in the form of an open Spanish fan.

FAI

315 - FAISAN À LA CHOUCROUTE * GIBIER

Photo Pheasant with sauerkraut.

PHEASANT WITH SAUERKRAUT * GAME

INGREDIENTS: pheasant. To cook: raw sauerkraut (fermented cabbage cut into strips), apple, garlic, carrots, onions, goose fat, pork bard, quince jelly, orange zest, dry white wine, poultry stock, bouquet garni, juniper berries, cloves, cinnamon.

RECIPE: the ingredients simmer for 2 hours 15 mins and the pheasant then added to finish cooking in the oven. Served hot.

FAL

316 - FALUE - RECETTE DE LA RÉGION DE NORMANDIE * PÂTISSERIE

Photo Brioche bun from the Normandy region.

BRIOCHE BUN FROM THE NORMANDY REGION * CAKE

INGREDIENTS: flour, butter, cream, eggs, yeast, sugar.

RECIPE: all the ingredients are mixed then left to prove before dividing up the dough and baking. Served cold.

FAR

317 - FAR BRETON * PÂTISSERIE DE BRETAGNE

Photo Butter cake with prunes and raisins.

BUTTER CAKE - A SPECIALITY FROM BRITTANY

INGREDIENTS: for the mixture: flour, butter, sugar, milk, eggs. Garnish: vanilla sugar, Malaga raisins prunes.

RECIPE: the ingredients are mixed and then added to the garnish and cooked together. Served cold or warm.

318 - FAR DU POITOU * LÉGUMES

Photo Poitou stuffed cabbage or lettuce.

POITOU STUFFED CABBAGE OR LETTUCE * VEGETABLES

INGREDIENTS: for the chopped vegetable: lettuce, sorrel, green cabbage and spinach leaves, bacon, vegetable stock, parsley and chervil. For the stuffing: breadcrumbs, eggs, cream. RECIPE: All the green vegetables are chopped and mixed with the herbs, the stuffing prepared and then mixed with the vegetables. A little stuffing is placed on cabbage and lettuce leaves that are closed like a bag and cooked in a pot in vegetable stock for 4 hours. Served hot.

319 - FAR AUX PRUNEAUX * PÂTISSERIE

Photo Butter cake with prunes.

BUTTER CAKE WITH PRUNES * CAKE
INGREDIENTS: for the shortcrust pastry: flour, butter, sugar, eggs. For the filling: eggs, butter, flour, milk, cream, lemon zest, vanilla pod, prunes (dried plums).
RECIPE: the rich shortcrust is prepared, then the filling. Baked for 50'. Served warm or cold topped.

FAU

320 - FAUX-FILET SAUCE AU POIVRE * VIANDE

Photo Sirloin steak with pepper sauce.

SIRLOIN STEAK WITH PEPPER SAUCE * MEAT
INGREDIENTS: sirloin steak, peppercorns. For the pepper sauce: butter, flour, cream.
RECIPE: the peppercorns are sauteed in butter and cream added. The steak is cooked separately. Served hot.

321 - FAUX-FILET MARCHAND DE VIN * VIANDE

Photo Sirloin steak with red wine sauce.

SIRLOIN STEAK WITH RED WINE SAUCE * MEAT
INGREDIENTS: sirloin steak, oil. For the sauce: shallots, butter, full-bodied red wine, meat stock, flour, parsley.
RECIPE: the sauce is prepared and cooked separately to coat the cooked steak. Served hot.

FEN

322 - FENOUIL À LA VAPEUR COULIS DE TOMATE * LÉGUMES

Photo Fennel with tomato sauce.

STEAMED FENNEL WITH TOMATO SAUCE * VEGETABLES
INGREDIENTS: fennel bulb, tomato.
RECIPE: the fennel is steamed and served hot with a tomato sauce.

FET

323 - FETTUCINE ALLA CARBONARA * PÂTES - SPÉCIALITÉ ITALIENNE

Photo Ribbon noodles with cream and bacon sauce.

RIBBON PASTA WITH CREAM AND BACON SAUCE - AN ITALIAN SPECIALITY * PASTA
INGREDIENTS: Italian pasta, diced bacon, egg yolk, cream, grated Italian Parmesan cheese, parsley.
RECIPE: the pasta is boiled, the bacon cooked and mixed together with cream, herbs and Parmesan. An egg yolk is placed in its shell. Served hot.

FEU

324 - FEUILLES DE CHÊNE OU SALADE AUX FOIES DE VOLAILLE * ABATS

Photo Poultry livers salad.

POULTRY LIVERS WITH OAK LEAF OR OTHER LETTUCE * OFFAL
INGREDIENTS: lettuce, poultry livers, butter. To season: garlic, cider vinegar, oil.
RECIPE: the livers are browned. The seasoning is mixed and served with the hot livers.

325 - FEUILLES DE VIGNE * LÉGUMES - SPÉCIALITÉ GRECQUE

Photo Stuffed vine leaves.

STUFFED VINE LEAVES - A GREEK SPECIALITY * STARTER
INGREDIENTS: fresh vine leaves. To cook: lemons, sprigs of coriander, chicken stock, olive oil. For the stuffing: minced shoulder of lamb, rice, onion, chopped mint, olive oil, nutmeg, cinnamon.
RECETTE: the rice, onion and meat are sautéed in oil and then the other ingredients added and cooked; the leaves are stuffed, rolled and cooked further. Served cold.

326 - FEUILLETÉ D'ASPERGES * ENTRÉE

Photo Asparagus in pastry.

ASPARAGUS IN PASTRY * STARTER
INGREDIENTS: pastry: flour, butter, water, filling: cooked asparagus. Sauce: cream.
RECIPE: the pastry is made with the ingredients, left to rest and folded over several times before baking with the asparagus in the middle. Served hot.

327 - FEUILLETÉ AU CHÈVRE * ENTRÉE

Photo Goat's cheese in pastry.

GOAT'S CHEESE IN PASTRY * STARTER

INGREDIENTS: flaky pastry, small goat's cheeses, thyme.

RECIPE: a cheese is enclosed in pastry squares with a few sprigs of thyme and baked in the oven. Served hot.

328 - FEUILLETÉ AU JAMBON ET AUX CHAMPIGNONS * ENTRÉE

Photo Ham and mushrooms in pastry.

HAM AND MUSHROOMS IN PASTRY * STARTER

INGREDIENTS: flaky pastry, ham, cultivated mushrooms, egg yolk, oil. For the cheese sauce: milk, butter, flour, eggs, grated Comté cheese.

RECIPE: the sauce is prepared and cooked with all the other ingredients. The flaky pastry is divided to form several layers alternating the sauce, ham and mushrooms, then cooked. Served hot.

329 - FEUILLETÉ AU ROQUEFORT * ENTRÉE

Photo Roquefort cheese in pastry.

ROQUEFORT CHEESE IN PASTRY * STARTER

INGREDIENTS: flaky pastry, Roquefort cheese (see Roquefort n° 929), cream.

RECIPE: the cheese is mashed with a fork with the cream and placed in the centre of a square of pastry which is closed, baked and served hot with a green salad.

330 - FEUILLETÉ À LA SAUCISSE * ENTRÉE

Photo Mini sausage roll.

SAUSAGE ROLL * STARTER

INGREDIENTS: flaky pastry, small Strasbourg sausages.

RECIPE: small pieces of sausage are enclosed in a square of flaky pastry and baked in the oven. Served hot.

331 - FEUILLETÉ À LA VIANDE * ENTRÉE

Photo Meat in pastry.

MEAT IN PASTRY * STARTER
INGREDIENTS: flaky pastry, minced beef, cultivated mushrooms, tomatoes, onions, Parmesan cheese, lemon, egg yolk, thyme.
RECIPE: the ingredients are all mixed and then placed in the centre of a square of pastry. Served hot.

FEV

332 - FÈVES FRAÎCHES EN SALADE * LÉGUMES

Photo Broad bean.

FRESH BROAD BEAN SALAD
* VEGETABLES
INGREDIENTS AND RECIPE: the broad beans are boiled, seasoned with olive oil, yoghurt, lemon juice, shallots and herbs, served cold.

333 - FÈVES EN PURÉE * LÉGUMES

Photo Broad bean puree.

BROAD BEAN PUREE * VEGETABLES
INGREDIENTS: broad beans. To cook: vegetable broth. For the puree: sprig of savory, butter, cream, parsley, nutmeg.
RECIPE: the beans are cooked in the stock, pureed and mixed with the other ingredients. Served hot.

FIC

334 - FICELLE PICARDE * ENTRÉE

Photo Picardy pancake.

PICARDY PANCAKE * STARTER
INGREDIENTS: pancake batter, flour, egg, milk. For the white sauce: butter, flour, milk. For the filling: mushrooms, shallots, slices of ham, cream. For the topping: butter, grated cheese.
RECIPE: the pancake batter is prepared. The filling ingredients are cooked and each pancake filled with the sauce and baked in the oven. Served hot.

335 - FILET DE BŒUF EN CROÛTE * VIANDE

Photo Beef wellington.

BEEF WELLINGTON * MEAT
INGREDIENTS: piece of fillet of beef, flaky pastry.
RECIPE: the flaky pastry is spread over the fillet before cooking for 40'. Served hot or cold.

336 - FILET DE BŒUF AU ROQUEFORT * VIANDE

Photo Fillet of beef with Roquefort cheese.

FILLET OF BEEF WITH ROQUEFORT CHEESE * MEAT
INGREDIENTS: butter, fillet of beef. Sauce: Roquefort cheese (see n° 929), cream.
RECIPE: the fillet is browned in the butter and the mashed cheese mixed with the cream before cooking. Served hot.

337 - FILET DE BŒUF ROSSINI * VIANDE

Photo Fillet of beef Rossini.

FILLET OF BEEF ROSSINI * MEAT
INGREDIENTS: tournedos steak, soft bread, foie gras, butter, Madeira wine.
RECIPE: the bread, steak and foie gras are browned in butter and served hot.

338 - FILET DE CHEVREUIL AUX POIRES * GIBIER

Photo Fillet of venison.

FILLET OF VENISON WITH PEARS * GAME
INGREDIENTS: venison. For the marinade: red wine, juniper berries, mustard seed, bay leaf. For the garnish: pears, cranberry blueberry jelly.
RECIPE: the venison is marinated in the refrigerator, browned in butter and cooked in the oven. The cream, pears and cranberry jelly are added at the end of cooking. Served hot.

339 - FILET DE CHAPON AU JUS DE BOUILLABAISSE * POISSON

Photo Fillet of red scorpionfish in stewed juices.

FILLET OF RED SCORPIONFISH IN STEWED JUICES * FISH
INGREDIENTS: red scorpionfish, fish stock, potatoes, coriander.
RECIPE: the scorpionfish and potatoes are cooked separately in fish stock and served hot.

340 - FILET DE CABILLAUD PANÉ * POISSON

Photo Breadcrumbed fillets of cod.

BREADCRUMBED FILLETS OF COD * FISH
INGREDIENTS: cod, lemon, egg, breadcrumbs, butter.
RECIPE: the fish is sprinkled with lemon, covered with the ingredient mixture and cooked in butter. Served hot.

341 - FILET DE CABILLAUD SAUCE AU BEURRE * POISSON

Photo Fillet of cod with butter sauce and sun-dried tomatoes.

FILLET OF COD WITH BUTTER SAUCE * FISH
INGREDIENTS: cod, butter. For the sauce: butter, lemon.
RECIPE: the cod is cooked in butter and the sauce prepared. Served hot.

342 - FILET DE COLIN PANÉ * POISSON

Photo Breadcrumbed fillet of hake with pasta.

BREADCRUMBED FILLETS OF HAKE * FISH
INGREDIENTS: fillet of hake, breadcrumbs, beaten egg, butter.
RECIPE: the fillet is dipped in egg and breadcrumbs and then cooked in butter. Served hot.

343 - FILET D'ÉGLEFIN * POISSON

Photo Fillet of haddock with polenta.

FILLET OF HADDOCK * FISH
INGREDIENTS AND RECIPE: olive oil, butter. The fillet is cooked. Served hot.

344 - FILET DE FLÉTAN * POISSON

Photo Fillet of halibut.

FILLET OF HALIBUT * FISH
INGREDIENTS AND RECIPE: butter, lemon juice. The fillet is cooked. Served hot.

345 - FILETS DE HARENG MARINÉS POMMES À L'HUILE * POISSON

Photo Fillets of herring.

MARINATED FILLETS OF HERRING WITH POTATO SALAD * FISH
INGREDIENTS: fillets of herring, shallots, olive oil, cider vinegar, bay leaf, juniper berries, cloves.
RECIPE: the fillets are marinated with the ingredients for 3 days. Served cold.

346 - FILET DE LIEU NOIR AU BEURRE FONDU * POISSON

Photo Fillet of coley with butter and lemon.

FILLET OF COLEY WITH MELTED BUTTER * FISH
INGREDIENTS: fillet of coley. To cook: butter, lemon juice.
RECIPE: the coley fillet is cooked. Served hot.

347 - FILET DE LIEU AU BEURRE D'HERBES * POISSON

Photo Fillet of pollock with herb butter.

FILLET OF POLLOCK WITH HERB BUTTER * FISH
INGREDIENTS: fillet of pollock. For the herb butter: parsley.
RECIPE: all the ingredients are cooked separately. Served hot.

348 - FILET DE LIEU À LA FLORENTINE * POISSON

Photo Fillet of pollock with spinach.

FILLET OF POLLOCK WITH SPINACH * FISH
INGREDIENTS: fillet of pollock. To garnish: spinach, onions, lemon. For the topping: cheese. To cook: dry white wine, oil, grated nutmeg.
RECIPE: the pollock is cooked with the ingredients then baked in the oven with the other ingredients, served hot

349 - FILET DE LOUP SAUCE AU BEURRE * POISSON

Photo Fillet of sea bass with butter sauce.

FILLET OF SEA BASS WITH BUTTER SAUCE * FISH
INGREDIENTS AND RECIPE: butter, the fillet is cooked in butter. Served hot.

350 - FILET DE LOUP AU JUS DE TAPENADE * POISSON

Photo Fillet of sea bass with tapenade.

FILLET OF SEA BASS WITH TAPENADE * FISH
INGREDIENTS: fillet of sea bass, tapenade, butter. To cook: olive oil, cream, cherry tomatoes, basil, cep mushrooms.
RECIPE: the fillet is cooked in butter then all the other ingredients added, served hot.

351 - FILET MIGNON DE PORC RÔTI * VIANDE

Photo Roast pork tenderloin.

ROAST PORK TENDERLOIN * MEAT
INGREDIENTS: pork tenderloin, butter, onions, garlic, olive oil.
RECIPE: the fillet is roasted in the oven with the ingredients. Served hot.

352 - FILET MIGNON DE PORC SAUCE MARCHAND DE VIN * VIANDE

Photo Pork tenderloin with red wine sauce.

PORK TENDERLOIN WITH RED WINE SAUCE * MEAT
INGREDIENTS: pork tenderloin, see Red wine sauce n° 786.
RECIPE: the fillet is cooked and the sauce prepared. Served hot.

352-1 - FILET MIGNON DE VEAU * VIANDE

Photo Veal tenderloin.

VEAL TENDERLOIN * MEAT
INGREDIENTS: veal tenderloin, butter. Sauce: cream
RECIPE: the sauce is added after cooking. Served hot.

353 - FILET DE RASCASSE AU CRESSON * POISSON

Photo Fillet of rockfish.

FILLET OF ROCKFISH WITH WATERCRESS * FISH
INGREDIENTS: rockfish fillets, chopped watercress, butter, dry white wine, cream.
RECIPE: the fillet and watercress are cooked in butter, served hot.

354 - FILET DE SANDRE RÔTI * POISSON

Photo Fillet of zander in butter with sun-dried tomatoes.

ROAST FILLET OF ZANDER * FISH
INGREDIENTS AND RECIPE: the fillet is cooked in butter, the lemon juice added and it is served immediately.

355 - FILET DE SOLE MEUNIÈRE * POISSON

Photo Fillet of sole in butter.

FILLET OF SOLE IN BUTTER SAUCE * FISH
INGREDIENTS: sole, butter, flour.
RECIPE: the floured sole is browned in butter and served hot.

FLA

356 - FLAGEOLETS * LÉGUMES

Photo Flageolets beans.

FLAGEOLETS BEANS * VEGETABLES
RECIPE: the beans are cooked in stock after soaking overnight. Served hot.

357 - FLAMEKUCHE OU TARTE FLAMBÉE - SPÉCIALITÉ D'ALSACE

Photo Cream, bacon and onion tart.

CREAM , BACON AND ONION TART - A SPECIALITY FROM ALSACE
INGREDIENTS: bread dough base, sliced onions cooked in butter, diced bacon, cream.
RECIPE: the dough is spread with the ingredients and baked. Served hot.

358 - FLAMICHE AUX POIREAUX * LÉGUMES - SPÉCIALITÉ D'ARTOIS

Photo Leek pie.

LEEK PIE - A VEGETABLE SPECIALITY FROM ARTOIS
INGREDIENTS: flaky pastry. Garnish: sliced white of leeks, butter. For the stuffing: cream, eggs, pepper, nutmeg.
RECIPE: the garnish ingredients are cooked in butter, placed on the pastry with the cream and beaten egg yolks, covered with a pastry lid and baked in the oven. Served hot.

359 - FLAN * PÂTISSERIE

Photo Vanilla custard tart.

CUSTARD TART * PASTRY
INGREDIENTS: shortcrust pastry. To garnish: eggs, sugar, butter, milk, vanilla pod.
RECIPE: the shortcrust pastry is cooked with the mixed ingredients, raisins may be added. Served cold.

360 - FLAN AU CARAMEL * DESSERT

Photo Caramel custard cream.

CARAMEL CUSTARD CREAM * DESSERT
INGREDIENTS: eggs, sugar, liquid cream.
RECIPE: the caramel is put into the base of the ramekin and the filling added; it is cooked together in a bain marie for 1 hour 15'. Served cold.

FOI

361 - FOIE GRAS AU NATUREL MI-CUIT * ABATS

Photo Foie gras.

PART-COOKED FOIE GRAS * OFFAL
RECIPE: the foie gras sinews are removed; it is seasoned with pepper and salt, paprika, port or Armagnac brandy, barely cooked and refrigerated. Served cold.

362 - FOIE GRAS « D'OIE » FRAIS POÊLÉ AUX RAISINS * ABATS

Photo Slices of foie gras pan-fried with grapes.

FRESH FOIE GRAS PAN-FRIED WITH GRAPES * OFFAL

INGREDIENTS: slices of foie gras, grapes, Sauterne wine.

RECIPE: the liver is cooked for 2', the grapes are cooked in the wine, served hot.

363 - FOIE GRAS DE CANARD POÊLÉ ABRICOTS ET PAIN D'ÉPICE * ABATS

Photo Pan-fried duck with apricots and gingerbread.

PAN-FRIED DUCK FOIE GRAS WITH APRICOTS AND GINGERBREAD * OFFAL

RECIPE: see N° 362

364 - FOIE DE VEAU PERSILLÉ * ABATS

Photo Parsleyed calf's liver.

PARSLEYED CALF'S LIVER * OFFAL

INGREDIENTS: sliced calf's liver, butter, parsley, vinegar.

RECIPE: the liver is cooked and the vinegar added. Served hot with parsley.

365 - FOIES DE VOLAILLE EN SALADE * ABATS

Photo Poultry liver salad.

POULTRY LIVER SALAD * OFFAL

INGREDIENTS: poultry livers. To cook: goose fat, sherry vinegar.

RECIPE: the poultry livers are cooked in the fat, the vinegar added and served hot.

366 - FOND D'ARTICHAUT * LÉGUMES

Photo Artichoke heart with vinaigrette sauce, whole artichoke.

ARTICHOKE HEART * VEGETABLES
INGREDIENTS: artichoke. To serve: vinaigrette sauce (n° 803). Served hot or cold.

367 - FONDANT AU CHOCOLAT * PÂTISSERIE

Photo Chocolate cake.

CHOCOLATE CAKE * PASTRY
INGREDIENTS: cooking chocolate, eggs, sugar, flour, butter.
RECIPE: the ingredients are mixed and then baked. Served cold or warm.

368 - FONDUE BOURGUIGNONNE * VIANDE SPÉCIALITÉ DE BOURGOGNE

Photo Meat fondue.

MEAT FONDUE - A SPECIALITY FROM BURGUNDY
INGREDIENTS: meat cut into large cubes, gherkins, ketchup, mayonnaise, béarnaise and tartare sauce.
RECIPE: everyone cooks a piece of meat on a fork in a chafing dish of hot oil, served with the various sauces. Served hot.

369 - FONDUE SAVOYARDE * FROMAGE - SPÉCIALITÉ DE SAVOIE

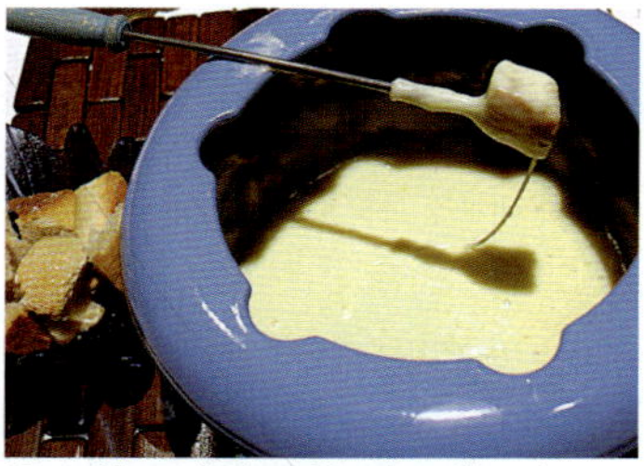

Photo Cheese fondue with cubes of bread.

CHEESE FONDUE - A SAVOY SPECIALITY
INGREDIENTS: Savoy cheeses: Gruyère, Beaufort, Emmenthal, garlic, dry white wine, Kirsch liqueur, grated nutmeg. To serve: cubes of dry bread.
RECIPE: the cheeses are mixed, cooked in a pot rubbed with garlic, the wine, kirsch and nutmeg are then added. Served hot.

FOR

370 - FORÊT NOIRE * PÂTISSERIE

Photo Black forest gateau.

BLACK FOREST GATEAU * CAKE
INGREDIENTS: dark chocolate, butter, egg yolks, stiffly beaten egg whites, sugar, flour, ground almonds, baking powder. To garnish: griotte cherries, gelatine, sugar, cream, Kirsch liqueur, lemon juice.
RECIPE: the ingredients are mixed and the pastry baked in the oven, cut into 3 slices crossways; the cherries and whipped, sweetened cream are spread over each slice. Served cold.

FOU

371 - FOUACE * PÂTISSERIE - SPÉCIALITÉ D'ALBI * REPRIS DANS LE ROMAN « GARGANTUA DE RABELAIS »

Photo Bun cake.

BUN CAKE - A SPECIALITY FROM ALBI * MENTIONED IN THE NOVEL "GARGANTUA" BY RABELAIS
INGREDIENTS: for the mixture: fresh baker's yeast, milk, flour, eggs, sugar, orange flower water, butter. To garnish: egg yolks, orange flower water, sugar.
RECIPE: all the dough ingredients are hand mixed for 30' and it is then left to prove overnight. It is shaped into a crown and baked for 1 hour. When removed from the oven, it is brushed with the garnish mixture. Served cold.

372 - FOUÉE POITEVINE * PÂTISSERIE - SPÉCIALITÉ DU POITOU

BUN CAKE WITH CREAM
A POITOU SPECIALITY CAKE
INGREDIENTS: flour, butter, egg, yeast, sugar, milk. To garnish: cream, sugar.
RECIPE: the dough ingredients are mixed and it is proved twice until it has doubled in volume; it is then folded into 3 and baked. Garnished with cream and caster sugar Sprinkled with cinnamon before serving.

373 - FOUGASSE - SPÉCIALITÉ DE PROVENCE

Photo Olive oil bread.

OLIVE OIL BREAD - A SPECIALITY FROM PROVENCE
INGREDIENTS: for the dough: flour, baker's yeast. To garnish: anchovies in oil, olive oil, butter, warm water.
RECIPE: the yeast and flour are mixed with the ingredients, left to prove for 30' and then baked for 30'. Served warm.

FRA

374-1 - FRAISES À LA CRÈME CHANTILLY - FRUITS

Photo Strawberries with whipped cream.

STRAWBERRIES WITH WHIPPED CREAM * FRUIT
Served cold.

374-2 - FRAISES AU SUCRE - FRUITS

Photo Strawberries with sugar.

STRAWBERRIES WITH SUGAR * FRUIT
Served cold.

374-3 - FRAISES DES BOIS - FRUITS

Photo Wild strawberries.

WILD STRAWBERRIES * FRUIT
Served cold.

375 - FRAISIER * PÂTISSERIE

Photo Strawberry cream sponge.

STRAWBERRY CREAM SPONGE * CAKE
INGREDIENTS: strawberries, ground almonds, sugar, flour, butter, egg yolks, stiffly beaten egg whites, cream, milk, Grand Marnier liqueur.
RECIPE: the mixture is baked in the oven, the pastry sprinkled with Grand Marnier, cut in two and filled with strawberries and cream. Served cold.

376 - FRAMBOISES ET « CHANTILLY » - FRUITS

Photo Raspberries.

RASPBERRIES WITH WHIPPED CREAM * FRUIT
Served cold.

FRI

377 - FRIANDS À LA VIANDE * ENTRÉE

Photo Meat pastry.

MEAT PASTRY * STARTER
INGREDIENTS: flaky pastry, minced meat, nutmeg.
RECIPE: the meat is cooked in the pastry. Served hot.

378 - FRIANDS * PÂTISSERIE

Photo Almond sponge.

ALMOND SPONGE * CAKE
INGREDIENTS AND RECIPE: soft sponge mixture: flour, butter, milk, eggs, ground almonds, served cold.

379 - FRICADELLES D'AGNEAU OU BOULETTES DE VIANDE D'AGNEAU * VIANDE

Photo Lamb meatballs.

LAMB MEATBALLS * MEAT
INGREDIENTS: minced shoulder of lamb, bread, crushed garlic, onion sauteed in butter, egg, dry white wine, cream, parsley, oregano.
RECIPE: the ingredients are mixed, shaped into balls and fried in the oil, served hot.

380 - FRICADELLES DE BŒUF * VIANDE

Photo Beef meatballs.

BEEF MEATBALLS * MEAT
RECIPE: see N°380, the lamb is replaced with beef. Served hot.

381 - FRICADELLES DE VOLAILLE * VOLAILLE - SPÉCIALITÉ D'ALSACE

Photo Poultry burgers.

POULTRY BURGERS - A SPECIALITY FROM ALSACE
INGREDIENTS: minced, cooked poultry flesh, egg yolks, butter, chopped shallots sautéed in butter, soft bread soaked in milk. For the sauce: butter, nutmeg.
RECIPE: all the ingredients are mixed, rolled into a flat, round shape and cooked in butter. Served hot.

382 - FRICANDEAU * VIANDE

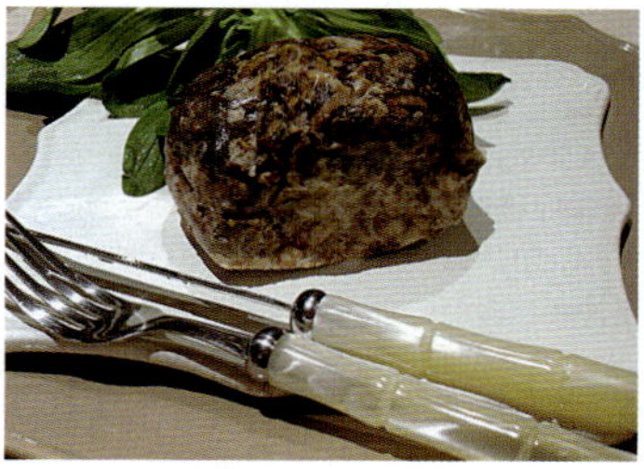

Photo Braised veal.

BRAISED VEAL * MEAT
INGREDIENTS: mixture of lean and fat pork with herbs and spices in a pork caul.
RECIPE: the ingredients are cooked in the oven. Served cold.

383 - FRICASSÉE DE POULET DE BRESSE * VOLAILLE SPÉCIALITÉ DE BOURGOGNE

Photo Bresse chicken fricasee, morel mushrooms.

BRESSE CHICKEN FRICASEE - A POULTRY FROM BURGUNDY
INGREDIENTS: for the preparation: Bresse chicken cut into pieces, onion sautéed in butter. To cook: flour, butter, wine, poultry stock, shallots, clove, nutmeg. For the sauce: morel mushrooms cooked in butter (see n° 521), lemon juice, cream.
RECIPE: the pieces of chicken are prepared and combined with the ingredients to cook. The sauce is added, served hot.

384 - FRISÉE À LA LYONNAISE * SALADE

Photo Warm endive salad with bacon and eggs.

WARM ENDIVE SALAD WITH BACON AND EGGS * SALAD
INGREDIENTS: curly endive, fried diced bacon, poached eggs, croutons, vinaigrette sauce.
RECIPE: the eggs, bacon and vinegar are served hot on the endive.

385 - FRITURE D'ÉPERLANS * POISSON

Photo Fried smelts.

FRIED SMELTS * FISH
INGREDIENTS: smelts, flour, cooking oil.
RECIPE: the fish are fried in oil and served immediately.

FRO

386 - FROMAGE BLANC À LA CRÈME * FROMAGE

Photo Fromage blanc with cream.

FROMAGE BLANC WITH CREAM * CHEESE
INGREDIENTS AND RECIPE: fromage blanc and cream. Served cold.

387 - FROMAGE DE CHÈVRE SUR LIT DE SALADE VERTE

Photo Goats cheese on a bed of green salad.

GOAT'S CHEESE ON A BED OF GREEN SALAD
Served cold.

FRU

388 - FRUITS ROUGES AU VIN * DESSERT - FRUITS

Photo Red fruit in wine.

RED FRUIT IN WINE * FRUIT DESSERT
INGREDIENTS: fruit. To cook: red wine, cinnamon, sugar.
RECIPE: the ingredients are cooked in the wine. Served cold.

GAL

389 - GALANTINE DE LAPIN

Photo Rabbit galantine.

RABBIT GALANTINE
INGREDIENTS: to macerate: rabbit and liver, shoulder of pork, bacon, ham, veal bone. For the cooking stock: celery, shallots, onion, carrots, garlic, water. For the stuffing: liver, fillet of rabbit, bacon, egg, brandy, cultivated mushrooms, chilli, cardamom. RECIPE: the ingredients are macerated for 12 hours. The stuffing and cooking stock are prepared, the mixture layered in a terrine dish and cooked for 1 hour in a bain marie. Served cold.

390 - GALANTINE DE VEAU * VIANDE

VEAL GALANTINE * MEAT
INGREDIENTS: to macerate: fillet of veal, pork meat with fat removed, calf's liver, bread, egg yolk, cream. For the stuffing: mushrooms, shallots, garlic, calf's liver, brandy, Cointreau liqueur, cream, butter, parsley, ham.
RECIPE: the ingredients are macerated for 12 hours, mixed with the stuffing and cooked in a terrine dish for 50'. Served cold.

391 - GALETTE BRETONNE AU JAMBON * ŒUFS

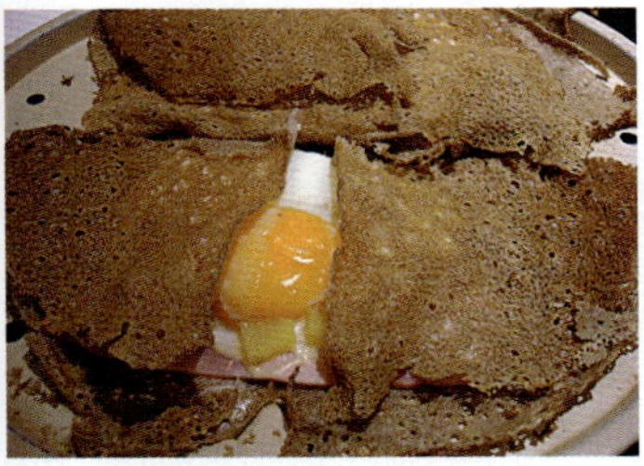

Photo Ham pancake with a fried egg.

HAM PANCAKES * EGGS
INGREDIENTS: panpastry batter: buck wheat flour, water, milk, egg. Filling: ham, bacon, egg.
RECIPE: the batter is left to rest for 4 hours. Each pancake is filled and served hot.

392 - GALETTE BRETONNE AUX NOIX DE SAINT-JACQUES * ŒUFS

Photo Scallop pancake.

SCALLOP PANCAKE * EGGS
RECIPE: see N°391 The ham, bacon and egg are replaced with scallops, butter, garlic, cream and parsley. Served hot.

393 - GALETTE DE POMMES DE TERRE * LÉGUMES

Photo Potato and onion cake.

POTATO AND ONION CAKE
* VEGETABLES
INGREDIENTS: potatoes, grated onion, egg, flour. To cook: butter, oil.
RECIPE: the ingredients are cooked and served hot.

394 - GALETTE DES ROIS PROVENÇALE * PÂTISSERIE SPÉCIALITÉ DE PROVENCE

Photo Provençal twelfth night bun cake.

TWELFTH NIGHT BUN CAKE - A SPECIALITY FROM PROVENCE
INGREDIENTS: bun mixture: flour, sugar, yeast, milk, egg, butter. Garnish: raisins, crystallised lemon and orange, nibbed almonds, cinnamon, large pieces of sugar.
RECIPE: the dough is left to prove before adding the garnish and baking. Sprinkled with sugar. Served cold.

395 - GALETTE DES ROIS - GÂTEAU DES ROIS - DÉBUT JANVIER * PÂTISSERIE

Photo Twelfth night cake.

TWELFTH NIGHT CAKE - A JANUARY SPECIALITY
INGREDIENTS: flaky pastry, filling, called "frangipane": butter, milk, egg, sugar, ground almonds, rum. Traditionally, the person who finds the hidden bean is king or queen and wears a paper crown.
RECIPE: the pastry is cooked with the frangipane filling and served warm.

GAM

396 - GAMBAS GRILLÉES * CRUSTACÉS

Photo Grilled gambas prawns with garlic and butter.

GRILLED GAMBAS PRAWNS * SHELLFISH
INGREDIENTS: raw gambas, garlic, olive oil, lemon, parsley.
RECIPE: the gambas are grilled then served with crushed garlic mixed with butter and chopped parsley. Served hot with the shell peeled off before eating.

GAN

397 - GANACHE * PÂTISSERIE

Photo Chocolate cream pastry.

CHOCOLATE CREAM * PASTRY
Shortcrust pastry, chocolate. Served cold.

GAR

398 - GARBURE BÉARNAISE * PLAT COMPLET - SPÉCIALITÉ DU BÉARN

Photo Goose, beef and vegetable stew.

GOOSE, BEEF AND VEGETABLE STEW
A ONE-DISH SPECIALITY FROM BÉARN
INGREDIENTS: meat: goose legs, beef. Vegetables: potatoes, cabbage, French beans, white beans, turnip, carrot, half an onion, regional cheese, bay leaf, sage, parsley.
RECIPE: the meat is cooked in fat then stewed with the vegetables. At the end of cooking, the dish is put in the oven, topped with bread covered with grated cheese and browned. Served hot.

399 - GARDIANE DE TAUREAU * VIANDE SPÉCIALITÉ DE CAMARGUE

Photo Cattle-herder stew.

CATTLE-HERDER STEW – A SPECIALITY FROM CAMARGUE * MEAT
INGREDIENTS: boned blade and knuckle of beef, tomatoes, red wine, onions, carrots, garlic, flour, sage and herbs.
RECIPE: The meat is marinated for 12 hours and then cooked. Served hot.

GAS

400 - GASPACHO * POTAGE - SPÉCIALITÉ DU SUD

Photo Gaspacho soup.

GASPACHO - A SPECIALITY COLD SOUP FROM THE SOUTH
INGREDIENTS: tomatoes, cucumber, green and yellow pepper, onions, garlic, soft bread, oil, sherry vinegar, chopped chervil, basil.
RECIPE: chopped cucumber and tomatoes are added to the ingredients macerated for 24 hours; the soup is then blended. Served cold.

GAT

401 - GÂTEAU AUX NOIX * PÂTISSERIE SPÉCIALITÉ DU DAUPHINÉ

Photo Walnut cake.

WALNUT CAKE OR TART - A SPECIALITY FROM DAUPHINÉ
INGREDIENTS: walnuts. Mixture: flour, sugar, eggs, baking powder, butter, rum, cream, icing sugar, Armagnac brandy.
RECIPE: the mixture cooked for 35', served cold.

402 - GÂTEAU BASQUE * PÂTISSERIE - SPÉCIALITÉ DU BÉARN

Photo Custard cream cake.

CUSTARD CREAM CAKE - A SPECIALITY FROM BÉARN
INGREDIENTS: mixture: flour, butter, sugar, eggs. Cream filling: milk, sugar, egg yolks, flour, ground almonds, vanilla, butter.
RECIPE: the mixture is left to rest for 30'. The cooked cream is added and the pastry cooked for 30'. Served cold.

403 - GÂTEAU MOELLEUX AU CHOCOLAT * PÂTISSERIE

Photo Soft-centre chocolate cake.

SOFT-CENTRE CHOCOLATE CAKE
* CAKE
INGREDIENTS: flour, eggs, butter, cream, chocolate.
RECIPE: the ingredients are mixed and baked. Served warm, with soft chocolate oozing from the centre.

404 - GÂTEAU DE FOIES DE VOLAILLE * ABATS SPÉCIALITÉ DU POITOU

Photo Potted poultry liver paté.

POTTED POULTRY LIVER PATÉ - AN OFFAL SPECIALITY FROM POITOU
INGREDIENTS: poultry livers, milk, brandy, garlic, butter. Stuffing: shallots, egg yolks, cream, butter, sugar, allspice, thyme, bay leaf.
RECIPE: the livers are marinated in milk, drained and sprinkled with brandy; the stuffing is precooked, blended with the livers and baked in ramekins in the oven in a bain marie for 30'. Served cold.

405 - GÂTEAU DE RIZ * DESSERT

Photo Creamed rice dessert.

CREAMED RICE DESSERT * DESSERT
INGREDIENTS: rice, raisins, crystallised fruit, egg yolks, stiffly beaten egg whites, sugar, milk, rum.
RECIPE: the crystallised fruit and raisins are soaked in rum, the rice cooked in milk, the yolks and sugar mixed and added to the fruit and rice and then the dessert cooked in the oven for 40'. Served cold, topped with caramel.

406 - GÂTEAU DE SEMOULE * DESSERT

Photo Creamed semolina dessert.

CREAMED SEMOLINA DESSERT * DESSERT
INGREDIENTS: semolina, milk, vanilla, butter, egg yolks, stiffly beaten egg whites, sugar.
RECIPE: the semolina is cooked in milk, mixed with the other ingredients and cooked in the oven. Served cold.

407 - GÂTEAU ROULÉ * PÂTISSERIE

Photo Swiss roll with raspberry jam filling.

SWISS ROLL * CAKE
INGREDIENTS: flour, eggs, butter, sugar, milk.
RECIPE: the ingredients are mixed, baked on a tray and, when cooked, filled with jam or cream and rolled. Served cold.

GAU

408 - GAUFRE * PÂTISSERIE

Photo Waffles with icing sugar.

WAFFLES * CAKE
INGREDIENTS: waffle batter: flour, baking powder, sugar, milk.
RECIPE: the ingredients are mixed, the batter cooked in a waffle iron, served hot.

409 - GAUFRE À LA CHANTILLY * PÂTISSERIE

Photo Waffles with whipped cream.

WAFFLES WITH WHIPPED CREAM (N° 239) * CAKE
INGREDIENTS AND RECIPE: see n° 408. Served hot.

410 - GAUFRE AU CHOCOLAT * PÂTISSERIE

Photo Waffles with chocolate.

WAFFLES WITH CHOCOLATE * CAKE
INGREDIENTS AND RECIPE: see n° 408. Served hot.

GEL

411 - GELÉE SALÉE

Photo Aspic jelly.

ASPIC JELLY
For savoury dishes: clarified meat juices, solidified by cooling. Served cold.

412 - GELÉE SUCRÉE

Photo Jellies.

SWEET JELLIES
For desserts: fruit juice cooled with sugar solidified by cooling, called fruit jellies. Quince jelly. Served cold.

GEN

413 - GÉNOISE * PÂTISSERIE

Photo Genoese sponge.

GENOESE SPONGE * CAKE
INGREDIENTS: sponge mixture: flour, cornflour, sugar, egg yolks, stiffly beaten egg whites. Cream: chocolate or whipped cream or jam.
RECIPE: the sponge is baked and cut into 3, filled with whipped cream and jam or chocolate. Served cold.

GIG

414 - GIGOT D'AGNEAU AUX HERBES * VIANDE

Photo Leg of lamb with herbs.

LEG OF LAMB WITH HERBS * MEAT
INGREDIENTS: leg of lamb. To cook: onion, garlic, parsley, basil, thyme, chopped rosemary, olive oil.
RECIPE: the lamb is covered with the mixture, cooked and served hot.

415 - GIGOT D'AGNEAU RÔTI * VIANDE

Photo Roast leg of lamb.

ROAST LEG OF LAMB * MEAT
INGREDIENTS: leg of lamb with the bone, olive oil, white wine. To rub over the lamb: thyme, slivers of garlic.
RECIPE: the meat is studded with garlic and then cooked. Served sliced, hot or cold.

416 - GIGOT À LA BRAYAUDE * VIANDE - SPÉCIALITÉ DU LIMOUSIN

Photo Leg of lamb with potatoes.

LEG OF LAMB WITH POTATOES
A SPECIALITY FROM LIMOUSIN * MEAT
INGREDIENTS: leg of lamb. Herbs: garlic, thyme, crumbled bayleaf. Garnish: sliced potatoes, butter, bouillon.
RECIPE: the lamb is coated with herbs and cooked above the potatoes, bouillon and butter mixture, served hot.

417 - GIGOT DE 11 HEURES * VIANDE - SPÉCIALITÉ DE PROVENCE

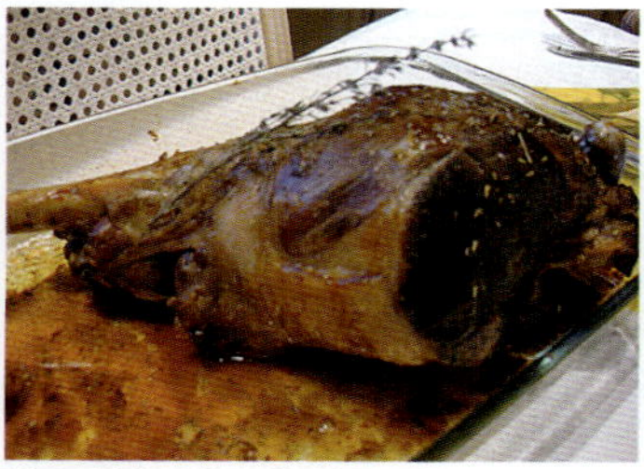

Photo 11-hour leg of lamb.

11-HOUR LEG OF LAMB - A MEAT
SPECIALITY FROM PROVENCE
INGREDIENTS: leg of lamb. To macerate: garlic, bay leaf, thym, carrots, onions, oil, brandy. To cook: tomatoes, sticks of celery, oil, white wine, bouquet garni.
RECIPE: the lamb is marinated for 24 hours and cooked for 5 hours with all the ingredients. The whole leg of lamb is served hot.

418 - GIGOTON D'AGNEAU : PETIT GIGOT * VIANDE

SMALL LEG OF LAMB * MEAT
INGREDIENTS AND RECIPE: see n° 415. Served hot.

GIR

419 - GIROLLES SAUTÉES * LÉGUMES

Photo Sauteed girolle mushrooms.

SAUTEED GIROLLE MUSHROOMS * VEGETABLES
INGREDIENTS: girolles (chanterel family wild mushrooms), garlic, olive oil, parsley
RECIPE: the mushrooms are cooked followed by the garlic and parsley and served hot.

GLA

420 - GLACE * DESSERT GLACÉ

Photo Ice cream, lemon, strawberry.

ICE CREAM * ICED DESSERT
INGREDIENTS: eggs, sugar, milk, cream,
RECIPE: the egg and sugar mixture is added to the cream and milk and put to freeze in an ice-cream maker. Served iced.

GNO

421 - GNOCCHI À LA PARISIENNE * ENTRÉE

Photo Gnocchi with white sauce.

GNOCCHI WITH WHITE SAUCE * STARTER
INGREDIENTS: choux pastry: flour, butter, eggs, water. For the garnish: grated cheese, Béchamel (white) sauce, butter, flour, milk and small dumplings. RECIPE: the choux pastry (see n° 173) is cooked, the garnish placed in the centre and the dish baked in the oven for 20'. Served immediately.

422 - GNOCCHI DE POMMES DE TERRE * LÉGUMES

Photo Potato gnocchi.

POTATO GNOCCHI * VEGETABLES
INGREDIENTS: cooked potatoes, flour, egg yolks, butter, grated Parmesan cheese.
RECIPE: the mashed potato is mixed with the flour and egg yolks, formed into small balls, cooked in boiling water and baked in the oven for 10'. Served hot.

423 - GNOCCHI À LA ROMAINE * LÉGUMES

Photo Gnocchi with egg and cheese.

GNOCCHI WITH EGG AND CHEESE
* VEGETABLES
INGREDIENTS: semolina, Parmesan cheese, egg yolks, milk.
RECIPE: the semolina is cooked in milk and water. Parmesan cheese and egg yolks are added. Served cooked sprinkled with Parmesan cheese. Served hot.

GOU

424 - GOUGÈRE * ENTRÉE

Photo Cheese choux pastry puff.

CHEESE CHOUX PASTRY PUFF
* STARTER
INGREDIENTS: grated Gruyère cheese, flour, water, eggs, butter, nutmeg.
RECIPE: butter and flour are added to the boiling water, eggs, Gruyère and nutmeg. Large balls of pastry sprinkled with cheese are cooked and served hot.

425 - GOULASH * VIANDE

Photo Goulash.

GOULASH * MEAT
INGREDIENTS: cubed beef, potatoes, sliced carrots, tomatoes, onion, meat stock, paprika.
RECIPE: the meat and onions are browned in fat and cooked in the meat stock with the vegetables for 45'. Served hot.

GOY

426 - GOYÈRE VALENCIENNOISE * FROMAGE SPÉCIALITÉ DES FLANDRES

Photo Valenciennes cheese tart.

VALENCIENNES CHEESE TART
A SPECIALITY FROM FLANDERS
INGREDIENTS: shortcrust or flaky pastry, cheese, eggs, Maroilles (n° 924) and Emmenthal cheese, butter, nutmeg.
RECIPE: pastry round, covered with the melted cheese, butter and beaten egg and cooked for 30'. Served hot.

427 - GRANITÉ DE PASTÈQUE * DESSERT GLACÉ

WATER MELON GRANITE * ICED DESSERT
INGREDIENTS: water melon, sugar, lemon juice.
RECIPE: the water melon is pureed, mixed with the ingredients and refrigerated until served ice.

428 - GRAS DOUBLE À LA LYONNAISE * ABATS SPÉCIALITÉ DE LYON

Photo Tripe and onions.

TRIPE AND ONIONS, A LYON SPECIALITY * OFFAL
INGREDIENTS: precooked strips of tripe, sliced onions, parsley, sherry vinegar, oil, white wine.
RECIPE: the tripe is cooked for 3′ in oil with the onions; the vinegar and parsley is added at the end and served hot.

429 - GRATIN D'AUBERGINES AUX TOMATES * LÉGUMES SPÉCIALITÉ DE PROVENCE

Photo Baked aubergine and tomatoes.

BAKED AUBERGINE AND TOMATOES
A SPECIALITY FROM PROVENCE * VEGETABLES
INGREDIENTS: round slices of aubergine and tomatoes, garlic, butter, thyme, parsley.
RECIPE: aubergines and tomatoes are layered in a dish, cooked with thyme, garlic, and parsley and topped with cheese to brown. Served hot.

430 - GRATIN DE COURGETTES AU PARMESAN * LÉGUMES

Photo Baked courgettes with Parmesan cheese.

BAKED COURGETTES WITH PARMESAN CHEESE * VEGETABLES
INGREDIENTS: sliced courgettes. Sauce base: shallots, garlic, butter, meat stock. Herbs: thyme, basil, topping: grated Parmesan, breadcrumbs
RECIPE: the sauce base is sautéed to cover the herbs and courgettes and cooked for 40′ with the breadcrumbs and Parmesan. Served hot.

431 - GRATIN DAUPHINOIS * LÉGUMES

Photo Sliced potato baked in cream.

SLICED POTATO BAKED IN CREAM
* VEGETABLES
INGREDIENTS: sliced potatoes. To cook: garlic, butter, milk, cream, grated nutmeg.
RECIPE: the potatoes are covered with the other ingredients and baked for 1 hour in the oven. Served hot.

432 - GRATIN AUX FRUITS ROUGES * DESSERT - FRUITS

Photo Baked red fruit.

BAKED RED FRUIT * FRUIT DESSERT
INGREDIENTS: red fruit, raspberries, redcurrants. Cream: sugar, egg yolks, lemon zest, vanilla pod, ground almonds.
RECIPE: the fruit is coated with the cream and browned for 7'. Served warm.

433 - GRATIN DE MACARONIS * PÂTES

Photo Macaroni cheese.

MACARONI CHEESE * PASTA
INGREDIENTS: macaroni pasta. White sauce: butter, flour, cream milk. To garnish: grated Gruyère cheese.
RECIPE: the pasta is mixed with white sauce and baked in the oven to brown. Served hot.

434 - GRATIN DE POLENTA * PÂTES

Photo Baked polenta.

BAKED POLENTA * PASTA
INGREDIENTS: polenta (type of cornmeal), cream, milk, egg, grated Gruyère cheese.
RECIPE: all the ingredients are cooked and served hot.

GRA

435 - GRATINÉE À L'OIGNON * POTAGE

Photo French onion soup.

FRENCH ONION SOUP * SOUP
INGREDIENTS: sliced onions. To cook: white wine, flour. For the topping: grated Gruyère, toasted bread.
RECIPE: the ingredients are cooked for 20', baked in the oven to brown and served hot.

436 - GRATINÉE D'OIGNONS EN CROÛTE DE BEAUFORT * POTAGE SPÉCIALITÉ DE LYON

Photo Onion soup with cheese crouton.

ONION SOUP WITH CHEESE CROUTONS * SOUP - A SPECIALITY FROM LYON
INGREDIENTS: sliced onions, butter, garlic, white wine, meat stock, golden croutons, Beaufort cheese (see cheese n° 908).
RECIPE: the onions are browned in butter, added to the wine and stock, cooked for 20' and the soup topped with croutons and Beaufort, served hot.

GRE

437 - GRENADINS DE VEAU * VIANDE

Photo Tiny veal escalopes.

TINY VEAL ESCALOPES * MEAT
INGREDIENTS: tiny veal escalopes, onions, garlic, oil.
RECIPE: the escalopes are sauteed in oil and the onions and garlic added. Served hot.

438 - GRENOUILLES SAUTÉES (CUISSES DE) SPÉCIALITÉ DE BOURGOGNE

Photo Sautées frog's legs.

SAUTEED FROG'S LEGS - A SPECIALITY OF BURGUNDY
INGREDIENTS: frog's legs dusted with flour, butter, lemon, chopped parsley.
RECIPE: the frog's legs are browned in butter, sprinkled with lemon and served hot.

GRO

439 - GROSEILLES * FRUITS

REDCURRANT * FRUIT

Photo Redcurrant.

HAC

440 - HACHIS PARMENTIER - PLAT COMPLET * VIANDE

COTTAGE PIE - A ONE-DISH MEAL * MEAT
INGREDIENTS: mashed potatoes. Filling: minced beef, onion, egg, butter, parsley, grated nutmeg. Topping: grated Gruyère cheese.
RECIPE: the filling is placed between layers of mashed potato, baked in the oven for 30', browned and served immediately.

Photo Cottage pie.

HAD

441 - HADDOCK * POISSON

SMOKED HADDOCK * FISH
INGREDIENTS AND RECIPE: haddock cooked quickly in milk, drained, served with cream and potatoes.

Photo Smoked haddock.

HAM

442 - HAMPE DE BŒUF * VIANDE

BEEF SKIRT * MEAT
INGREDIENTS: beef skirt, butter. Served hot.

Photo Beef skirt.

HAR

443 - HARENGS MARINÉS POMMES À L'HUILE * POISSON

Photo Marinated herring with potato salad.

MARINATED HERRING WITH POTATO SALAD * FISH
INGREDIENTS: filleted herrings, onions, flour, oil, vinegar, lemon, bay leaf, peppercorns.
RECIPE: the herring is dusted with flour and sautéed in oil. The ingredients are boiled and poured over the herrings which are left for 24h. Served cold.

444 - HARICOTS À LA PROVENÇALE * LÉGUMES

Photo Beans provençal style.

BEANS PROVENCAL STYLE * VEGETABLES
INGREDIENTS: beans. To cook: tomatoes, onion, garlic, olive oil, raspberry vinegar, capers, bay leaf, rosemary, thyme, parsley.
RECIPE: the dried beans are soaked for 12 hours, boiled and then cooked with the ingredients for 1 hour 30 mins. Served hot.

445 - HARICOTS VERTS EN PERSILLADE * LÉGUMES

Photo French beans with parsley.

FRENCH BEANS WITH PARSLEY * VEGETABLES
INGREDIENTS: French beans, garlic, butter, parsley.
RECIPE: the beans are cooked in boiling water, then in butter with the parsley; served hot. French beans with parsley

HOM

446 - HOMARD À L'AMÉRICAINE * CRUSTACÉS

Photo Lobster in tomato and brandy sauce.

LOBSTER IN TOMATO AND BRANDY SAUCE * SHELLFISH
INGREDIENTS: lobsters. To cook: oil, butter. Sauce: lobster cooking juices, carrots, tomatoes, onions, shallots, garlic, butter, oil, fish stock, dry white wine, brandy, tarragon, chervil, parsley.
RECIPE: the lobsters are cooked in their shells in oil and butter then simmered with the sauce ingredients for 20'; the creamy part of the lobster and coral are mixed with butter, sieved, and incorporated into the sauce which is cooked for 5'. The lobster is coated with the sauce and served hot.

447 - HOMARD À LA NAGE * CRUSTACÉS

COOKED COLD LOBSTER * SHELLFISH
INGREDIENTS: lobster, lemon, herbs, sprigs of dill.
RECIPE: the live lobsters are boiled for 20' in water with lemon and herbs, drained and split in two lengthways. Served cold with melted salted butter and slices of lemon.

448 - HOMARD THERMIDOR * CRUSTACÉS

Photo Lobster thermidor.

LOBSTER THERMIDOR
* SHELLFISH
INGREDIENTS: lobster. To cook: carrot, onion, olive oil, lemon, dry white wine. Herb butter: butter, shallots, garlic, chopped parsley. Sauce: cream, tarragon mustard, flour, Calvados applejack brandy, chopped herbs (chervil, chives, tarragon).
RECIPE: the live lobsters are boiled with the ingredients for 15', the shell removed and browned in the oven with the herb butter. The sauce is prepared and served separately with the lobster. Served hot.

HUI

449 - HUÎTRES CHAUDES AU CHAMPAGNE * MOLLUSQUES

Photo Warm oysters in champagne sauce.

WARM OYSTERS IN CHAMPAGNE SAUCE
* SHELLFISH
INGREDIENTS: shucked oysters. Sauce: egg yolks, butter, champagne, wine vinegar, lemon juice.
RECIPE: each oyster is coated with the sauce in its shell, baked in the oven and served hot.

450 - HUÎTRES CHAUDES ET LEUR FLAN * MOLLUSQUES SPÉCIALITÉ DE NORMANDIE

Photo Warm oysters with savoury custard.

WARM OYSTERS WITH SAVOURY CUSTARD
- A SPECIALITY FROM NORMANDY
INGREDIENTS: oysters. Shallot butter: butter, shallots, garlic, chopped chervil, lemon juice, soft bread without crust. Custard: egg yolks, cream, chervil, butter.
RECIPE: the shallot butter ingredients are blended to garnish each oyster before browning in the oven. The savoury custard is steamed in ramekins for 20'. Served hot separately.

451 - HUÎTRES CHAUDES AU GRILL * MOLLUSQUES

Photo Warm grilled oysters.

WARM GRILLED OYSTERS * SHELLFISH
INGREDIENTS: shucked oysters. Sauce: cultivated mushrooms, butter, flour, cream, dry white wine, chopped parsley. Topping: breadcrumbs, butter.
RECIPE: the oysters are poached in their liquid and white wine. They are returned to their shells, coated with the sauce, flashed under the grill and served hot.

452 - HUÎTRES AU NATUREL - VINAIGRE À L'ÉCHALOTE, CITRON, BEURRE, PAIN * MOLLUSQUES

Photo plain oysters with shallot vinegar, lemon.

PLAIN OYSTERS WITH SHALLOT VINEGAR, LEMON, BUTTER AND BREAD
* SHELLFISH
Served cold.

ILE

453 - ILE FLOTTANTE * DESSERT

Photo Floating island.

FLOATING ISLAND * DESSERT
INGREDIENTS: the floating island: stiffly beaten egg whites, vanilla sugar. Garnish: liquid caramel. Custard sauce: egg yolks, sugar, milk, vanilla pod.
RECIPE: the custard sauce is cooked. The floating island is cooked for 45' in a bain marie and then coated with custard sauce and caramel. Served cold.

JAM

454 - JAMBON BRAISÉ * CHARCUTERIE

Photo Braised ham.

BRAISED HAM * COOKED MEATS AND SIMILAR
INGREDIENTS: whole ham, sugar, garlic, cloves.
RECIPE: the ham is soaked for 12 hours, dried, roasted in the oven for 2 ½ hours and served hot in fairly thick slices.

455 - JAMBON VENDÉEN AUX MOGETTES * CHARCUTERIE SPÉCIALITÉ DE VENDÉE

Photo Vendée ham with mogette beans.

VENDEE HAM WITH MOGETTE BEANS - A COOKED MEAT SPECIALITY FROM VENDÉE
INGREDIENTS: Vendée ham, oil. To cook: Vendée mogette beans, water, clove of garlic, onion, bouquet garni.
RECIPE: the ham is brushed with oil and grilled; after soaking for 12 hours, the beans are cooked with the ingredients. Served hot.

456 - JAMBONNEAU AU CHOU * CHARCUTERIE

Photo Ham shank with cabbage.

HAM SHANK WITH CABBAGE * COOKED MEATS AND SIMILAR
INGREDIENTS: ham shank, cabbage. To cook: carrot, turnip, leek, stalk of celery, onion, garlic, dry white wine, bay leave, poultry stock, thyme.
RECIPE: the ingredients are cooked together for 2 hours. Served hot.

JAR

457 - JARDINIÈRE DE LÉGUMES PRINTANIERS * LÉGUMES

Photo Mixed spring vegetables.

MIXED SPRING VEGETABLES * VEGETABLES
INGREDIENTS: French beans, new carrots, peas, potatoes, sugar snap peas, onions, butter, herbs.
RECIPE: each vegetable is cooked separately, then together with the butter, served hot.

458 - JARRET DE PORC GRILLÉ * CHARCUTERIE

Photo Knuckle of pork in jelly.

GRILLED KNUCKLE OF PORK * MEAT
INGREDIENTS: knuckle of pork, bay leaf, clove.
RECIPE: the knuckle is boiled with all the ingredients for 1 hour, then grilled, served hot.

459 - JARRET DE VEAU RÔTI * VIANDE

Photo Roast knuckle of veal with sliced vegetables.

ROAST KNUCKLE OF VEAL * MEAT
INGREDIENTS: knuckle of veal. To cook: carrots, stalk of celery, leek, garlic, oil, dry white wine, lemon, onions. Sauce: flour, cream, tomato puree, basil, chopped parsley.
RECIPE: the veal, wine and vegetables are cooked in the oven for 1 hour . The sauce is cooked for 15' and served hot separately.

JOU

460 - JOUE DE PORC BRAISÉE * ABATS

Photo Braised cheek of pork.

BRAISED CHEEK OF PORK * OFFAL
INGREDIENTS: pork cheeks. To cook: chopped carrots, onions, diced celery stalk, tomatoes, wine, oil, butter.
RECIPE: the cheeks are cooked over a high heat, the vegetables, wine, tomatoes and water added and cooked for 1 hour. Served hot.

JUL

461 - JULIENNE DE LÉGUMES * LÉGUMES

Photo Sliced vegetables.

FINELY-SLICED VEGETABLES * VEGETABLES
INGREDIENTS: carrots, courgettes, stalk of celery, onions, garlic, oil.
RECIPE: the vegetables cut into matchsticks are fried in butter for 5' and served hot.

KOU

462 - KOUGLOF * PÂTISSERIE - SPÉCIALITÉ D'ALSACE

Photo Kugelhopf cake.

KUGELHOPF CAKE
* A SPECIALITY FROM ALSACE
INGREDIENTS: proved dough: flower, milk, yeast. Other mixture: flour, eggs, butter, sugar, milk. Additions: Malaga raisins soaked in Kirsch liqueur, flaked almonds, sugar.
RECIPE: the raisins are macerated in the Kirsch for 12 hours. The dough is proved and then combined with the other mixture. The almonds are placed in the base of a mould before the mixture to be baked. Served cold sprinkled with icing sugar.

463 - LANGOUSTE GRILLÉE * CRUSTACÉS

Photo Grilled crawfish.

GRILLED CRAWFISH * SHELLFISH
INGREDIENTS AND RECIPE: crawfish, butter. The crawfish is grilled with butter. Served hot.

464 - LANGOUSTE MAYONNAISE * CRUSTACÉS

Photo Crawfish with mayonnaise.

CRAWFISH WITH MAYONNAISE * SHELLFISH
The crawfish is cooked in court-bouillon. Served cold.

465 - LANGOUSTINES SAUTÉES AU GINGEMBRE * CRUSTACÉS

Photo Raw Dublin Bay Prawns.

DUBLIN BAY PRAWNS SAUTEED WITH GINGER * SHELLFISH
INGREDIENTS: shelled Dublin Bay Prawn tails, spinach, carrots. Sauce: cream, wine. To cook: butter, fresh grated ginger.
RECIPE: the vegetables are steamed, combined with the other ingredients and cooked further. Served hot.

466 - LANGUE DE BŒUF BOURGUIGNONNE * ABATS

Photo Ox tongue in a wine sauce.

OX TONGUE IN A WINE SAUCE * OFFAL
INGREDIENTS: ox tongue. To cook: water, leek, onion, bouquet garni, bay leaf, juniper berries, spicy paprika. Sauce: butter, flour, red Burgundy wine, cream.
RECIPE: the ingredients and sauce are cooked separately, hot dish.

467 - LANGUE DE BŒUF SAUCE GRIBICHE * ABATS

Photo Ox tongue with gribiche sauce.

OX TONGUE WITH GRIBICHE SAUCE * OFFAL
INGREDIENTS: ox tongue, carrots, leek, stalk of celery, onions, garlic, bouquet garni, cloves. Gribiche sauce: onion, boiled eggs, oil, vinegar, mustard, gherkins, capers, chopped herbs.
RECIPE: the meat is cooked for 4 hours with the chopped vegetables, served hot, the sauce prepared with all the cold ingredients mashed with a fork is served separately.

468 - LANGUE DE BŒUF SAUCE PIQUANTE * ABATS

Photo Ox tongue with sharp sauce.

OX TONGUE WITH SHARP SAUCE * OFFAL
INGREDIENTS: ox tongue, carrots, leek, stalk of celery, chopped onions and garlic, bouquet garni, cloves. To cook: butter, flour, dry white wine, bouquet garni. Sharp sauce: shallots, gherkins, capers, dry white wine, vinegar, parsley, tarragon, chervil.
RECIPE: the meat is cooked for 4 hours with the chopped vegetables and cooking sauce. The sharp sauce is prepared and the dish served hot.

LAP

469 - LAPEREAU AU PAILLÉ DE POMMES SPÉCIALITÉ DE NORMANDIE

Photo Rabbit with straw potatoes.

RABBIT WITH STRAW POTATOES - A MEAT SPECIALITY FROM NORMANDY
INGREDIENTS: saddles of rabbit, butter. Mushroom duxelles: chopped mushrooms, lemon, shallots, butter, straw potatoes (see N° 580)
RECIPE: the rabbit is cooked in butter and cider with the shallots and mushrooms, cut into pieces and presented on straw potatoes with a little sauce, served hot.

470 - LAPIN À LA BRESSANE

Photo Rabbit with wine and cream sauce.

RABBIT WITH A WINE AND CREAM SAUCE
INGREDIENTS: jointed rabbit. To cook: smoked bacon, butter. Flour : onion, garlic, butter, flour, dry white wine, old wine vinegar, grated nutmeg. Sauce: cream, egg yolks.
RECIPE: the rabbit is browned with the cooking ingredients then cooked a further 1 hour, the sauce is served hot with the rabbit.

471 - LAPIN CHASSEUR

Photo Rabbit with red wine and mushroom sauce.

RABBIT WITH RED WINE AND MUSHROOM SAUCE
INGREDIENTS: leg of rabbit. Marinade: thyme, bay leaf, oil. Sauce: cultivated mushrooms, butter, flour. To cook: shallots, butter, meat stock, red Burgundy wine, parsley.
RECIPE: the rabbit is rubbed with thyme, bay leaf and oil and left for 12 hours. The legs and ingredients are cooked for 30'. The precooked mushrooms, butter and flour are added. The rabbit is served hot accompanied by the sauce.

472 - LAPIN À LA FLEUR DE THYM OU À LA PROVENÇALE

Photo Rabbit with thyme.

RABBIT WITH THYME / PROVENCAL STYLE
INGREDIENTS: saddle of rabbit, potatoes, courgettes, tomato, olive oil, thyme.
RECIPE: the saddle is browned in butter with the thyme and baked in the oven with all the ingredients chopped into pieces, served hot.

473 - LAPIN À LA GRAINE DE MOUTARDE

Photo Rabbit with grain mustard.

RABBIT WITH GRAIN MUSTARD
INGREDIENTS: jointed rabbit. To cook: bacon, butter, oil, grain mustard. Sauce: cream, cooking juices.
RECIPE: all the ingredients are cooked and the sauce served hot with the rabbit.

474 - LAPIN À LA MOUTARDE

Photo Rabbit with mustard.

RABBIT WITH MUSTARD
INGREDIENTS: see n° 473, the sauce is made with ordinary mustard. Served hot.

LAP

475 - LAPIN À LA TOMATE

Photo Rabbit with a wine and tomato sauce.

RABBIT WITH A WINE AND TOMATO SAUCE
INGREDIENTS: jointed rabbit, tomatoes, pine nuts, garlic, butter, oil, dry white wine, bay leaf, rosemary, sage, grated nutmeg.
RECIPE: the rabbit is browned with all the ingredients and cooked for 20' with the tomatoes and pine nuts. Served hot.

476 - LAPIN AUX OLIVES

Photo Rabbit with olives.

RABBIT WITH OLIVES
INGREDIENTS: jointed rabbit. To cook: flour, butter, oil, red wine, chopped carrot, parsley. Sauce: olives.
RECIPE: the rabbit is browned and then simmered with all the ingredients; the olives are added at the end of cooking, served hot.

LAS

477 - LASAGNES * PÂTES - SPÉCIALITÉ ITALIENNE

Photo Lasagne.

LASAGNE - AN ITALIAN PASTA SPECIALITY
INGREDIENTS: minced beef, chopped bacon, carrots, chopped celery and onions, butter, meat stock. At the end of cooking: tomato puree. White sauce: butter, flour, nutmeg, milk. To garnish: Mozzarella cheese, butter, grated Parmesan cheese. RECIPE: the cooking ingredients are mixed, browned and cooked. The white sauce is prepared and alternate layers of lasagne pasta, meat, white sauce and the cheeses placed in a dish, baked and browned in the oven. Served immediately.

LEN

478 - LENTILLES AUX ÉCHALOTES * SALADE

Photo Lentils with shallots.

LENTILS WITH SHALLOTS * SALAD
INGREDIENTS: lentils, shallots, garlic, oil, raspberry vinegar, vegetable stock, thyme, chopped parsley.
RECIPE: the lentils, garlic and thyme are cooked in the stock. Served cold, sprinkled with vinegar and parsley.

479 - LENTILLES D'ACCOMPAGNEMENT D'UN PLAT * LÉGUMES

Photo Lentils.

LENTILS AS THE GARNISH FOR A DISH * VEGETABLES
INGREDIENTS: lentils, very finely chopped, celeriac, carrots, white of leek. To cook: onions, garlic, butter, coriander.
RECIPE: the vegetables are cooked, drained and served hot.

LIE

480 - LIEU AU BEURRE FONDU * POISSON

Photo Pollock with melted butter.

POLLOCK WITH MELTED BUTTER * FISH
INGREDIENTS: pollock. To cook: chopped carrot, leek and onion, bay leaf, tarragon, fish stock. Sauce: butter, lemon.
RECIPE: the ingredients are boiled. The fish is poached and served hot with boiled potatoes.

481 - LIEU AU BEURRE D'HERBES ET DE CITRON * POISSON

Photo Pollock with lemon herb butter and boiled potatoes.

POLLOCK WITH LEMON HERB BUTTER * FISH
INGREDIENTS: fillet of pollock, butter, lemon juice, parsley.
RECIPE: the pollock is cooked in melted butter and served hot with lemon juice.

482 - LIÈVRE CHASSEUR * GIBIER

Photo Hare with red wine and mushroom sauce.

HARE WITH RED WINE AND MUSHROOM SAUCE * GAME
INGREDIENTS: saddle of hare. Marinade: lemon juice, garlic, brandy, bacon, carrot, shallots, lemon, full-bodied red wine, bay leaf, crushed thyme, cloves, sugar. Sauce: grapes, cream, cooking juices. RECIPE: the saddle and ingredients are marinated for 5 hours and then cooked in the oven for 40'. The sieved cooking juices are added to the sauce. Served hot.

483 - LIÈVRE À LA ROYALE * GIBIER

Photo Stuffed hare with truffles.

STUFFED HARE WITH TRUFFLES * GAME
INGREDIENTS: hare. Stuffing: blood, liver, heart and lungs of the hare, poultry livers, bacon, breadcrumbs, stock, chopped onion sautéed in butter, garlic, chopped truffles, parsley. To cook: red wine. Presentation sauce: game stock, Armagnac brandy, truffles.
RECIPE: the hare is stuffed, cooked for 2 hours, cut into pieces and served hot with the sauce.

LIM

484 - LIMANDE - SOLE EN ROULADE * POISSON

Photo Rolled stuffed lemon sole.

ROLLED STUFFED LEMON SOLE * FISH
INGREDIENTS: lemon sole fillets. Stuffing: sliced cultivated mushrooms, bay leaf, onion, shallots, butter. Sauce: egg yolks, wine.
RECIPE: the stuffing is cooked for 30′ blended with one sole fillet and added to the egg yolks and cream. The fillets and stuffing are cooked, the fillet coated with the sauce and served hot.

LIN

485 - LINZERTORTE * PÂTISSERIE

Photo Bakewell tart.

BAKEWELL TART * PASTRY
INGREDIENTS: ground almonds, raspberry jam, flour, sugar, vanilla sugar, cocoa, egg, butter, Kirsch liqueur.
RECIPE: the butter, egg and Kirsch liqueur are mixed and allowed to rest for 1 hour. The pastry (flour and butter) is rolled out, spread with jam and strips of pastry placed around the edge. The tart is cooked for 1 hour. Served cold.

LOT

486 - LOTTE À L'AMÉRICAINE * POISSON

Photo Monkfish in tomato and brandy sauce.

MONKFISH IN TOMATO AND BRANDY SAUCE * FISH
INGREDIENTS: pieces of monkfis. To cook: carrots, onion, shallots, garlic, butter, oil, flour, fish stock, dry white wine, brandy, bouquet garni, tarragon. Sauce: butter, flour.
RECIPE: the monkfish is browned and cooked with the ingredients for 20′. The sauce is added, the dish cooked 5′ and served hot.

LOU

487 - LOUP FARCI * POISSON

Photo *Stuffed sea bass.*

STUFFED SEA BASS * FISH
INGREDIENTS: sea bass. Stuffing: cultivated mushrooms, breadcrumbs, shallots, butter, egg, cream, lemon juice, sprigs of chervil, nutmeg.
RECIPE: the stuffing ingredients are cooked and placed in the fish which is sprinkled with lemon juice, cooked for 35′ and served hot.

MAC

488 - MACARONS * PÂTISSERIE

Photo Raspberry, coffee, chocolate and vanilla macaroons.

MACAROONS * CAKE
INGREDIENTS: stiffly beaten egg whites, ground hazelnuts, sugar, flour. Flavouring: chocolate, vanilla or coffee.
RECIPE: All the ingredients are mixed and small spoonfuls of the mixture baked in the oven. Served cold.

489 - MACÉDOINE DE FRUITS * FRUITS

Photo Diced fruit salad.

DICED FRUIT SALAD * FRUIT
RECIPE: different kinds of raw or cooked fruit in syrup (water, sugar, lemon juice, liqueur). Served cold.

490 - MACÉDOINE DE LÉGUMES * LÉGUMES

Photo Russian salad.

RUSSIAN SALAD * VEGETABLES
INGREDIENTS: peas, sweetcorn, red peppers, carrots, courgettes, onions, garlic, chives, mayonnaise.
RECIPE: the vegetables are diced and cooked separately then mixed with mayonnaise. Served cold.

491 - MACHE AUX LARDONS * SALADE

Photo Lamb's lettuce with bacon.

LAMB'S LETTUCE WITH BACON * SALAD
INGREDIENTS: lamb's lettuce, hard-boiled eggs, lean, pan-fried bacon. Dressing: onions, garlic, oil, vinegar.
RECIPE: the ingredients are mixed and served cold.

MAD

492 - MADELEINES * PÂTISSERIE

Photo Fairy cakes.

FAIRY CAKES * CAKE
INGREDIENTS: flour, baking powder, sugar, butter, milk, eggs.
RECIPE: sugar, eggs and milk are mixed, added to the flour to rise and the cakes cooked in small individual moulds. Served cold.

MAG

493 - MAGRET DE CANARD SAUCE À L'ORANGE * VOLAILLE

Photo Duck breasts with ceps.

DUCK BREASTS WITH ORANGE SAUCE * POULTRY
INGREDIENTS: duck breasts, orange zest, shallots, oil, Grand Marnier liqueur, sugar.
RECIPE: the duck breasts are cooked with the shallots and other ingredients, sprinkled with orange juice and served hot.

494 - MAGRET DE CANARD SAUCE AU VIN * VOLAILLE

Photo Duck breasts with wine sauce.

DUCK BREASTS WITH WINE SAUCE * POULTRY
INGREDIENTS: duck breasts. Wine sauce: shallots, butter, red wine, chopped parsley, flour.
RECIPE: the duck breasts are browned, the inside remaining pink, and coated with the wine sauce. Served hot.

MAN

494-1 - MANCHONS DE CANARD AUX CÈPES * VOLAILLE

Photo Duck drumsticks with ceps.

DUCK DRUMSTICKS WITH CEPS * POULTRY
INGREDIENTS: duck drumsticks. To cook: goose fat, carrots, tomatoes, poultry stock, garlic. For the garnish: goose fat, cep mushrooms.
RECIPE: the drumsticks are cooked and served hot with the sautéed ceps.

MAQ

495 - MAQUEREAU AUX HERBES ET AU RAIFORT * POISSON

Photo Mackerel with herbs and horseradish.

MACKEREL WITH HERBS AND HORSERADISH * FISH
INGREDIENTS: whole mackerel, tomatoes. To cook: oil, parsley, rosemary, thyme, sage. Sauce: cream, lemon juice, grated horseradish.
RECIPE: the mackerel and herb sauce are cooked in a foil case for 15′ then served hot.

496 - MAQUEREAUX AU VIN * POISSON

Photo Mackerel in wine.

MACKEREL IN WINE * FISH
INGREDIENTS: whole, gutted mackerel, carrot, lime and lemon, onion, dry white wine, bay leaf, fennel seeds, cloves.
RECIPE: the mackerel covered with the chopped ingredients are cooked for 4′ and served cold.

MAR

497 - MARRONS ENTIERS CUITS * LÉGUMES

Photo Cooked chestnuts.

WHOLE COOKED CHESTNUTS * VEGETABLES
Served hot.

498 - MATEFAIMS * PÂTISSERIE

Photo Apple pancake.

APPLE PANCAKE * CAKE
INGREDIENTS: sliced apples, flour, egg yolks, sugar, butter, milk, lemon, brandy.
RECIPE: the ingredients are mixed and cooked for 10′.

499 - MATELOTE D'ANGUILLES * POISSON

Photo Eel stew.

EEL STEW * FISH
INGREDIENTS: pieces of eel, garlic. For the sauce base: oil, flour. To cook: bay leaf, thyme, parsley, grated nutmeg. Sauce: eggs, beer mixed with the cooking juices. Garnish: browned croutons.
RECIPE: the eel pieces are browned in the oil and cooked with all the other ingredients. Served hot with croutons.

500 - MATELOTE DE BROCHET REIMOISE * POISSON SPÉCIALITÉ DE CHAMPAGNE

Photo Pike stew.

PIKE STEW - A CHAMPAGNE SPECIALITY * FISH
INGREDIENTS: pike cut into slices. Court bouillon stock: onions, shallots, garlic, champagne. Garnish: croutons fried in butter. Sauce: butter.
RECIPE: the pike is cooked in the court bouillon and served hot with the butter, cooking juices and croutons.

501 - MATELOTE AUX TROIS POISSONS * POISSON

Photo Three-fish stew.

THREE-FISH STEW * FISH
INGREDIENTS: sliced eel, trout, pike or barbel, cultivated mushrooms, onions, garlic, butter, cream, flour, lemon juice, dry white wine, brandy, bouquet garni.
RECIPE: The fish is browned in butter and cooked with the ingredients. Served hot.

MED

502 - MÉDAILLONS DE VEAU * VIANDE

Photo Veal medallions, rosti, potato, mushrooms.

VEAL MEDALLIONS * MEAT
INGREDIENTS: round slices of veal, butter, sugar.
RECIPE: the slices of veal are cooked in butter. Served hot.

MEL

503 - MELON AU JAMBON DE PARME * ENTRÉE

Photo Melon with Parma ham.

MELON WITH PARMA HAM * STARTER
INGREDIENTS: Parma ham, melon.
RECIPE: a slice of ham is wrapped around each slice of melon. Served cold.

504 - MELON AU PORTO * ENTRÉE

Photo Melon with port.

MELON WITH PORT * STARTER
INGREDIENTS: melon, red port.
RECIPE: the centre of the melon is filled with port. Served cold.

505 - MELON SURPRISE * DESSERT

Photo Melon surprise.

MELON SURPRISE * DESSERT
INGREDIENTS: melon, strawberries, raspberries, diced apple and peach, lemon juice, port, sugar.
RECIPE: The fruit is sprinkled with lemon and sugar. Served cold.

506 - MERINGUE * DESSERT

Photo Meringues.

MERINGUES * DESSERT
INGREDIENTS: egg whites, sugar.
RECIPE: stiffly beaten egg whites cooked for 1 hour. Served cold.

507 - MERLAN BONNE FEMME * POISSON

Photo Whiting with wine sauce.

WHITING WITH WINE SAUCE * FISH
INGREDIENTS: whiting. To cook: cultivated mushrooms, onions, shallots, garlic, butter, wine, bay leaf, parsley.
RECIPE: The ingredients are cooked and added to the whiting which is baked in the oven. Served hot.

508 - MERLAN EN COLÈRE * POISSON

Photo Fried whiting with lemon and herbs.

FRIED WHITING WITH LEMON AND HERBS * FISH
INGREDIENTS: whiting, lemon, flour, oil, chopped herbs, parsley.
RECIPE: the whiting are floured, fried seasoned with salt and served hot.

509 - MERLAN EN FILETS * POISSON

Photo Fillets of whiting.

FILLETS OF WHITING * FISH
INGREDIENTS AND RECIPE: fillets of whiting, butter. The fillets are cooked. Served hot.

510 - MERLU FRIT * POISSON

Photo Fried hake.

FRIED HAKE * FISH
INGREDIENTS AND RECIPE: the hake is coated with flour and breadcrumbs and cooked in oil. Served hot.

511 - MERLU PANÉ * POISSON

Photo Breadcrumbed hake.

BREADCRUMBED HAKE * FISH
INGREDIENTS AND RECIPE: the fish is dipped in beaten egg and breadcrumb and then cooked. Served hot.

MIG

512 - MIGNARDISES * PÂTISSERIE

Photo Sweet titbits.

SWEET TITBITS
Served cold with tea or coffee.

512-1 - MIGNON DE VEAU AUX MORILLES * VIANDE

Photo Veal tenderloin with mushrooms.

VEAL TENDERLOIN WITH MORELS * MEAT
INGREDIENTS: sliced veal tenderloin, butter, morel mushrooms, cream.
RECIPE: the veal is cooked in butter, the morels cooked in cream and added. Served hot.

513 - MILLEFEUILLE * PÂTISSERIE

Photo Custard cream slice.

CUSTARD CREAM SLICE * CAKE
INGREDIENTS: several strips of flaky pastry. Custard cream: egg yolks, flour, sugar, hot milk, vanilla pod.
RECIPE: the pastry is cooked, the custard cream filling added and served cold.

MIN

514 - MINESTRONE * POTAGE - SPÉCIALITÉ D'ITALIE

Photo Minestrone soup.

MINESTRONE - A SOUP FROM ITALY
INGREDIENTS: Savoy cabbage, cooked separately: bacon, onions, carrots, leek, celeriac. Other vegetables: potatoes, celeriac, French beans, large kidney beans, carrots, courgettes, white of leeks, onions, garlic, tomato puree. For the garnish: grated Parmesan cheese, chopped parsley, small precooked pasta.
RECIPE: the assembled ingredients are cooked for 30' in stock, poured into a tureen and served hot.

MIQ

515 - MIQUE DE MAÏS * LÉGUMES - SPÉCIALITÉ DE GASCOGNE

Photo Corn dumpling.

CORN DUMPLING - A VEGETABLE SPECIALITY FROM GASCONY
INGREDIENTS: fine corn meal. Preparation: goose fat, lean pieces of pork belly, chopped garlic. To cook: stock.
RECIPE: the precooked preparation is added to the corn meal and cooking finished in the hot stock; served hot with a salad.

MIX

516 - MIXES - GRILL * VIANDE

Photo Mixed grill.

MIXED GRILL * MEAT
INGREDIENTS: lamb chops, chipolata sausages, bacon, tomatoes, oil, thyme.
RECIPE: the meat and tomatoes are grilled and served hot with sauces.

MOE

517 - MOELLE (TARTINE) * ABATS

Photo Marrow on toasted bread.

BEEF MARROW ON A SLICE OF BREAD * OFFAL
INGREDIENTS AND RECIPE: the marrow is cooked in the bone in court bouillon then removed and served hot on toasted bread.

518 - MOELLEUX AU CHOCOLAT * PÂTISSERIE

Photo Soft-centre chocolate cake.

SOFT-CENTRE CHOCOLATE CAKE * CAKE
INGREDIENTS: melted chocolate, butter, egg yolks, sugar, almonds, stiffly beaten egg whites
RECIPE: All the ingredients are mixed and baked, served hot. Melted chocolate should ooze from the centre.

MOG

519 - MOGETTES À LA CRÈME * LÉGUMES - SPÉCIALITÉ DU POITOU

Photo Mogette beans with cream.

MOGETTE BEANS WITH CREAM
A POITOU SPECIALITY * VEGETABLES
INGREDIENTS: white beans. To cook: onion, water, bouquet garni, butter, nutmeg, cloves. At the end of cooking: cream, chopped parsley, butter. RECIPE: the beans are cooked and served hot with the ingredients to be added at the end of cooking.

MOK

520 - MOKA AU CAFÉ * PÂTISSERIE

Photo Chocolate and coffee gateau.

CHOCOLATE AND COFFEE GATEAU * CAKE
INGREDIENTS: biscuit base: flour, sugar, butter, egg yolks, chocolate, cinnamon, stiffly beaten egg whites, butter cream: sugar, butter, egg yolks, coffee extract, cream, softened butter.
RECIPE: the biscuit base is cooked for 1 hour and then covered with butter cream. Served cold.

MOR

521 - MORILLES À LA CRÈME * CHAMPIGNONS - SPÉCIALITÉ D'ALSACE

Photo Morels with cream.

MORELS MUSHROOMS WITH CREAM * MUSHROOM - A SPECIALITY FROM ALSACE
INGREDIENTS: morels. To cook: shallots, butter, lemon. Presentation: cream, nutmeg.
RECIPE: the morels are cooked for 10' with the cooking ingredients and served hot with the presentation ingredients.

522 - MORUE À L'AIL ET AUX TOMATES * POISSON

Photo Salt cod with garlic and tomatoes.

SALT COD WITH GARLIC AND TOMATOES * FISH
INGREDIENTS: salt cod. To cook: tomatoes, onions, garlic, olive oil, thyme. Presentation: chopped parsley, chopped coriander leaves.
RECIPE: the ingredients are cooked and served hot with the presentation ingredients.

MOU

523 - MOUCLADE D'AUNIS * MOLLUSQUES

Photo Mussels with wine and cream sauce.

MUSSELS WITH WINE AND CREAM SAUCE * SHELLFISH
INGREDIENTS: small mussels. To cook: shallots, butter, white wine, bouquet garni. Sauce: butter, flour, parsley, nutmeg. Presentation: lemon juice, cream.
RECIPE: the mussels are cooked for 5' and served in their shells with the precooked sauce. Served hot with the cooking juices.

524 - MOUCLADE * MOLLUSQUES

Photo Mussels in wine and cream.

MUSSELS IN WINE AND CREAM * SHELLFISH
INGREDIENTS: mussels, carrot, stalk of celery, white of leek, shallots, garlic, butter, dry white wine, bay leaf, crumbled thyme, parsley. Presentation: cream.
RECIPE: the ingredients are cooked in water, the cream added to the cooking juices and served immediately.

525 - MOULES FARCIES * MOLLUSQUES

Photo Stuffed mussels.

STUFFED MUSSELS * SHELLFISH
INGREDIENTS: mussels. To cook: shallots, garlic, dry white wine. Stuffing: tomatoes, garlic, breadcrumbs, olive oil, wine, parsley.
RECIPE: the cooked mussels are stuffed and flashed under the grill to brown. Served immediately.

526 - MOULES À LA JULIENNE DE LÉGUMES * MOLLUSQUES

Photo Mussels with matchstick vegetables.

MUSSELS WITH MATCHSTICK VEGETABLES * SHELLFISH
INGREDIENTS: mussels. Cooking vegetables cut into matchsticks: leeks, carrots, shallots, butter, egg yolk. Presentation: cream, egg yolk, dry white wine, vermouth.
RECIPE: the vegetables are cooked with the mussels which are served hot with the presentation elements.

527 - MOULES MARINÉES À L'ESCABÈCHE * MOLLUSQUES

Photo Mussels with pungent sauce.

MUSSELS WITH PUNGENT SAUCE * SHELLFISH
INGREDIENTS: mussels. Escabeche sauce: tomatoes, onion, garlic, olive oil, red wine vinegar, bay leaf, chopped parsley.
RECIPE: the mussels are cooked in water, removed from their shells and refrigerated with the precooked escabeche sauce for 3 hours. Served cold.

528 - MOULES MARINIÈRES * MOLLUSQUES

Photo Mussels mariner style.

MUSSELS MARINER STYLE * SHELLFISH
INGREDIENTS: mussels. To cook: carrot, shallots, garlic, butter, dry white wine, thyme, bay leaf, parsley.
RECIPE: the ingredients are cooked for 10' and served hot with the sieved cooking juices.

529 - MOULES MARINIÈRES À LA BRETONNE * MOLLUSQUES

Photo Mussels Breton mariner style.

MUSSELS BRETON MARINER STYLE * SHELLFISH
INGREDIENTS: Breton mussels, dry white wine. To cook: shallots, bouquet garni, butter. The sauce: butter, flour, sieved cooking juices, lemon juice. ¨Presentation: chopped parsley, bouquet garni.
RECIPE: the ingredients are cooked for 5'. The mussels are coated in the cooked sauce and served hot.

530 - MOULES (SOUPE DE) * POTAGE - MOLLUSQUES

Photo Mussel soup.

MUSSEL SOUP * SOUP - SHELLFISH
INGREDIENTS: small mussels. To cook: onion, celery stalk, butter, dry white wine, brandy, sprigs of chervil, chopped shallots, thyme. Presentation: butter, white of leeks, cream.
RECIPE: the ingredients are cooked and the precooked presentation ingredients added. Served hot.

531 - MOUSSAKA * SPÉCIALITÉ GRECQUE - PLAT COMPLET

Photo Moussaka.

MOUSSAKA - A ONE-DISH MEAL AND GREEK SPECIALITY
INGREDIENTS: minced lamb, aubergines, tomatoes. To cook: onions, garlic, olive oil, parsley, oregano leaves. To brown: grated Parmesan cheese. RECIPE: the meat and cooking ingredients are cooked in oil. The aubergine is cooked separately. The meat, aubergines and tomatoes are layered, the top sprinkled with Parmesan cheese and the dish baked in the oven. Served hot.

532 - MOUSSE AU CHOCOLAT * DESSERT

Photo Chocolate mousse.

CHOCOLATE MOUSSE * DESSERT
INGREDIENTS: melted dark chocolate, sugar, egg yolks, stiffly beaten egg whites, cream.
RECIPE: the ingredients are mixed and refrigerated for 4 hours, served cold.

533 - MOUSSE AU CHOCOLAT BLANC * DESSERT

Photo White chocolate mousse.

WHITE CHOCOLATE MOUSSE * DESSERT
INGREDIENTS: chocolate, sugar, egg yolks, stiffly beaten egg whites, cream.
RECIPE: identical to the previous dish but with white chocolate. Served cold.

534 - MOUSSE AU CITRON * DESSERT

Photo Lemon mousse.

LEMON MOUSSE * DESSERT
INGREDIENTS: lemon zest, sugar, desiccated coconut, butter, egg yolks, stiffly beaten egg whites, lemon juice, sheet of gelatine.
RECIPE: the ingredients are mixed and refrigerated for 2 hours. Served cold.

535 - MOUSSE D'AVOCAT AUX CREVETTES * ENTRÉE

Photo Avocado mousse with prawns.

AVOCADO MOUSSE WITH PRAWNS * STARTER
INGREDIENTS: avocados. Mousse: shallots, oil, lemon juice, sprigs of chervil. Presentation: cooked shelled prawns.
RECIPE: the avocados are blended, the mixture returned to the avocado skins with the prawns and chervil on top, refrigerated and served.

536 - MOUSSE DE FOIES DE VOLAILLE * ENTRÉE

Photo Poultry liver mousse.

POULTRY LIVER MOUSSE * STARTER
INGREDIENTS: poultry livers. Marinade: Armagnac brandy. To cook: shallots, butter, crushed green and pink peppercorns.
RECIPE: the livers are marinated, cooked in butter for 7′ with the shallots and marinade juice, blended and refrigerated in a terrine dish for 12 hours. Served cold.

537 - MOUSSE DE POISSON DE SAUMON * POISSON

Photo Salmon mousse.

SALMON MOUSSE * FISH
INGREDIENTS: pieces of salmon fillet. To cook: butter, olive oil, lemon juice, eggs, dry white sherry, dill. Sauce: whipped cream.
RECIPE: the cooked fillets are pureed with the cream, served cold.

538 - MOUSSE DE TURBOT * POISSON

Photo Turbot mousse.

TURBOT MOUSSE * FISH
INGREDIENTS: turbot fillets. To cook: saffron, butter, egg yolks, cream. Marinade: lemon juice.
RECIPE: the turbot fillets are marinated for 10′ then mixed with the ingredients to cook, served cold.

539 - MOUSSELINE DE LÉGUMES * LÉGUMES

Photo Pureed vegetables in cream.

PUREED VEGETABLES IN CREAM * VEGETABLES
INGREDIENTS: carrots or broccoli. Puree: milk, whipped cream, thyme, bay leaf, chives, grated nutmeg.
RECIPE: the vegetables are pureed after cooking. Served hot.

MOZ

540 - MOZZARELLA À L'HUILE D'OLIVE * FROMAGE DE BUFFLE SPÉCIALITÉ ITALIENNE

Photo Mozzarella.

MOZARELLA WITH OLIVE OIL - AN ITALIAN BUFFALO CHEESE SPECIALITY
Served cold.

MYS

541 - MYSTÈRE * DESSERT GLACÉ MERINGUÉ

Photo Meringue ice cream.

MERINGUE ICE CREAM * MERINGUE ICE CREAM DESSERT
INGREDIENTS AND RECIPE: vanilla ice cream with a meringue centre, covered in caramelised hazelnut crisp.

NAG

542 - NAGE DE COQUILLAGES À LA DIEPPOISE * MOLLUSQUES

Photo Shellfish in lemon butter sauce.

SHELLFISH IN LEMON BUTTER SAUCE * SHELLFISH
INGREDIENTS: cockles, mussels. To cook: lemon juice, butter, cider, chopped chervil and chives.
RECIPE: the cockles and mussels are cooked in the cider and taken out of their shells; the juices are sieved, mixed with the lemon and butter. Served hot coated with sauce.

NAV

543 - NAVARIN DE MOUTON PRINTANIER * VIANDE

Photo Mutton casserole with spring vegetables.

MUTTON CASSEROLE WITH SPRING VEGETABLES * MEAT
INGREDIENTS: cubed mutton. To garnish: potatoes, turnips, carrots, French beans, peas. To cook: onions, garlic, oil, butter, flour, tomato puree, bouquet garni, chopped parsley, water.
RECIPE: the meat is browned, all the ingredients added and cooked for 1 hour. Served hot.

544 - NAVARIN AUX POMMES * VIANDE

Photo Lamb casserole with potatoes.

LAMB CASSEROLE WITH POTATOES * MEAT
INGREDIENTS: cubed stewing lamb. To cook: oil, flour, tomato puree, garlic, butter, potatoes.
RECIPE: the lamb is browned in oil, the other ingredients added and the casserole cooked for 1 hour. Served hot.

545 - NAVETS GLACÉS * LÉGUMES

Photo Glazed turnips.

GLAZED TURNIPS * VEGETABLES
INGREDIENTS: turnips cut into large dice. To cook: water, butter, sugar.
RECIPE: the turnips are cooked for 25' with the ingredients until the water has evaporated. Served immediately with roast duck or roast pork.

546 - NOISETTES DE VEAU * VIANDE

Photo Veal cutlet.

VEAL CUTLET * MEAT
INGREDIENTS: veal, butter, onions.
RECIPE: the cutlets are cooked in butter with the onion. Served hot.

546-1 - NOIX * FRUITS

Photo Walnuts.

WALNUTS * NUTS

546-2 - NOIX DE VEAU À L'ÉTOUFFÉE * VIANDE

Photo Braised cushion of veal.

BRAISED CUSHION OF VEAL * MEAT
INGREDIENTS: cushion of veal. Sauce: cream, chopped dill, mild paprika, lemon. To cook: vegetable stock, bay leaf, chopped basil.
RECIPE: the veal is cooked in a foil case for 1 hour with its ingredients, the cooking juices filtered to make the sauce and served hot.

547 - NOIX DE SAINT-JACQUES RÔTIES * MOLLUSQUES

Photo Roasted scallops.

ROASTED SCALLOPS - SHELLFISH
INGREDIENTS: scallops, butter, parsley.
RECIPE: the scallops are cooked in butter and served hot.

548 - NOIX DE SAINT-JACQUES AUX ENDIVES BRAISÉES * MOLLUSQUES

Photo Scallops with braised chicory.

SCALLOPS WITH BRAISED CHICORY * SHELLFISH
INGREDIENTS: scallops, butter, parsley. To garnish: chicory
RECIPE: see N°547. The chicory is braised in butter. Served hot.

NOU

549 - NOUGAT GLACÉ * DESSERT GLACÉ

Photo Iced nougat with blueberries.

ICED NOUGAT * ICED DESSERT
INGREDIENTS: diced crystallised fruit. To macerate: Kirsch liqueur. Nougatine: sugar, single cream, water. Presentation: ground almonds. Meringue: egg whites, sugar. To garnish: whipped cream
RECIPE: the whipped cream, macerated crystallised fruit and powdered nougatine are added to the cooked meringue and refrigerated for 12 hours, served icy cold.

550 - ŒUF AU PLAT * ENTRÉE

Photo Fried egg.

FRIED EGG * STARTER
INGREDIENTS: egg, butter.
RECIPE: the egg is cooked in butter. Served hot.

551 - ŒUFS BROUILLÉS * ENTRÉE

Photo Scrambled egg.

SCRAMBLED EGG * STARTER
INGREDIENTS: beaten eggs, butter, cream, chopped chives.
RECIPE: the mixture is stirred in a buttered pan over a bain marie saucepan and served immediately.

552 - ŒUFS BROUILLÉS AUX TRUFFES * ENTRÉE

Photo Truffled scrambled egg.

TRUFFLED SCRAMBLED EGG * STARTER
INGREDIENTS: eggs, truffle shavings, butter, cream, truffle juice.
RECIPE: the eggs and ingredients are beaten and cooked in the bain marie in butter, served immediately. May be presented in an egg shell.

553 - ŒUFS BROUILLÉS AU LARD * ENTRÉE

Photo Scrambled egg with bacon.

SCRAMBLED EGG WITH BACON * STARTER
INGREDIENTS: eggs, lean slices of bacon. To garnish: slices of toast, butter, strong mustard. To cook: milk, chopped chives.
RECIPE: the bacon is browned, the eggs cooked with the milk, constantly stirred and served hot topped with the bacon.

554 - ŒUF COCOTTE AU JAMBON * ENTRÉE

Photo Eggs cooked with ham.

EGGS COOKED WITH HAM * STARTER
INGREDIENTS: eggs, egg yolks, diced ham, pieces of Gouda cheese, cream, chives, mild paprika.
RECIPE: the ham and gouda are put into dishes with an egg on the top; the ingredients and extra yolks are beaten and poured into the dishes to cook. Served hot.

555 - ŒUF À LA COQUE * ENTRÉE

Photo Soft-boiled eggs with "soldiers".

SOFT-BOILED EGGS * STARTER
INGREDIENTS: eggs, sliced bread, salted butter.
RECIPE: the eggs are boiled for 3' and served in egg cups. Served hot.

556 - ŒUFS DURS MAYONNAISE * ENTRÉE

Photo Egg mayonnaise.

EGG MAYONNAISE * STARTER
INGREDIENTS: eggs, mayonnaise (n° 792-1).
RECIPE: the eggs are boiled for 8', cut in two and served cold.

557 - ŒUF EN GELÉE * ENTRÉE

Photo Eggs in jelly.

EGGS IN JELLY * STARTER
INGREDIENTS: eggs, tomato, slivers of truffle (optional), ham, wine vinegar, gelatine softened in meat stock, tarragon leaves, chopped chervil.
RECIPE: the ingredients are layered, refrigerated for 3 hours and served cold.

558 - ŒUFS EN MEURETTE * ENTRÉE

Photo Eggs in a brown sauce.

EGGS IN A BROWN SAUCE * STARTER
INGREDIENTS: egg, buttered toast. To cook: chopped shallots, butter, vinegar. Brown sauce: poultry giblets, red wine, flour.
RECIPE: the brown sauce is cooked for 30′ and sieved, the egg boiled for 4′, served hot on buttered toast, coated with the brown sauce.

559 - ŒUF MIROIR * ENTRÉE

Photo Mirror egg.

MIRROR EGG * STARTER
RECIPE: the egg is broken into a special buttered dish and cooked. Served hot, the yolk should be runny.

560 - ŒUF MOLLET * ENTRÉE

Photo Coddled eggs with salad.

CODDLED EGGS * STARTER
RECIPE: the eggs are boiled for 6′ and cold water poured over. Served hot, the yolk should be runny.

561 - ŒUFS À LA NEIGE * DESSERT

Photo Snow eggs.

SNOW EGGS * DESSERT
INGREDIENTS: custard sauce: egg yolks, vanilla sugar, sugar, milk, salt. For the eggs: stiffly beaten egg whites. For the caramel: sugar, water.
RECIPE: the custard sauce is cooked. The egg whites are placed on the custard, coated with caramel and served cold.

OIE

562 - OIE AUX AIRELLES * VOLAILLE

GOOSE WITH CRANBERRIES * POULTRY
INGREDIENTS: goose. Sauce: filtered cooking juices, cranberry jelly, red wine, grated nutmeg, sugar.
RECIPE: the goose is cooked for 2 hours, stuffed with the chopped goose heart and liver, jointed and served hot with the sauce separate.

563 - OIE DE NOËL * VOLAILLE

Photo Christmas goose.

CHRISTMAS GOOSE * POULTRY
INGREDIENTS: goose, chestnuts, flour, poultry stock.
RECIPE: the chestnuts cooked in stock and the goose roasted in the oven for 4 hours are served hot.

OME

564 - OMELETTE AU BROCCIU * ŒUFS, FROMAGE SPÉCIALITÉ DE CORSE

Photo Brocciu cheese omelette.

BROCCIU CHEESE OMELETTE
A CORSICAN SPECIALITY * EGGS
INGREDIENTS: eggs, Brocciu cheese, olive oil.
RECIPE: the eggs are beaten with the cheese, cooked in oil and the omelette folded. Served hot.

565 - OMELETTE AUX CÈPES * ŒUFS - SPÉCIALITÉ DE GASCOGNE

Photo Cep omelette.

CEP OMELETTE, A SPECIALITY FROM GASGONY * EGGS
INGREDIENTS: eggs, butter, cep mushrooms, goose fat, garlic, chopped parsley, butter.
RECIPE: the ceps are cooked in goose fat with the beaten eggs, served hot.

566 - OMELETTE FORESTIÈRE * ŒUFS, CHAMPIGNONS

Photo Wild mushroom omelette.

WILD MUSHROOM OMELETTE * EGGS
INGREDIENTS: wild mushrooms (girolles, ceps, oyster), eggs, butter.
RECIPE: mushrooms browned in butter cooked with the beaten eggs.

567 - OMELETTE AU FROMAGE * ŒUFS

Photo Cheese omelette.

CHEESE OMELETTE * EGGS
INGREDIENTS: eggs, Emmenthal cheese, garlic, butter.
RECIPE: the ingredients are mixed and cooked for 8' if the omelette is to be slightly runny (baveuse). Served immediately.

568 - OMELETTE LYONNAISE * ŒUFS - SPÉCIALITÉ DE LYON

Photo Onion omelette.

ONION OMELETTE - A SPECIALITY FROM LYON * EGGS
INGREDIENTS: eggs, sliced onion, parsley, butter, vinegar.
RECIPE: the beaten egg is added to the onion cooked in butter, the vinegar is heated and poured over the hot omelette as it is served.

569 - OMELETTE AU LARD ET AUX POMMES DE TERRE * ŒUFS

Photo Bacon and potato omelette.

BACON AND POTATO OMELETTE * EGGS
INGREDIENTS: eggs, lean chopped bacon, diced Gruyère cheese, sliced potato, oil, parsley.
RECIPE: the bacon and potatoes are cooked separately, added to the beaten egg and mixed with the Gruyère to finish cooking. Served immediately.

570 - OMELETTE DE LA MÈRE POULARD * ŒUFS

SPECIAL NORMANDY OMELETTE * EGGS
similar to an ordinary omelette as above.
Ingredients: eggs, butter.
RECIPE: the beaten egg is cooked in butter and constantly stirred except for the last few minutes, then served with the sides turned in.

571 - OMELETTE AUX MORILLES * ŒUFS

Photo Morel omelette.

MOREL OMELETTE * EGGS
INGREDIENTS: eggs, morel mushrooms, butter, cream, chopped chives and chervil.
RECIPE: the morels are browned in butter for 6'. The ingredients are mixed and cooked for 8' if the omelette is to be runny (baveuse), the morels added, the omelette folded and served hot.

572 - OMELETTE NIVERNAISE * ŒUFS - SPÉCIALITÉ DU NIVERNAIS

Photo Ham and sorrel omelette.

HAM AND SORREL OMELETTE
A SPECIALITY FROM NIVERNAIS * EGGS
INGREDIENTS: eggs, butter, chopped sorrel, ham and chives.
RECIPE: the sorrel and ham are cooked in butter, mixed with the beaten egg. Served hot.

573 - OMELETTE PÉRIGOURDINE * ŒUFS

Photo Mushroom omelette.

TRUFFLE AND MUSHROOM OMELETTE
* EGGS
INGREDIENTS: beaten eggs, ceps, girolles, horn of plenty mushrooms, truffles, garlic, goose fat, chopped parsley.
RECIPE: the omelette is cooked, the mushrooms cooked in the fat and added with the truffle. Served hot.

574 - OMELETTE SOUFFLÉE AU CITRON * DESSERT

Photo Lemon soufflé omelette.

LEMON SOUFFLÉ OMELETTE * DESSERT
INGREDIENTS: egg yolks, sugar, butter, vanilla sugar, flour, stiffly beaten egg whites. To garnish: whipped crème fraîche, juice and zest of lemon.
RECIPE: The ingredients are mixed, cooked, the filling inserted and folded in two.

ONG

575 - ONGLET À L'ÉCHALOTE * VIANDE

Photo Skirt with shallots.

SKIRT WITH SHALLOTS * MEAT
INGREDIENTS: beef skirt, butter, shallots.
RECIPE: the shallots and meat are cooked in butter and served hot.

576 - ONGLET DE VEAU AU PAPRIKA * VIANDE

Photo Veal skirt with paprika.

VEAL SKIRT WITH PAPRIKA * MEAT
INGREDIENTS: diced skirt, paprika, poultry stock, chopped tomato, garlic and onions, olive oil, cream.
RECIPE: the meat, garlic and onions are browned, the paprika added with the stock and tomato and cooked for 1 hour. Served hot with cream

ORA

577 - ORANGE GIVRÉE * DESSERT GLACÉ

Photo Orange sorbet.

SORBET SERVED IN AN ORANGE * ICED DESSERT
INGREDIENTS: oranges, caster sugar, icing sugar, stiffly beaten egg whites, lemon, apricot jam.
RECIPE: the orange and lemon pulp is removed, chopped and mixed with the juice of the two fruits and the sugar and egg, then put back into the orange skin. The jam is mixed with hot water to coat the skin before it is rolled in sugar. Put in the freezer.

OSS

578 - OSSO BUCCO * VIANDE - SPÉCIALITÉ ITALIENNE

Photo Osso bucco.

OSSO BUCCO - AN ITALIAN SPECIALITY * MEAT

INGREDIENTS: slices of knuckle of veal with the bone, onion, garlic, butter, flour, dry white wine, meat stock, orange and lemon zest, chopped marjory, grated nutmeg.

RECIPE: The floured meat is cooked in butter with the onion, garlic, wine and fruit zests and cooked for 1 hour. Served hot.

PAE

579 - PAËLLA * PLAT COMPLET - SPÉCIALITÉ ESPAGNOLE

Photo Paella.

PAELLA - A ONE-DISH MEAL AND SPANISH SPECIALITY

INGREDIENTS: chicken, pieces of pork fillet, sliced chorizo sausage, mussels, gambas prawns, rice, black olives, tomatoes, peas, lemon, onions, garlic, olive oil, dry white wine, poultry stock, saffron. RECIPE: the meats are all cooked separately, the ingredients added and cooked together in the oven for 20'. Served hot. (squid and other fish may be added).

PAI

580 - PAILLÉ DE POMMES DE TERRE * LÉGUMES SPÉCIALITÉ DE NORMANDIE

Photo Straw potatoes.

STRAW POTATOES * VEGETABLES
A SPECIALITY FROM NORMANDY

INGREDIENTS: potatoes and apples grated to resemble straw, flour, eggs, butter, parsley and chives.

RECIPE: the ingredients are mixed and cooked in oil, served hot.

581 - PAIN D'ÉPICES * PÂTISSERIE

Photo Spiced cake.

SPICED CAKE * CAKE

INGREDIENTS: for the mixture: water, honey, sugar, rum. Different types of flour: rye, wheat. Spices: cinnamon, nutmeg, lemon and orange zest. RECIPE: The water, honey, sugar and rum are mixed and incorporated into the flour and spices. It is allowed to rest for 48 hours, cooked for 1 hour and served cold.

582 - PAIN PERDU * DESSERT

Photo French toast.

FRENCH TOAST * DESSERT
INGREDIENTS: dry bun bread soaked in hot milk, sugar, vanilla. To cook: butter and beaten eggs.
RECIPE: the bread is dipped in the egg yolks, cooked in butter and served hot with sugar.

583 - PAIN DE POISSON * POISSON

Photo Fish terrine.

FISH TERRINE * FISH
INGREDIENTS: pieces of lemon sole and salmon fillets, precooked spinach, butter, egg yolk, cream, lemon juice, dry white vermouth, dill.
RECIPE: the fish is blended with the cream, vermouth and egg yolk and layered with the spinach to cook. Served warm or cold in slices.

584 - PAIN AUX NOIX * PAIN - SPÉCIALITÉ NIÇOISE

Photo Walnut bread.

WALNUT BREAD - A BREAD SPECIALITY FROM NICE
INGREDIENTS: flour, walnut oil, water, yeast, baking powder, shelled walnuts (n° 546-1).
RECIPE: the flour and yeast are mixed with the water, oil and walnuts, left for 3 hours to prove and baked for 30'. Served with cheese.

585 - PAIN AUX RAISINS * PAIN - SPÉCIALITÉ NIÇOISE

Photo Raisin bread.

RAISIN BREAD - A BREAD SPECIALITY FROM NICE
INGREDIENTS: flour, sugar, raisins, yeast, baking powder, water.
RECIPE: the flour is kneaded with water and sugar to form a dough to which the raisins are added, proved for 3 hours and baked for 30'.

585-1 - PAIN DE SEIGLE * PAIN

Photo Rye bread.

RYE BREAD * BREAD
INGREDIENTS: rye flour, water, yeast.

PAL

586 - PALERON BRAISÉ DE BŒUF * VIANDE

Photo Braised flank of beef.

BRAISED FLANK OF BEEF * MEAT
INGREDIENTS: cubed beef, cabbage, sliced onions and carrots, tomatoes, potatoes, white wine, bay leaf, thyme.
RECIPE: the meat is browned, the ingredients added and cooked for 2 hours; the cabbage and potatoes are boiled. Served together hot.

587 - PALETS AUX AMANDES * PÂTISSERIE

ALMOND BISCUITS * BISCUIT
INGREDIENTS: flour, caster sugar, vanilla sugar, blanched almonds, butter, egg yolk, Calvados applejack brandy.
RECIPE: the ingredients are mixed, the dough cut into rounds and cooked for 10′. Served cold.

588 - PALETS BRETONS * PÂTISSERIE DE BRETAGNE

Photo Breton biscuits.

BRETON BISCUITS * BISCUITS FROM BRITTANY
INGREDIENTS: flour, sugar, eggs, butter, milk.
RECIPE: the ingredients are mixed, shaped into balls, flattened and baked for 10′. Served cold.

589 - PALETS AUX FIGUES * PÂTISSERIE

FIG BISUITS * BISCUIT
INGREDIENTS: figs, hazelnuts, cinnamon, diced crystallised orange and lemon, flour, baking powder, honey, sugar, butter, eggs. To macerate: rum, Kirsch liqueur.
RECIPE: the figs are macerated for 1 hour, mixed with the other ingredients and baked for 25', then cut into squares. Served cold.

590 - PALETS GRENOBLOIS * PÂTISSERIE DE GRENOBLE

Photo Grenoble biscuits.

GRENOBLE BISCUITS * BISCUITS FROM GRENOBLE
INGREDIENTS: dough: flour, sugar, chopped hazelnuts, butter, egg yolk, lemon zest, ground cinnamon, garnish: stiffly beaten egg white
RECIPE: the ingredients are mixed, the dough cut into rounds, topped with the egg white and hazelnuts put in the centre. Baked for 15', served cold.

591 - PALETTE DE PORC À LA DIABLE * VIANDE

Photo Blade of pork.

BLADE OF PORK WITH MUSTARD * MEAT
INGREDIENTS: blade of pork, sliced potatoes and onions, butter, thyme, meat stock, caul.
RECIPE: alternate layers of potato, onions and thyme with the pork on top, cooked with the stock for 1 hour 30 mins. Served hot.

592 - PALOURDES * MOLLUSQUES

Photo Clams.

CLAMS * FRESH SHELLFISH
Served cold.

PAM

593 - PAMPLEMOUSSE AU SUCRE * FRUITS

Photo Grapefruit with sugar.

GRAPEFRUIT WITH SUGAR * FRESH FRUIT
Served cold.

PAN

594 - PAN BAGNAT * PLAT COMPLET - SPÉCIALITÉ NIÇOISE

Photo Tuna salad roll.

TUNA OR ANCHOVY SALAD ROLL
A ONE-MEAL SPECIALITY FROM NICE
INGREDIENTS: bread roll, tomatoes, green peppers, spring onions (local green variety), black olives, anchovies or tuna, olive oil, basil. Other ingredients: hard-boiled egg, vinegar, onions, bread rubbed with garlic.
RECIPE: the tomatoes, peppers, onions, olives and anchovies are layered and sprinkled with olive oil and chopped basil. Served cold.

595 - PANNEQUETS BERRICHONS * LÉGUMES SPÉCIALITÉ DE POMMES DE TERRE DU BERRY

Photo Potato cream pancakes.

POTATO CREAM PANCAKES - A SPECIALITY FROM BERRY * VEGETABLES
INGREDIENTS: peeled boiled potatoes, flour, milk, cream, eggs, nutmeg.
RECIPE: the potatoes are mashed, added to the flour, egg and cream and left to rest for 1 hour. Spoonfuls are cooked in hot butter forming panpastrys. Served hot.

PAP

596 - PAPILLOTE DE CABILLAUD AUX PETITS LÉGUMES * POISSON

Photo Cod in foil with tiny vegetables.

COD IN FOIL WITH TINY VEGETABLES * FISH
INGREDIENTS: cod tail, sliced bacon. To cook: sliced into matchsticks: leeks, onions, carrots, butter, mustard, lemon juice, parsley.
RECIPE: the cod is spread with mustard and cooked in a closed foil case with the ingredients for 40'. Served hot.

PAP

597 - PAPILLOTE DE POISSON AU CHOU * POISSON

Photo Fish cooked in cablage leaves.

FISH COOKED IN CABBAGE LEAVES * FISH
INGREDIENTS: pureed fillet of cod. Garnish: Savoy cabbage. To cook: sesame oil, eggs, mustard, cream, lemon juice, dry white wine, vegetable stock, chopped basil.
RECIPE: cabbage blanched for 10'. The fillets are blended with the ingredients and cooked for 30' in cabbage leaves. Served hot.

598 - PAPILLOTE DE SÉBASTES (RASCASSES) * POISSON

Photo Redfish in foil.

REDFISH IN FOIL * FISH
Served hot.

599 - PAPILLOTE DE TRUITE AUX HERBES * POISSON

Photo Trout in foil with herbs.

TROUT IN FOIL WITH HERBS * FISH
INGREDIENTS: trout, stuffing: lemon, shallots, butter, lemon juice, sage, basil, chives.
RECIPE: the fish is stuffed and baked in foil for 20'. Served immediately.

PAR

600 - PARFAIT AU CAFÉ * DESSERT GLACÉ

COFFEE PARFAIT * ICED DESSERT
INGREDIENTS: icing sugar, egg yolks, whipped cream, coffee liqueur.
RECIPE: the ingredients are mixed, frozen for 5 hours. Served cold.

601 - PARIS BREST * PÂTISSERIE

Photo Custard puff crown.

CUSTARD PUFF CROWN * CAKE
INGREDIENTS: for the choux pastry: flour, butter, nibbed almonds, water, eggs, custard cream, eggs, milk, flour, butter, praline, icing sugar
RECIPE: the pastry is shaped into a ring, sprinkled with almonds and baked for 20'. The crown is sliced through the middle and filled with custard cream. Served cold.

602 - PARMENTIER DE CANARD * VOLAILLE

Photo Duck cottage pie.

DUCK COTTAGE PIE * POULTRY
INGREDIENTS: mashed potatoes. Filling: minced duck, onion, egg, butter, parsley, grated nutmeg, topping: grated Gruyère cheese.
RECIPE: the mash is spread in a buttered dish, topped with the filling and then the rest of the mash, finishing with the grated cheese. Browned for 30' and served immediately.

PAT

602-1 - PÂTES AU FOIE GRAS ET CÈPES * PÂTES

Photo Pasta with foie gras and ceps.

PASTA WITH FOIE GRAS AND CEPS * PASTA
INGREDIENTS: fresh pasta, pieces of foie gras, goose fat to cook the cep mushrooms.
RECIPE: the cooked and drained pasta is served with the ceps and foie gras, served hot.

603 - PÂTÉ DE CAMPAGNE * CHARCUTERIE

Photo Country pâté.

COUNTRY PÂTÉ * COOKED MEATS AND SIMILAR
INGREDIENTS: minced veal, pork, bacon and pig's liver, eggs, soft bread, milk, onion, clove of garlic, chopped parsley and thyme.
RECIPE: the bread is soaked in the milk, mixed with ingredients and cooked for 1 hour. Served cold.

604 - PATTES DE CRABES * CRUSTACÉS

Photo Crab's claws.

CRAB'S CLAWS * SHELLFISH
INGREDIENTS AND RECIPE: the crabs are cooked in court bouillon; only the claws are served to be cracked open. Served cold with mayonnaise.

605 - PÂTÉ EN CROÛTE * CHARCUTERIE

Photo French pork pie.

FRENCH PORK PIE * COOKED MEATS AND SIMILAR
INGREDIENTS: shortcrust pastry, minced pork fillet and blade, bacon, egg yolks, sherry jelly. Herbs: crumbled thyme, garlic, chopped marjory, juniper berries.
RECIPE: the meat with the herbs is refrigerated for 8 hours. A buttered terrine dish is lined with shortcrust pastry, the meat added and cooked for 50'. Served cold.

606 - PÂTES FRAÎCHES À LA CARBONARA * PÂTES SPÉCIALITÉ ITALIENNE

Photo Fresh pasta with bacon and cream sauce.

FRESH PASTA WITH BACON AND CREAM SAUCE - AN ITALIAN PASTA SPECIALITY
INGREDIENTS: ribbon pasta, diced bacon, cream, egg yolks.
RECIPE: the pasta is boiled for 7', added to the browned bacon and cream and presented with an egg yolk in its shell. Served hot.

607 - PÂTES FRAÎCHES À LA BOLOGNAISE * PÂTES SPÉCIALITÉ ITALIENNE

Photo Fresh pasta Bolognese.

FRESH PASTA BOLOGNESE - AN ITALIAN PASTA SPECIALITY
INGREDIENTS: ribbon pasta. Bolognese sauce: butter, minced meat, onions, mushrooms, tomato sauce, basil, Parmesan cheese.
RECIPE: the sauce is cooked and added to the boiled pasta with the Parmesan cheese. Served hot.

607-1 - PÂTÉ LYONNAIS À LA VIANDE ET SAUCISSE * ENTRÉE

Photo Lyon pastry.

LYON MEAT AND SAUSAGE PASTRY * STARTER
Served hot.

PAU

608 - PAUPIETTES DE DINDE * VOLAILLE

Photo Stuffed turkey rolls.

STUFFED TURKEY ROLLS * POULTRY
INGREDIENTS: turkey escalopes. Stuffing: cream, chervil, thyme, onion, butter, sausage meat, egg yolk. To cook: poultry stock. Sauce: crème fraiche.
RECIPE: the vegetables are browned in butter, laid on the escalope, rolled into olives and cooked for 20', served hot.

609 - PAUPIETTES DE SOLE AUX HERBES * POISSON

Photo Sole rolls stuffed with herbs.

SOLE ROLLS STUFFED WITH HERBS * FISH
INGREDIENTS: sole fillets. Garnish: matchsticks of fennel, wild rice, dry white wine, vegetable stock. Stuffing: butter, chopped lemon grass, sauce: cream, lemon juice, dill, parsley.
RECIPE: the fillets are rolled around the stuffing. The garnish is cooked, the fish coated with sauce and served immediately.

610 - PAUPIETTE DE VEAU AUX MORILLES * VIANDE

Photo Veal rolls with morels.

VEAL ROLLS WITH MORELS * MEAT
INGREDIENTS: thin veal escalopes, bacon, shallots, butter, oil, parsley. Morel mushroom sauce: morels, cream, watercress.
RECIPE: the escalope, covered with another escalope and bacon, is rolled, tied with string and cooked for 8'. The sauce is cooked, served hot.

611 - PAVÉ DE RUMSTECK AU BLEU OU SAUCE AU ROQUEFORT * VIANDE

Photo Rump steak with blue cheese sauce.

RUMP STEAK WITH BLUE CHEESE SAUCE * MEAT
INGREDIENTS: Rump steak, butter. Sauce: cream, Roquefort or Bleu d'Auvergne cheese.
RECIPE: the steak is grilled and served hot with the sauce.

612 - PAVÉ DE RUMSTECK SAUCE AU POIVRE * VIANDE

Photo Rump steak with pepper sauce.

RUMP STEAK WITH PEPPER SAUCE * MEAT
INGREDIENTS: rump steak, butter. Pepper sauce: green peppercorns, lamb stock base.
RECIPE: grilled rump steak served hot with the cooked sauce.

613 - PAVÉ DE SANDRE * POISSON

Photo Thick fillet of zander.

THICK FILLET OF ZANDER * FISH
INGREDIENTS: fillet of zander, oil, butter.
RECIPE: the zander is cooked quickly. Served immediately.

614 - PÊCHES ESCOFFIER * DESSERT - FRUITS

Photo Escoffier peaches.

ESCOFFIER PEACHES * FRUIT DESSERT
INGREDIENTS: halved peach. Sauce: cream, Grand Marnier liqueur. Garnish: nougat ice cream, whipped cream. Cooking syrup: orange juice and zest, sugar, vanilla pod.
RECIPE: peaches poached for 10' in syrup, served cold with whipped cream and nougat ice cream.

615 - PÊCHE MELBA * DESSERT GLACÉ - FRUITS

Photo Peach Melba with whipped cream.

PEACH MELBA * FRUIT DESSERT
INGREDIENTS: yellow peaches, vanilla ice cream, sugar, lemon juice.
RECIPE: halved peach served with a scoop of vanilla ice cream, toasted flaked almonds, whipped cream.

PER

616 - PERDREAU BRAISÉ AUX LENTILLES * GIBIER

Photo Braised partridge with lentils.

BRAISED PARTRIDGE WITH LENTILS * GAME
INGREDIENTS: partridge. To cook the lentils: lean bacon, carrots, leek. To cook the partridge: onions, dry white wine, meat stock, bay leaf, sauce: cream.
RECIPE: the lentils and ingredients are cooked for 1 hour 30 mins. The partridge is cooked for 1 hour and the cream added to the cooking juices. Served hot.

617 - PERDREAU AU CHOU VERT * GIBIER

Photo Partridge with green cabbage.

PARTRIDGE WITH CABBAGE * GAME
INGREDIENTS: partridge, lean bacon, cabbage, carrots, butter, small onions, bay leaf.
RECIPE: the partridge is placed on the vegetables cooked in butter and stock and cooked for 30'. Served hot.

618 - PERDREAU FARCI * GIBIER

Photo Stuffed partridge with cabbage.

STUFFED PARTRIDGE * GAME
INGREDIENTS: partridge. Stuffing: bacon, dry bread, raisins, onions, poultry stock.
RECIPE: the stuffed partridge is cooked for 30' and served hot.

619 - PERSIL * AROMATES

Photo Parsley.

PARSLEY * HERB

619-1 - PETITS POIS AU LARD * LÉGUMES

Photo Peas with bacon.

PEAS WITH BACON * VEGETABLES
INGREDIENTS AND RECIPE: the peas are cooked with the butter and the bacon. Served hot.

620 - PETIT SALÉ AU CHOU * VIANDE

Photo Salt pork with cabbage.

SALT PORK WITH CABBAGE * MEAT
INGREDIENTS: salt pork, cabbage, sliced onions, smoked bacon, garlic.
RECIPE: the cabbage is boiled for 5' then cooked for 1 hour 30 mins with all the other ingredients and served hot.

621 - PETIT SALÉ AUX LENTILLES * VIANDE

Photo Salt pork with lentils.

SALT PORK WITH LENTILS * MEAT
INGREDIENTS: pork, bacon, sausages. To cook the lentils: carrots, onions, bouquet garni.
RECIPE: the meat and lentils are cooked separately then combined to finish cooking, served hot.

622 - PETIT SALÉ À LA TOULOUSAINE * VIANDE

Photo Salt pork with beans.

SALT PORK WITH BEANS * MEAT
INGREDIENTS: salt pork. To cook: water, dried white beans, carrots, onions, oil, bay leaf, parsley.
RECIPE: the beans are soaked for 12 hours and cooked with the ingredients for 1 hour. Served hot.

623 - PETIT BABA AU RHUM * PÂTISSERIE

Photo Rum baba.

INDIVIDUAL RUM BABA * CAKE
INGREDIENTS: dough: flour, yeast, sugar, butter, eggs, cream, milk, water, rum, lemon zest.
RECIPE: the flour, yeast, sugar and milk are mixed with the beaten egg and warm butter, rested, baked for 20' in moulds, soaked in the rum mixture while still hot and served cold decorated with whipped cream.

624 - PETITS FARCIS À LA PROVENÇALE * LÉGUMES SPÉCIALITÉ DE PROVENCE

Photo Stuffed vegetables.

STUFFED VEGETABLES - A SPECIALITY FROM PROVENCE
INGREDIENTS: tomatoes, courgettes, onions. Stuffing: vegetable pulp, shallots, garlic, ham or meat, sausage meat, eggs, bread soaked in milk, grated cheese, butter, cream, olive oil, parsley. Topping: breadcrumbs
RECIPE: the vegetables are hollowed out, filled with the mixture, cooked for 30' and served hot browned.

PIE

625 - PIED DE PORC À LA SAINTE MENEHOULD * ABATS

Photo Golden pig's foot.

GOLDEN PIG'S FEET * OFFAL
INGREDIENTS: pig's feet, bacon bard. To cook the pig's feet: water, carrots, onions, garlic, wine, bay leaf, thyme, parsley, tarragon, clove. Breadcrumb mixture: egg yolk, breadcrumbs.
RECIPE: the pig's feet are halved, barded and cooked for 5 hours, then rolled in breadcrumbs to brown. Served hot.

626 - PIED DE PORC FARCI * ABATS

Photo Stuffed pig's foot.

STUFFED PIG'S FEET * OFFAL
INGREDIENTS: pig's feet, stuffing: chine, fat bacon, calf's liver, shallots, spinach, parsley.
RECIPE: the feet are stuffed and cooked in stock for 1 hour 30 mins. Served hot.

627 - PIED DE PORC VINAIGRETTE * ABATS

Photo Pig's foot with vinaigrette dressing.

PIG'S FEET WITH VINAIGRETTE DRESSING * OFFAL
INGREDIENTS: pig's feet. To cook: water, carrots, onions, garlic, wine, bay leaf, thyme, parsley, tarragon, vinaigrette dressing: oil, vinegar, parsley.
RECIPE: the halved pig's feet are cooked for 5 hours and served cold with the vinaigrette dressing.

628 - PIEDS ET PAQUETS * ABATS

Photo Sheep's feet and tripe.

SHEEP'S FEET AND TRIPE * OFFAL
INGREDIENTS: sheep's feet and tripe, ham. To cook: fat bacon, tomatoes, carrots, leek, onions, garlic, meat stock, dry white wine, parsley, bouquet garni, clove, nutmeg.
RECIPE: the ingredients are cooked for 8 hours. Served hot.

PIG

629 - PIGEON AUX PETITS POIS * VOLAILLE

Photo Pigeon with peas.

PIGEON WITH PEAS * POULTRY
INGREDIENTS: pigeon. To cook: lean bacon, shelled peas, lettuce heart, shallots, butter, wine, parsley.
RECIPE: the ingredients are cooked separately from the pigeons and combined to finish cooking. Served hot.

630 - PILAF D'AGNEAU * VIANDE

Photo *Lamb pilaff.*

LAMB PILAFF * MEAT
INGREDIENTS: meat, lamb kidneys and liver. Garnish: rice, onions, olive oil. Sauce: meat stock, pine nuts, chilli, cinnamon, raisins, tomatoes, peppercorns.
RECIPE: the meat and onions are browned in butter and the stock and rice added to cook. Served immediately.

631 - PILAF DE FOIES DE VOLAILLE * ABATS

Photo *Poultry liver pilaff.*

POULTRY LIVER PILAFF * OFFAL
INGREDIENTS: diced poultry livers, rice, onion, butter, cream, vegetable stock, dry white wine, parsley.
RECIPE: the livers are cooked in butter and the other ingredients added to finish cooking. Served hot.

PIN

632 - PINTADE FARCIE * VOLAILLE

Photo *Stuffed guinea fowl.*

STUFFED GUINEA FOWL * POULTRY
INGREDIENTS: guinea fowl, stuffing: poultry livers, lean bacon, oyster mushrooms, onion, butter, oil, brandy, breadcrumbs, bay leaf, tarragon.
RECIPE: the guinea fowl is stuffed and cooked for 40'. Served hot.

633 - PINTADE À LA NORMANDE * VOLAILLE

Photo *Guinea fowl with Applejack brandy sauce.*

GUINEA FOWL WITH APPLEJACK BRANDY SAUCE * POULTRY
INGREDIENTS: guinea fowl. To cook: bacon bard, apples, butter, thyme, cider, Calvados applejack brandy, sugar. Sauce: cream.
RECIPE: the guinea fowl is cooked for 45', served hot with the sauce.

PIN

634 - PINTADE AU CHOU * VOLAILLE

Photo Guinea fowl with cabbage.

GUINEA FOWL WITH CABBAGE * POULTRY
INGREDIENTS: guinea fowl, cabbage. To cook: sliced bacon, carrots, onions, stock.
RECIPE: the cabbage is blanched for 20', drained and cooked with the guinea fowl and ingredients for 30'. Served hot.

PIP

635 - PIPERADE * OMELETTE AUX LÉGUMES - SPÉCIALITÉ DU BÉARN

Photo Scrambled egg with pepper, ham and tomato.

SCRAMBLED EGG WITH PEPPER, HAM AND TOMATO - A SPECIALITY OF BÉARN
INGREDIENTS: scrambled eggs. Vegetables: tomatoes, pepper, onions, Bayonne raw ham, goose fat, garlic, oil, butter, Espelette chilli pepper.
RECIPE: the vegetables are sautéed and added to the scrambled egg to cook. Served hot.

PIS

636 - PISSALADIÈRE * LÉGUMES - SPÉCIALITÉ DE NICE

Photo Mediterranean onion pizza.

MEDITERRANEAN ONION PIZZA - A VEGETABLE SPECIALITY FROM NICE
INGREDIENTS: bread dough. Garnish: sliced onions, garlic, small black olives, anchovies, olive oil, thyme.
RECIPE: the onions, garlic and thyme are sautéed in oil to garnish the dough with the anchovies and black olives; it is baked for 20'. Served hot.

637 - PISSENLITS AU LARD * SALADE

Photo Dandelion salad with bacon.

DANDELIONS WITH BACON * SALAD
INGREDIENTS: dandelion leaves (slightly bitter taste), diced smoked bacon. Vinaigrette dressing: shallots, garlic, hard-boiled egg, vinegar, mustard.
RECIPE: The bacon is cooked and the vinaigrette dressing and browned croutons served over the salad.

PIT

638 - PITHIVIERS * PÂTISSERIE - SPÉCIALITÉ D'ORLÉANS

Photo Pithiviers almond tart.

PITHIVIERS ALMOND TART
A SPECIALITY FROM ORLÉANS
INGREDIENTS: flaky pastry. Cream filling: ground almonds, sugar, flour, butter, eggs, rum.
RECIPE: the centre of the pastry is filled with the cream and cooked, served warm.

PLA

639 - PLATEAU DE FRUITS DE MER * CRUSTACÉS, MOLLUSQUES

Photo Seafood platter.

SEAFOOD PLATTER * SHELLFISH
INGREDIENTS: consists of cupped and/or flat oysters, small and large clams, whelks, winkles, brown shrimp, prawns, firm-flesh clams.

PLE

640 - PLEUROTES SAUTÉES À L'AIL * CHAMPIGNONS

Photo Oyster mushrooms sautéed with garlic.

OYSTER MUSHROOMS SAUTEED WITH GARLIC * MUSHROOMS
INGREDIENTS: oyster mushrooms, garlic, olive oil, butter, lemon, parsley.
RECIPE: the mushrooms and garlic are cooked in butter, the lemon juice added and served hot.

PLI

641 - PLIE AU LARD * POISSON

Photo Plaice with bacon.

PLAICE WITH BACON * FISH
INGREDIENTS: plaice. Garnish: bacon, cultivated mushrooms, onions, butter. To cook: flour. Sauce: lemon juice, chopped parsley, butter.
RECIPE: the plaice and garnish are cooked separately and served hot with the sauce.

642 - PLIE AUX HERBES * POISSON

Photo Plaice with herbs.

PLAICE WITH HERBS * FISH
INGREDIENTS: plaice. Garnish: potatoes, butter. Sauce: cream, lemon juice, chopped herbs.
RECIPE: the plaice are cooked for 5' with the sauce, the precooked potatoes browned in butter, served hot.

POC

643 - POCHOUSE * POISSON

Photo Poached freshwater fish.

POACHED FRESHWATER FISH * FISH
INGREDIENTS: freshwater fish, onions, garlic, Burgundy Aligote white wine, bouquet garni. To cook: butter, flour, fish stock. Sauce: egg yolks, cream, cooking juice. Garnish: slice of country bread.
RECIPE: some pieces of fish are cooked in butter with the garlic and onions and the seasoned wine. Other pieces are poached and cooked in the cooking sauce. Served hot together with the sauce.

644 - POCHOUSE VERDUNOISE * POISSON SPÉCIALITÉ DE BOURGOGNE

Photo Poached freshwater fish verdun style.

POACHED FRESHWATER FISH VERDUN STYLE - A FISH SPECIALITY FROM BURGUNDY
INGREDIENTS: freshwater fish (eel, pike, carp, perch). To cook: onions, shallots, garlic, bouquet garni, oil, Burgundy Aligoté wine. Sauce: butter, flour, cooking juices. Garnish: bread, garlic.
RECIPE: the fish and ingredients are cooked, the sauce and garlic croutons added when served hot.

POE

645 - POÊLÉE D'AUBERGINES ET DE VEAU AUX TOMATES * VIANDE

Photo Veal with aubergines and tomatoes.

VEAL WITH AUBERGINES AND TOMATOES * MEAT AND VEGETABLE
INGREDIENTS: aubergines, boned shoulder of veal, tomatoes, onions, garlic, butter, sesame oil, meat stock.
RECIPE: the ingredients are cooked separately and the tomatoes and garlic added later. Served hot.

646 - POÊLÉE DE CHAMPIGNONS DES BOIS * CHAMPIGNONS

Photo Sauteed girolle and oyster mushrooms.

SAUTEED WILD MUSHROOMS
* MUSHROOMS
INGREDIENTS: girolles, ceps, butter.
RECIPE: the mushrooms are cooked in butter and served with garlic and parsley. Served hot.

POI

647 - POIRE BELLE-HÉLÈNE * FRUITS - DESSERT

Photo Pear and chocolate sundae.

PEAR AND CHOCOLATE SUNDAE
* FRUIT DESSERT
INGREDIENTS: pear halves, vanilla ice cream, dark chocolate, sugar, sweet wine, cinnamon, whipped cream.
RECIPE: The sweetened pears are poached in wine, coated with melted chocolate and served with vanilla ice cream and almonds.

648 - POIRE BOURDALOUE * PÂTISSERIE

Photo Pear and almond tart.

PEAR AND ALMOND TART * CAKE
INGREDIENTS: pears, shortcrust pastry. Frangipane filling: ground macaroons and almonds, sugar, flour, butter, eggs, milk, vanilla pod.
RECIPE: the pears are poached in syrup, drained, laid on the pastry with the frangipane filling and baked for 20'. Served cold or warm.

649 - POIRE SAUCE AU MIEL * DESSERT - FRUITS

Photo Pears with honey sauce.

PEARS WITH HONEY SAUCE * FRUIT DESSERT
INGREDIENTS: pears, lemon, honey sauce: sugar, honey, egg yolks, milk. Caramel: sugar, water.
RECIPE: the poached pears are coated with the honey sauce and caramel. Served warm.

650 - POIRE AU VIN ROUGE ET AUX ÉPICES * DESSERT - FRUITS

Photo Pears in red wine.

SPICY PEARS IN RED WINE * FRUIT DESSERT
INGREDIENTS: pears, liquid honey. Presentation sauce: whipped cream, vanilla. To cook: red wine, cloves, cinnamon, ginger, liquid honey.
RECIPE: the sauce is poured over the cooked pears. Served cold.

651 - POIREAUX EN GRATIN * LÉGUMES

Photo Leek cheese bake.

LEEK CHEESE BAKE * VEGETABLES
INGREDIENTS: white of leeks. White sauce: butter, flour, milk, grated nutmeg, cream. To brown: grated Emmenthal cheese.
RECIPE: the leeks are simmered for 20' and covered with the white sauce to brown. Served hot.

652 - POITRINE DE VEAU FARCIE * VIANDE - SPÉCIALITÉ DU POITOU

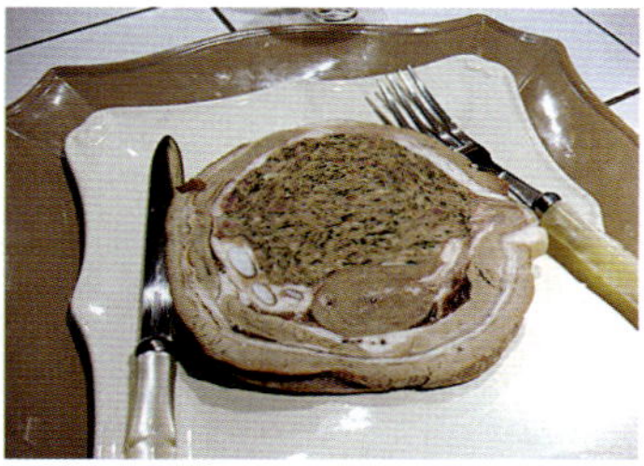
Photo Stuffed breast of veal.

STUFFED BREAST OF VEAL - A MEAT SPECIALITY FROM POITOU
INGREDIENTS: boned breast of veal. To cook: carrots, dry white wine, butter. Stuffing: spinach or Swiss chard, shallots, mushrooms, eggs, sausage meat, soft bread, milk, chopped parsley and tarragon, garlic. To cook: onions.
RECIPE: the breast of veal is filled with the mixed stuffing and cooked for 2 hours. Served hot or cold.

POM

653 - POMMES AU FOUR * FRUITS EN DESSERT

Photo Baked apples.

BAKED APPLES * FRUIT DESSERT
INGREDIENTS: Baking apples to fill: raisins, chopped hazelnuts, marzipan, lemon, vanilla sugar, Calvados applejack brandy, rum, cinnamon.
RECIPE: the apple is cored, the centre filled, baked for 30' in the oven and served hot. May be flamed with Calvados.

654 - POMMES AU FOUR * FRUITS - DESSERT - SPÉCIALITÉ DE LYON AUTRE VARIANTE

Photo Baked apples.

BAKED APPLES * FRUIT DESSERT - A LYON SPECIALITY - ANOTHER VARIATION
INGREDIENTS: apples, redcurrant jelly, butter, sugar.
RECIPE: the centre of the apples is filled with redcurrant jelly, sugar and butter, baked for 45' and served hot.

655 - POMMES DAUPHINE * LÉGUMES

Photo Dauphine potatoes.

DAUPHINE POTATOES * VEGETABLES
INGREDIENTS: mashed Bintje potatoes. Choux pastry: flour, butter, eggs, water. To cook: oil.
RECIPE: the choux pastry is mixed with the mashed potato and deep-fried in small portions. Served hot.

656 - POMMES DE TERRE BRESSANE * LÉGUMES

Photo Bresse baked potatoes.

BRESSE BAKED POTATOES * VEGETABLES
INGREDIENTS AND RECIPE: potatoes baked in the oven in fat with their skins. Served hot.

657 - POMMES DE TERRE À LA LYONNAISE * LÉGUMES

Photo Fried potatoes with onions.

FRIED POTATOES WITH ONIONS * VEGETABLES
INGREDIENTS: potatoes, sliced onions, butter, parsley.
RECIPE: pre-boiled potatoes, browned in a pan in butter with onions. Served immediately with chopped parsley.

658 - POMMES DE TERRE À LA SARLADAISE * LÉGUMES SPÉCIALITÉ DU PÉRIGORD

Photo Potatoes and ceps sautéed in goose fat.

POTATOES AND CEPS SAUTEED IN GOOSE FAT * VEGETABLES

INGREDIENTS: sliced potatoes, garlic, goose fat, cep mushrooms, parsley.

RECIPE: the potatoes and ceps are cooked in goose fat, garlic and parsley added and served hot.

659 - POMMES DE TERRE BOULANGÈRE * LÉGUMES

Photo Sliced potato bake.

SLICED POTATO BAKE * VEGETABLES

INGREDIENTS: Sliced potatoes, onions. To cook: carrots, leeks, celery, cultivated mushrooms, garlic, butter, meat stock, thyme.

RECIPE: the vegetables are cooked in the stock. Potatoes and onions are layered in a dish, covered with stock and baked for 1 hour 20 mins. Served hot.

660 - POMMES DE TERRE CRIQUE À LA LYONNAISE * LÉGUMES SPÉCIALITÉ DE LYON

Photo Lyon potato cake.

LYONS POTATO CAKE * VEGETABLES

INGREDIENTS: peeled grated potato, cooked sweetcorn, eggs, oil.

RECIPE: the ingredients are mixed, formed into cakes, fried for 3' and served hot.

661 - POMMES DE TERRE CUITES À LA DIABLE * LÉGUMES

Photo Potatoes baked in a "diable" dish.

POTATOES BAKED IN A DISH * VEGETABLES

INGREDIENTS: potatoes, a "diable" covered dish

RECIPE: the special dish is used to bake the potatoes for 1 hour without fat or water. Served hot.

662 - POMMES DE TERRE FARCIES

Photo *Stuffed potatoes (in the foreground).*

BAKED POTATOES
INGREDIENTS: potatoes. Stuffing: cooked meat, garlic, onions, eggs, milk, bread, cream, herbs.
RECIPE: the potatoes are stuffed and then cooked in fat. Served hot.

663 - POMMES DE TERRE EN PAPILLOTE * LÉGUMES

Photo *Foil-baked potatoes.*

FOIL-BAKED POTATOES * VEGETABLES
INGREDIENTS: potatoes, butter, parsley, chives, foil.
RECIPE: the potatoes are baked in the oven in a foil case. Served with butter, parsley, chives. Served hot.

664 - POMMES DE TERRE FARCIES AU ROQUEFORT * LÉGUMES

Photo *Baked potatoes with blue cheese.*

BAKED POTATOES WITH BLUE CHEESE * VEGETABLES
INGREDIENTS: potatoes. Filling: Roquefort cheese (n° 929), chopped chives.
RECIPE: preboiled potatoes, filled with a cheese mixture and baked in the oven. Served hot.

664-1 - POMMES DE TERRE RATE * LÉGUMES

Photo *Rate potatoes.*

RATE VARIETY POTATO * VEGETABLES
Based on the renowned mashed potato by Joël ROBUCHON. Served hot.

POM

665 - POMMES DE TERRE SAUTÉES * LÉGUMES

Photo Sauté potatoes.

SAUTE POTATOES * VEGETABLES
INGREDIENTS: potato cubes, oil.
RECIPE: the potatoes are browned and served hot.

POT

666 - POTAGE ARDENNAIS * POTAGE SPÉCIALITÉ DE LA CHAMPAGNE

Photo Ardennes chicory soup.

ARDENNES CHICORY SOUP - A SPECIALITY FROM CHAMPAGNE
INGREDIENTS: sliced potatoes, leeks, chopped chicory, butter, milk, toasted thin French sticks.
RECIPE: the leeks and chicory are cooked in butter, the potatoes and milk added and served hot with croutons and grated Gruyère cheese handed separately.

667 - POTAGE SAINT GERMAIN * POTAGE

Photo Pea and ham soup.

PEA AND HAM SOUP * SOUP
INGREDIENTS: peas, onion, green of leeks, lettuce, salt pork belly, butter, bouquet garni, stock. Garnish: peas, croutons sautéed in butter, chervil.
RECIPE: bacon cooked in butter, leeks, onions, lettuce, stock, peas are added and blended once cooked. Served hot.

668 - POT-AU-FEU * PLAT COMPLET

Photo Beef stewed with vegetables.

BEEF STEWED WITH VEGETABLES * A ONE-DISH MEAL
INGREDIENTS: fat and lean beef, marrow bone, leeks, carrots, celery, onions, bouquet garni.
RECIPE: the meat and vegetables are stewed for 4 hours. Served hot.

669 - POT-AU-FEU BASQUE * PLAT COMPLET - SPÉCIALITÉ BASQUE

Photo Salt pork stewed with vegetables.

SALT PORK STEWED WITH VEGETABLES
* A ONE-DISH MEAL, BASQUE SPECIALITY
INGREDIENTS: water, broad beans, a selection of chopped vegetables, blade of salt pork. To brown: cooking stock, grated cheese, thick slices of bread.
RECIPE: the ingredients are cooked, the cheese and bread added to brown and served hot.

670 - POT-AU-FEU DE POISSONS * PLAT COMPLET

Photo Fish stewed with vegetables.

FISH STEWED WITH VEGETABLES
* A ONE-DISH MEAL
INGREDIENTS: fish: pike, mullet, prawns. Vegetables: leek, carrots, stalk of celery, dry white wine, parsley, garnish: cauliflower, carrots, stalk of celery, shelled peas, shallots, parsley, tarragon.
RECIPE: the fish are poached in water, removed and the vegetables cooked with the wine; the fish are put back into the cooking stock once the vegetables are removed to finish cooking. Served immediately.

671 - POTÉE ALSACIENNE * PLAT COMPLET D'ALSACE

Photo Alsatian smoked pork stew.

ALSATIAN SMOKED PORK STEW
* A ONE-DISH MEAL FROM ALSACE
INGREDIENTS: smoked knuckle or shoulder of ham, thick slices of bacon, cut cabbage, carrots, onions, turnips, chopped leeks, bouquet garni, coriander. Juniper to finish cooking: large pieces of potato, garlic sausage.
RECIPE: the ingredients are stewed in water for 2 hours and the potatoes and sausage added for 20'. Served hot.

672 - POTÉE AUVERGNATE * PLAT COMPLET SPÉCIALITÉ D'AUVERGNE

Photo Auvergne pork stew.

AUVERGNE PORK STEW * A ONE-DISH MEAL
INGREDIENTS: blade of pork, half a knuckle of ham, sausages, carrots, turnips, cabbage, potatoes, onion, garlic, bouquet garni.
INGREDIENTS: the meat is cooked for 1 hour 30 mins, vegetables and herbs added and cooked for 30' longer. Served hot.

673 - POTÉE BÉARNAISE * PLAT COMPLET - SPÉCIALITÉ DU BÉARN

Photo Béarn beef and goose stew.

BÉARN BEEF AND GOOSE STEW * A ONE-DISH MEAL - A BÉARN SPECIALITY

INGREDIENTS: beef, goose leg. Vegetables step one: beans, leek, garlic, bay leaf. Step two: potatoes, cabbage, French beans, chopped carrots and turnips. To garnish: slices of bread, grated Gruyère cheese. RECIPE: the vegetables in step one are cooked with the meat and then the other vegetables. Presented in a dish with the toasted bread and Gruyère cheese. Served hot.

674 - POTÉE BOURGUIGNONNE * PLAT COMPLET SPÉCIALITÉ BOURGUIGNONNE

Photo Burgundy meat stew.

BURGUNDY MEAT STEW * A ONE-DISH MEAL - A BURGUNDY SPECIALITY

INGREDIENTS: knuckle of veal and pork, blade of pork, vegetables: potatoes, French beans, cabbage, carrots. To cook: chopped turnip, onion. Presentation: bread, grated Gruyère cheese.

RECIPE: the knuckle of veal is boiled for 1 hour with the onion. The other meat and vegetables are added, cooked for 20'. The broth, bread and cheese is served first, followed by the stewed meat and vegetables. Served hot.

675 - POTÉE CHAMPENOISE * PLAT COMPLET - SPÉCIALITÉ CHAMPENOISE

Photo Champagne stew.

CHAMPAGNE STEW * A ONE-DISH MEAL A CHAMPAGNE SPECIALITY

INGREDIENTS: knuckle of ham, smoked sausage, chicken, lean smoked bacon. Chopped vegetables: step one: beans, bay leaf, onion, cabbage, potatoes, carrots, leeks, garlic, soft bread, olive oil, crumbled thyme, chopped parsley. RECIPE: the step one ingredients are cooked for 1 hour, the other ingredients added and cooked for 30'. The dish is served with garlic bread. Served hot.

676 - POTÉE LORRAINE * PLAT COMPLET - SPÉCIALITÉ DE LORRAINE

Photo Lorraine pork stew.

LORRAINE PORK STEW * A ONE-DISH MEAL - A LORRAINE SPECIALITY

INGREDIENTS: knuckle or blade of pork, pork belly, cooking sausage, bard, carrots, turnips, leeks, green cabbage. Garnish: potatoes.

RECIPE: the ingredients are stewed for 2 hours 30 mins, the sausage added and cooked for a further 30 mins. The potatoes are cooked separately and served hot with the stew.

677 - POTÉE LYONNAISE * PLAT COMPLET - SPÉCIALITÉ DE LYON

Photo Lyon pork stew.

LYON PORK STEW * A ONE-DISH MEAL
A LYON SPECIALITY
INGREDIENTS: knuckle of pork, Lyon sausage, pork belly, cabbage, carrots, turnips RECIPE: all the ingredients are cooked together. Served hot.

POU

678 - POULARDE RÔTIE À LA NORMANDE * VOLAILLE SPÉCIALITÉ NORMANDE

Photo Roast chicken with cream and cider.

ROAST CHICKEN WITH CREAM AND CIDER
A POULTRY SPECIALITY FROM NORMANDY
INGREDIENTS: jointed chicken, butter. Vegetables: carrots. Sauce: dry cider, single cream, chopped parsley, tarragon, liquid honey. RECIPE: the chicken is browned in butter and cooked for 45' with the cider. The matchstick carrots are cooked in butter and honey. Served hot with the cooking juices mixed with cream.

679 - POULE AU POT * VOLAILLE - SPÉCIALITÉ DU BÉARN

Photo Stewed chicken.

STEWED CHICKEN - A POULTRY SPECIALITY FROM BÉARN
INGREDIENTS: chicken. Stuffing: breadcrumbs, liver, milk, Bayonne raw ham, shallots, garlic, egg, chopped parsley, chives, tarragon, vegetables: carrots, onions, leeks, bouquet garni.
RECIPE: the chicken skin is rubbed with lemon, the cavity stuffed, vegetables added and cooked together. The broth is served hot separately from the chicken and vegetables hot.

680 - POULE AU RIZ PARISIENNE * PLAT COMPLET

Photo Stewed chicken with rice.

STEWED CHICKEN WITH RICE
* A ONE-DISH MEAL
INGREDIENTS: chicken, rice, leeks, chopped carrots, onion, butter, oil, clove. Sauce: flour, butter, stock, egg yolk. RECIPE: the chicken and vegetables are stewed for 1 hour 30 mins. The rice is coloured in the oil then cooked in the cooking stock. The sauce is cooked for a few minutes. Served hot.

681 - POULET AUX ÉCREVISSES * VOLAILLE SPÉCIALITÉ DU DAUPHINÉ

Photo Chicken with crayfish.

CHICKEN WITH CRAYFISH - A POULTRY SPECIALITY FROM DAUPHINÉ
INGREDIENTS: jointed chicken, butter. Garnish: crayfish, shallots, tomatoes, oil, brandy, dry white wine. Stock: carrots, onion, white of leeks, garlic. Sauce: cream, chopped tarragon.
RECIPE: the chicken and vegetables are stewed. The cooked garnish is flamed. The vegetables are blended and added to the cream, chicken and crayfish. Served hot.

682 - POULET BASQUAISE * VOLAILLE - SPÉCIALITÉ DU BÉARN

Photo Chicken with peppers and tomatoes.

CHICKEN WITH PEPPERS AND TOMATOES A POULTRY SPECIALITY FROM BÉARN
INGREDIENTS: jointed chicken, Bayonne raw ham, tomatoes, peppers, onions, garlic, olive oil, chicken stock, paprika.
RECIPE: the chicken is browned in oil, the stock and other ingredients added and cooked for 30'. Served hot.

683 - POULET DE BRESSE AUX MORILLES * VOLAILLE

Photo Bresse chicken with morel mushrooms.

BRESSE CHICKEN WITH MOREL MUSHROOMS * POULTRY
INGREDIENTS: jointed chicken, morels, butter, oil, cream, Arbois yellow wine.
RECIPE: the chicken is browned in butter and cooked for 30'. The wine, morels and cream are added and cooked for 15'. Served hot.

684 - POULET FARCI * VOLAILLE

Photo Stuffed chicken.

STUFFED CHICKEN * POULTRY
INGREDIENTS: chicken, thyme, paprika. Stuffing: liver paté, cultivated mushrooms, butter, egg, breadcrumbs.
RECIPE: the chicken is coated with paprika and melted butter, stuffed and cooked for 50'. Served hot.

685 - POULET MARENGO * VOLAILLE

Photo Chicken Marengo.

CHICKEN MARENGO * POULTRY
INGREDIENTS: jointed chicken. To cook: black olives, chopped anchovies, chicken stock, cultivated mushrooms. Sauce: tomatoes, garlic, olive oil, chopped hard-boiled egg, lemon juice.
RECIPE: the chicken and ingredients are browned and cooked in the stock with the tomatoes and olives. Served hot, with the chopped egg garnish.

686 - POULET AUX OLIVES * VOLAILLE

Photo Chicken with olives.

CHICKEN WITH OLIVES * POULTRY
INGREDIENTS: Jointed chicken, black olives, tomatoes, garlic, olive oil, chicken stock, sprig of rosemary, basil.
RECIPE: The chicken is browned in oil and the tomatoes and olives added with the chicken stock to finish cooking. Served hot with basil.

687 - POULET RÔTI AU THYM * VOLAILLE

Photo Roast chicken with thyme.

ROAST CHICKEN WITH THYME * POULTRY
INGREDIENTS: chicken. Stuffing: white of leeks, butter, flour, egg, milk, chopped parsley. Garnish: crumbled thyme.
RECIPE: the cavity is filled with the cooked stuffing, the chicken sprinkled with thyme, cooked for 1 hour and served hot.

688 - POULET AU VINAIGRE * VOLAILLE

Photo Chicken with vinegar.

CHICKEN WITH VINEGAR * POULTRY
INGREDIENTS: chicken. To cook: chopped smoked bacon and onions, oil, butter, tomato puree, wine vinegar, bouquet garni.
RECIPE: The chicken is browned in oil and butter, the cooking sauce prepared and the chicken cooked for 45′ in the oven. Served hot.

POU

689 - POULET À LA NORMANDE * VOLAILLE

Photo Chicken with cider spirit sauce.

CHICKEN WITH CIDER SPIRIT SAUCE
* POULTRY
INGREDIENTS: chicken cut in 4, butter, cider spirit. To garnish: pieces of eating apple, water, butter. RECIPE: the chicken is browned in butter, pieces of apple put in the casserole with the chicken on top and the cider spirit and water added to cook. Served hot from the casserole.

690 - POUNTI * LÉGUMES ET VIANDE SPÉCIALITÉ DU CANTAL

Photo Pork and Swiss chard terrine.

PORK AND SWISS CHARD TERRINE - A MEAT AND VEGETABLE SPECIALITY FROM CANTAL
INGREDIENTS: boned pork, pork belly, Swiss chard leaves, sorrel, onion, parsley, butter, savoury custard: milk, whole eggs, flour, garnish: stoned prunes.
RECIPE: the browned onions are added to the other ingredients and cooked for 1 hour. Served hot.

PRA

691 - PRAIRES * MOLLUSQUES

Photo Clams.

CLAMS * SHELLFISH
Served cold.

PRO

692 - PROFITEROLES AU CHOCOLAT * DESSERT GLACÉ

Photo Chocolate profiteroles.

CHOCOLATE PROFITEROLES
* ICED DESSERT
INGREDIENTS: choux pastry: flour, butter, eggs, egg yolk, milk. The cream filling: vanilla, flour, sugar, egg yolks, milk, rum, vanilla pod. Sauce: dark chocolate cream.
RECIPE: portions of choux pastry are baked for 20', filled with vanilla cream and coated with hot chocolate sauce, variation: the vanilla cream may be replaced with a scoop of vanilla ice cream.

693 - PRUNEAUX À L'ARMAGNAC * FRUIT ALCOOLISÉ

Photo Prunes in Armagnac.

PRUNES IN ARMAGNAC BRANDY * FRUIT IN SPIRIT
INGREDIENTS: large prunes, sugar, aromatic China tea, Armagnac brandy.
RECIPE: the prunes are macerated for 2 hours in the prepared tea, drained, put in a jar with the sugar and Armagnac and kept for 2 months before serving cold.

694 - PRUNEAUX AU BOURGUEIL * FRUIT ALCOOLISÉ

Photo Prunes in Bourgueil wine.

PRUNES IN BOURGUEIL WINE * FRUIT IN SPIRIT
INGREDIENTS: prunes, orange, sugar, vanilla sugar, red Bourgueil wine, brandy.
RECIPE: the prunes, sliced orange, red wine, brandy and sugar are cooked for 15'. Served cold.

695 - PURÉE DE CÉLERI * LÉGUMES

Photo Celeriac puree.

CELERIAC PUREE * VEGETABLES
INGREDIENTS: celeriac, onion, cream, lemon juice, vegetable stock.
RECIPE: the onion and celeriac are cooked for 20' in the vegetable stock. The celery is blended with the cream. Served hot.

696 - PURÉE DE LENTILLES * LÉGUMES

Photo Lentil puree.

LENTIL PUREE * VEGETABLES
INGREDIENTS: lentils. To cook: onion, bouquet garni. Presentation: cream, butter.
RECIPE: the lentils are cooked for 1 hour 30 mins and blended to a puree. Served hot.

PUR

697 - PURÉE DE CAROTTES * LÉGUMES

Photo Carrot puree.

CARROT PUREE * VEGETABLES
INGREDIENTS AND RECIPE: the carrots and potatoes are boiled for 20', blended to a puree with butter. Served hot.

698 - PURÉE MOUSSELINE * LÉGUMES

Photo Potato puree.

POTATO PUREE * VEGETABLES
INGREDIENTS: mashed potatoes. To flavour: butter, milk, whipped cream or butter.
RECIPE: the puree is beaten with the ingredients over heat. Served hot.

QUA

699 - QUATRE-QUARTS BRETON * PÂTISSERIE

Photo Pound cake.

POUND CAKE * CAKE
INGREDIENTS: egg, caster sugar, melted butter, flour, baking powder, vanilla sugar.
RECIPE: all the ingredients are beaten in the above order and baked for 40'. Served cold.

QUE

700 - QUENELLES DE BROCHET SAUCE NANTUA * POISSON

Photo Pike quenelles with crayfish & brandy sauce.

PIKE QUENELLES WITH CRAYFISH AND BRANDY SAUCE * FISH
INGREDIENTS: pike quenelles with crayfish & brandy sauce see n° 795.
RECIPE: quenelles poached for 10' in water and baked in the oven with the prepared sauce. Served hot.

701 - QUEUE DE BŒUF RÔTIE AU FOUR * ABATS

Photo Roasted ox tail.

ROASTED OX TAIL * OFFAL
INGREDIENTS: ox tail, bouquet garni, carrots, onions, leeks.
RECIPE: the ox tail is cooked in stock for 3 hours, grilled and served hot.

702 - QUEUE DE BŒUF EN SALADE * ABATS

Photo Ox tail with vinaigrette dressing.

OX TAIL WITH VINAIGRETTE DRESSING * OFFAL
INGREDIENTS: pieces of ox tail, leeks, carrots, turnips, celery, onion, garlic, vinaigrette dressing, bouquet garni, chopped herbs.
RECIPE: the ox tail is boiled for 30'. The vegetables and flavouring are added and cooked for 4 hours. The meat is taken off the bone and served warm with the vinaigrette, herbs and chopped onion.

QUI

703 - QUICHE AUX ASPERGES * ENTRÉE, LÉGUMES

Photo Asparagus quiche.

ASPARAGUS QUICHE * STARTER, VEGETABLE
INGREDIENTS: pastry: flour, butter, egg. Filling: cooked green asparagus, grated Gruyère cheese, eggs, cream.
RECIPE: The pastry case is filled and baked in the oven for 30', served hot.

704 - QUICHE AUX CHAMPIGNONS * ENTRÉE

Photo Mini mushroom quiche.

MUSHROOM QUICHE * STARTER
INGREDIENTS: pastry: flour, butter. Filling: cultivated mushrooms, butter, eggs, cream.
RECIPE: the pastry case is filled and baked for 20'. Served hot.

705 - QUICHE AU JAMBON * ENTRÉE

Photo Mini-quiche with ham.

HAM QUICHE * STARTER
INGREDIENTS: shortcrust pastry: flour, butter, egg, filling, smoked ham. Grated Emmenthal cheese, eggs, cream.
RECIPE: The pastry case is cooked, the filling then added and baked further. Served hot.

706 - QUICHE LORRAINE - SPÉCIALITÉ DE LORRAINE * ENTRÉE

Photo Mini-quiche lorraine.

QUICHE LORRAINE - A STARTER SPECIALITY FROM LORRAINE
INGREDIENTS: shortcrust pastry: flour, butter. Filling: grated Emmenthal cheese, chopped bacon, butter, Comté cheese, eggs, cream, nutmeg.
RECIPE: the shortcrust pastry case is precooked, the filling added and baked for a further 30'. Served hot.

707 - QUICHE AUX MOULES * ENTRÉE AUX MOLLUSQUES

Photo Mussel quiche.

MUSSEL QUICHE * A SHELLFISH STARTER
INGREDIENTS: pastry: flour, butter, egg. Filling: cooked mussels, tomatoes, garlic, butter, eggs, cream, grated nutmeg.
RECIPE: the shortcrust pastry case is precooked, the filling added and baked for a further 20'. Served hot.

708 - QUICHE AUX PLEUROTES * ENTRÉE, CHAMPIGNONS

Photo Oyster mushroom quiche.

OYSTER MUSHROOM QUICHE * STARTER
INGREDIENTS: pastry: flour, butter, egg. Filling: oyster mushrooms, ham, grated Emmenthal cheese, eggs, cream, sprigs of chives.
RECIPE: The pastry case is filled and baked for 40'. Served hot.

709 - QUICHE AUX TOMATES BASILIC * ENTRÉE

Photo Tomato and basil quiche.

TOMATO AND BASIL QUICHE * STARTER
INGREDIENTS: flaky pastry. Garnish: chopped tomatoes, grated Gruyère cheese, butter, eggs, cream, basil.
RECIPE: the pastry case is filled and baked in the oven for 35'. Served hot.

RAB

710 - RÂBLE DE LIÈVRE AU GENIÈVRE * GIBIER

Photo Saddle of hare with juniper berries.

SADDLE OF HARE WITH JUNIPER BERRIES * GAME
INGREDIENTS: saddles of hare. Garnish: celeriac, carrot, onions, oil, full-bodied red wine, lemon juice, ground ginger, grated nutmeg, juniper berries. Sauce: filtered cooking juices, black grapes, cream, redcurrant jelly.
RECIPE: the meat is browned in oil, added to the garnish and baked in the oven. Hot dish.

711 - RÂBLE DE LIÈVRE RÔTI * GIBIER

Photo Roast saddle of hare.

ROAST SADDLE OF HARE * GAME
INGREDIENTS: saddle of hare, cultivated mushrooms, butter. Marinade: carrot, onion, garlic, oil, vinegar, full-bodied red wine, bay leaf, thyme. RECIPE: the hare is marinated for 24 hours and then cooked in the oven for 45'. The filtered marinade is cooked separately and added to the meat at the end of cooking. The mushrooms are cooked in butter. Served hot.

RAC

712 - RACLETTE * SPÉCIALITÉ À BASE DE FROMAGE

Photo Raclette.

RACLETTE - A MELTED CHEESE SPECIALITY
INGREDIENTS: slices of raclette cheese, air-dried Grisons meat, smoked raw ham, preboiled potatoes, cocktail onions, gherkins.
RECIPE: tiny "shovels" containing the cheese are heated in a special raclette machine and the melted cheese poured over hot potato.

713 - RAGOÛT D'AGNEAU AUX HARICOTS * VIANDE

Photo Lamb and bean casserole.

LAMB AND BEAN CASSEROLE * MEAT
INGREDIENTS: cubed lamb, beans. To cook: tomatoes, onions, olive oil, meat stock, bouquet garni, bay leaf, rosemary.
RECIPE: the beans are soaked overnight and cooked for 45' the next day. The meat is cooked for 1 hour with the ingredients, the beans and vinegar added and served together hot.

714 - RAGOÛT D'AGNEAU SAUCE AU VIN * VIANDE

Photo Lamb casserole with wine.

LAMB CASSEROLE WITH WINE * MEAT
INGREDIENTS: cubed neck of lamb. To cook: onions, garlic, olive oil, flour, full-bodied red wine. Sauce: chopped chives.
RECIPE: the meat is cooked for 40' and the sauce added. Served hot.

715 - RAGOÛT DE DINDE À LA BOURGUIGNONNE * VOLAILLE

Photo Turkey casserole with red wine.

TURKEY CASSEROLE WITH RED WINE * POULTRY
INGREDIENTS: cubed turkey escalopes. To cook: lean bacon, carrot, celery, onion, garlic, olive oil, flour, poultry stock, red wine, bay leaf, crumbled thyme, chopped marjory.
RECIPE: The ingredients are browned and cooked. Served hot.

716 - RAGOÛT DE MOUTON * VIANDE

Photo Mutton casserole.

MUTTON CASSEROLE * MEAT
INGREDIENTS: pieces of boned mutton shoulder, garlic, oil, butter, tomato puree, meat stock, rosemary.
RECIPE: the meat is browned in oil then cooked for 30' with the ingredients. Served hot.

717 - RAGOÛT DE HOMARD * CRUSTACÉS

LOBSTER CASSEROLE * SHELLFISH
INGREDIENTS: lobster. To cook: butter, oil, shallots, port, garnish: fillets of sole. To cook the fillets: spinach, fish stock. To cook the scallops: flour, egg, breadcrumbs, oyster, flaky pastry, breadcrumbs, spinach, shallots, butter, oil, egg, flour, cream, dry white wine, port, fish stock.
RECIPE: The lobster is browned then cooked for 15' with the other ingredients; each type of fish is cooked separately. The fish and shellfish are served hot, coated with the cream and cooking juices.

RAI

718 - RAIE AU BEURRE CITRONNÉ * POISSON

Photo Skate with lemon butter.

SKATE WITH LEMON BUTTER * FISH
INGREDIENTS: skate. To cook: carrots, celery, onions, garlic, butter, wine vinegar, lemon juice.
RECIPE: the boiled vegetables are added to the skate and melted butter and lemon juice poured over the fish. Served hot.

719 - RAIE AUX CÂPRES * POISSON

Photo Skate with capers.

SKATE WITH CAPERS * FISH
INGREDIENTS: skate. Court-bouillon stock: water, onion, wine vinegar.
RECIPE: the skate is poached in the court bouillon and melted butter and vinegar poured over the fish, sprinkled with capers.

RAS

720 - RASCASSE AU FOUR * POISSON

Photo Baked rockfish.

BAKED ROCKFISH * FISH
INGREDIENTS: gutted rockfish. Stuffing: breadcrumbs, garlic, to cook: olive oil, lemon juice, parsley.
RECIPE: the fish is stuffed, sprinkled with lemon juice and baked in a closed foil case for 40'. Served hot.

721 - RASCASSE SUR LIT DE LÉGUMES * POISSON

Photo Rockfish on a bed of vegetables.

ROCKFISH ON A BED OF VEGETABLES * FISH

INGREDIENTS: rockfish fillets, leeks, tomatoes, pureed watercress, shallots, butter, cream, lemon juice.

RECIPE: All the ingredients are browned and then baked together in the oven. Served immediately.

RAT

722 - RATATOUILLE * LÉGUMES

Photo Mediterranean vegetable stew.

MEDITERRANEAN VEGETABLE STEW * VEGETABLES

INGREDIENTS: red peppers, aubergines, courgettes, tomatoes, onions, garlic, olive oil, bouquet garni.

RECIPE: the vegetables are browned in oil separately then cooked together. Served hot sprinkled with basil.

RAV

723 - RAVIOLIS AU BŒUF * PÂTES

Photo Baked beef ravioli.

BEEF RAVIOLI * PASTA

INGREDIENTS: stuffing: cooked beef, oil, egg, thyme, parsley, marjory, onion. Ravioli pasta: flour, eggs, sauce and to bake: tomato sauce. To brown: grated Gruyère cheese.

RECIPE: each ravioli pasta square is stuffed, plunged into boiling water, drained and baked with the sauce in the oven. Served hot.

724 - RAVIOLIS AU SAUMON * PÂTES

Photo Salmon ravioli.

SALMON RAVIOLI * PASTA

INGREDIENTS AND RECIPE: see N°723, the meat is replaced with salmon and the tomato sauce with cream. Served hot.

REL

724-1 - RELIGIEUSE * PÂTISSERIE

Photo Religieuse.

RELIGIEUSE * CAKE
INGREDIENTS: choux pastry (flour, butter and sugar are added to boiling milk, quickly mixed and egg yolks added). RECIPE: this cake is baked then filled with custard cream flavoured to choice. The top is iced (icing sugar and water) with the same flavour as the inside of the religieuse. Served cold.

RIG

725 - RIGODON * DESSERT DE BOURGOGNE

BURGUNDY CREAM DESSERT
INGREDIENTS: custard cream: milk, sugar, beaten egg, vanilla or cinnamon, cut dry bun cake, chopped walnuts and hazelnuts.
RECIPE: the cream is cooked for 1 hour in a bain marie. Served cold.

RIL

726 - RILLETTES DE LAPIN

Photo Potted rabbit.

POTTED RABBIT
INGREDIENTS: jointed rabbit, calf's foot split in 2, carrots, celery, onions, olive oil, poultry stock, dry white wine, Armagnac brandy, bouquet garni, tarragon, coriander seeds, cloves.
RECIPE: the rabbit and calf's foot are browned in oil, cooked with the sliced vegetables, herbs, wine, Armagnac and meat stock, blended, put into a terrine dish and refrigerated for 24 hours. Served cold.

727 - RILLETTES D'OIE * VOLAILLE - SPÉCIALITÉ DU SUD-OUEST

Photo Potted goose.

POTTED GOOSE - A POULTRY SPECIALITY FROM SOUTHWEST
INGREDIENTS: goose, goose fat, casserole pork, lard, bouquet garni, garlic and onion.
RECIPE: The ingredients are cooked for 3 hours, the goose and pork are roughly shredded, put into pots with the cooking juices and melted lard and refrigerated. Served cold.

728 - RILLETTES DE PORC * VIANDE

Photo Potted pork.

POTTED PORK * MEAT
INGREDIENTS: pork belly, pieces of bacon, lard, bouquet garni.
RECIPE: the meat and lard are cooked for 5 hours, shredded and put into a pot with the melted lard. Served cold.

729 - RILLETTES DE SAUMON * POISSON

Photo Potted salmon.

POTTED SALMON * FISH
INGREDIENTS: pieces of smoked and fresh salmon, butter, dry white wine, olive oil, brandy.
RECIPE: the fresh salmon is cooked in wine then browned in oil and soaked in the brandy. The smoked salmon is minced, mixed with the other salmon and butter and refrigerated for 6 hours. Served cold.

RIS

730 - RIS DE VEAU À LA CRÈME ET AUX MORILLES * ABATS ET CHAMPIGNONS

Photo Calf's sweetbreads with cream and morels.

CALF'S SWEETBREADS WITH CREAM AND MORELS * OFFAL AND MUSHROOMS
INGREDIENTS: calfs sweetbreads, morel mushrooms, butter, vinegar, poultry stock, cream.
RECIPE: calfs sweetbreads cooked in water with vinegar added, sautéed in butter with the mushrooms and cooked in the added meat stock for 15'. The cream is added and the dish served hot.

731 - RISOTTO AUX CÈPES * RIZ ET CHAMPIGNONS

Photo Cep risotto.

CEP RISOTTO * MUSHROOM
INGREDIENTS: rice, chopped ceps, chicken stock butter, chopped onion.
RECIPE: the rice and ceps are browned in butter then cooked with the other ingredients. Served hot.

RIZ

732 - RIZ AU LAIT * DESSERT

Photo Rice pudding.

RICE PUDDING * DESSERT
INGREDIENTS: rice. To cook: milk, caster sugar, vanilla pod.
RECIPE: The ingredients are cooked for 35'. Served cold or warm.

733 - RIZ PILAF * RIZ

Photo Pilaff rice.

PILAFF RICE * VEGETABLES
INGREDIENTS: rice. To cook: water, onion, cloves, olive oil, butter.
RECIPE: the rice is sautéed in oil, the other ingredients added to the water and cooked for 18'. Served hot.

ROG

734 - ROGNONS DE BAUGE * ABATS - SPÉCIALITÉ D'ANJOU

Photo Kidneys with mushroom and mustard sauce.

KIDNEYS WITH MUSHROOM AND MUSTARD SAUCE - AN OFFAL SPECIALITY FROM ANJOU
INGREDIENTS: calf's kidneys cut into cubes, mustard, butter. To garnish, sliced mushrooms, butter, lemon. Sauce: shallots, Calvados applejack brandy, cream, tarragon.
RECIPE: the mushrooms and kidneys are cooked in butter separately, spread with mustard, the sauce added and cooked together. Served hot.

735 - ROGNONS BLANCS * ABATS D'AGNEAU

Photo Lamb sweetbreads.

LAMB SWEETBREADS * OFFAL
INGREDIENTS: testicles, refined, called "animella" in Italy, "choesels" in Brussels, "crilladillas" in Spain and "mountain oysters" in Kentucky.
RECIPE: dusted with flour and sauteed in butter. Served hot.

736 - ROGNONS DE VEAU À LA CRÈME * ABATS

Photo Calf's kidneys with cream sauce.

CALF'S KIDNEYS WITH CREAM SAUCE * OFFAL
INGREDIENTS: sliced calf's kidneys, onion, butter, flour, meat stock. Sauce: cream, egg yolk, brandy.
RECIPE: the onions and kidneys are browned, the stock added and cooked for 2', coated with sauce. Served hot.

737 - ROGNONS DE VEAU FLAMBÉS AU COGNAC * ABATS

Photo Calf's kidneys flamed in brandy.

CALF'S KIDNEYS FLAMED IN BRANDY * OFFAL
INGREDIENTS: sliced calf's kidneys, chopped onion and garlic, oil, butter, flour, mustard, cream, brandy.
RECIPE: the onion, garlic and kidneys are browned in oil then flamed in brandy. The cream, butter and mustard are added. Served hot.

738 - ROGNONS DE VEAU ENTIERS * ABATS

Photo Calf's kidney.

WHOLE CALF'S KIDNEYS * OFFAL
INGREDIENTS: calf's kidneys, butter, poultry stock, juniper spirit.
RECIPE: the kidneys are browned in butter for 5' then flamed in juniper spirit, the stock added and cooked for 15'. Served hot with the juices.

739 - ROGNONS DE VEAU À LA NORMANDE * ABATS

Photo Calf's kidneys with cream sauce.

CALF'S KIDNEYS WITH CREAM SAUCE * OFFAL
INGREDIENTS: sliced calf's kidneys, apple, onions, oil, butter, cream, Calvados applejack brandy, sugar.
RECIPE: the onions and kidneys are cooked slowly in the butter and oil and flamed in the Calvados. The cream and apple are added and cooked for a few minutes. Served hot.

ROS

740 - ROSBIF EN TRANCHES * VIANDE

Photo *Slices of roast beef.*

SLICES OF ROAST BEEF * MEAT
Served cold or hot.

741 - ROSTI * LÉGUMES

Photo *Rosti potato.*

ROSTI POTATO * VEGETABLES
INGREDIENTS: cooked potatoes, grated onion, butter.
RECIPE: the potatoes and onions are cooked in butter. Served hot.

742 - ROSTI GARNI * LÉGUMES

ROSTI POTATO WITH BACON AND EGG * VEGETABLES
INGREDIENTS: precooked, grated potato, mixed with flour, precooked spinach flavoured with nutmeg, lean bacon, egg, flour. RECIPE: the potato pastrys and bacon are cooked in butter and served with an egg on top. Served hot.

ROT

743 - RÔTI DE BŒUF SAUCE BÉARNAISE * VIANDE

Photo *Roast beef with béarnaise sauce.*

ROAST BEEF WITH BÉARNAISE SAUCE * MEAT
INGREDIENTS: fillet of beef, coated with garlic, oil, parsley, basil, chives. Sauce: shallots, egg yolks, butter, tarragon vinegar, dry white wine, beef stock, tarragon, chervil.
RECIPE: the meat is served hot or cold.

744 - RÔTI DE DINDONNEAU * VOLAILLE

Photo Roast turkey.

ROAST TURKEY * POULTRY
INGREDIENTS: boned turkey joint, smoked bacon, chopped onion, sauce: cream, flour, dry white wine.
RECIPE: the meat and onion are roasted in the oven in a foil case. The sauce is added to the cooking juices. Served hot.

745 - RÔTI DE PERDREAU SOUS LA CENDRE * VOLAILLE SPÉCIALITÉ D'ANJOU

Photo Partridge cooked in the ashes.

PARTRIDGE ROASTED IN THE ASHES
A POULTRY SPECIALITY FROM ANJOU
INGREDIENTS: partridge, butter, bard.
RECIPE: the partridge is cooked in a foil case in hot ashes for 20' and served hot.

746 - RÔTI DE PORC CONFIT * VIANDE

Photo Slow-roasted pork.

SLOW-ROASTED PORK * MEAT
INGREDIENTS: pork chine, chopped onions, garlic, pork fat.
RECIPE: the joint is slow-roasted with the ingredients. Served hot or cold.

747 - RÔTI DE PORC FROID À LA SAUCE TARTARE * VIANDE

Photo Roast pork with tartare sauce.

COLD ROAST PORK WITH TARTARE SAUCE * MEAT
INGREDIENTS: pork joint coated with garlic, mustard, thyme, marjory, tartare sauce (mayonnaise, chopped gherkin, parsley, chives, marjory, dill)
RECIPE: the coated meat is cooked for 1 hour 10 mins. Served cold sliced.

748 - RÔTI DE PORC AU ROMARIN * VIANDE

Photo Roast pork with rosemary.

ROAST PORK WITH ROSEMARY * MEAT
INGREDIENTS: pork joint coated with garlic, rosemary, thyme. To cook: celery, carrot, onion, oil, butter, dry white wine.
RECIPE: the joint and vegetables are browned separately in butter then cooked together with the wine for 1 hour. The cooking juices are sieved. Hot dish.

749 - RÔTI DE PORC À LA LIMOUSINE * VIANDE SPÉCIALITÉ DU LIMOUSIN

Photo Roast pork with red cabbage.

ROAST PORK WITH RED CABBAGE
A MEAT SPECIALITY FROM LIMOUSIN
INGREDIENTS: loin or chine of pork, lard, shredded red cabbage, precooked chestnuts, butter, sage.
RECIPE: the joint is rubbed with sage and cooked for 45'; the chestnuts and red cabbage are added to the cooking juices, served hot.

750 - RÔTI DE SANGLIER * GIBIER

Photo Roast wild boar.

ROAST WILD BOAR * GAME
INGREDIENTS: wild boar, bacon, oil, flour, red wine, meat stock, redcurrant jelly, juniper, clove, mild paprika. Sauce: flour, cider, cooking juices, redcurrant jelly.
RECIPE: the joint is rubbed with paprika, browned in the oil, barded and cooked for 1 hour. Served hot in slices with the sauce.

751 - RÔTI DE FILET DE VEAU * VIANDE

Photo Roast fillet of veal.

ROAST FILLET OF VEAL * MEAT
INGREDIENTS: fillet of veal coated with a mixture of butter, garlic, paprika, mustard, chopped thyme. Sauce: cooking juices, precooked cultivated mushrooms, tomatoes, wine, flour.
RECIPE: the joint is cooked in foil and served hot in slices with the sauce.

752 - RÔTI DE NOIX DE VEAU * VIANDE

Photo Roast cushion of veal.

ROAST CUSHION OF VEAL * MEAT
INGREDIENTS: cushion of veal. Marinade: shallots, garlic, white wine. To cook: oil, meat stock, bay leaf, thyme, rosemary. Sauce: sieved cooking juices, white wine, flour.
RECIPE: the veal is marinated for 24 hours and then roasted. The cooking and marinade juices are poured over the meat which is served sliced with the sauce.

ROU

753 - ROUGETS AU FENOUIL * POISSON - SPÉCIALITÉ DE PROVENCE

Photo Red mullet with fennel.

RED MULLET WITH FENNEL - A FISH SPECIALITY FROM PROVENCE
INGREDIENTS: red mullet. To cook: fennel stalks, lemon juice, olive oil and white wine, "rouille" sauce (crushed garlic, spices, egg yolk, olive oil).
RECIPE: the fish and ingredients are cooked. Served hot.

754 - ROULADE DE VEAU À LA CRÈME * VIANDE

Photo Veal rolls with cream sauce.

VEAL ROLLS WITH CREAM SAUCE * MEAT
INGREDIENTS: veal escalopes, lean bacon, cultivated mushrooms, chopped onions, oil. To cook: meat stock, dry white wine, sage. Sauce: cream, paprika, flour, cooking juices.
RECIPE: the escalopes are stuffed with the cooked mushrooms and onions, rolled and tied with string, browned and then cooked for 30' in the stock. Served hot with the sauce.

RUM

755 - RUMSTECK (OU PAVÉ DE) SAUCE AU BLEU OU AU ROQUEFORT * VIANDE

Photo Rump steak with blue cheese sauce.

RUMP STEAK WITH BLUE CHEESE SAUCE * MEAT
INGREDIENTS: slices of rump steak. Sauce: shallots, cream, blue cheese, butter.
RECIPE: the meat is grilled and served hot coated with the sauce.

SAB

756 - SABAYON DE SAINT-JACQUES * MOLLUSQUES

Photo *Scallops in light lemon cream sauce.*

SCALLOPS IN LIGHT LEMON CREAM SAUCE * SHELLFISH

INGREDIENTS: scallops. Sabayon sauce: cooking juices, lemon juice, egg yolks, cream, paprika. To cook: butter, lemon, wine, shallots, garlic, water. RECIPE: The scallops are browned in butter then cooked, the sabayon sauce prepared in the bain marie for 6', combined with the scallops and served hot.

SAL

757 - SALADE AUVERGNATE * SALADE SPÉCIALITÉ D'AUVERGNE

Photo *Ham and cheese salad.*

HAM AND CHEESE SALAD - A SPECIALITY FROM AUVERGNE

INGREDIENTS: lettuce, walnut oil, Fourme d'Ambert, Bleu d'Auvergne and Cantal cheeses, strips of Auvergne ham, walnuts, chopped hazelnuts, small pieces of bacon cooked in butter, vinaigrette dressing: walnut oil, vinegar.

RECIPE: the bacon pieces are served hot on the other ingredients.

758 - SALADE DE CALMARS * ENTRÉE, MOLLUSQUES

Photo *Squid salad.*

SQUID SALAD * FISH

INGREDIENTS: squid sauce: black olives, lettuce, tomatoes, garlic, olive oil, lemon juice, parsley, basil, oregano.

RECIPE: the squid are cooked in water and served warm or cold with the sauce.

759 - SALADE DE CHAMPIGNONS DE PARIS À LA CRÈME FRAÎCHE * SALADE, ENTRÉE

Photo *Mushroom salad with creme fraiche.*

MUSHROOM SALAD WITH CREME FRAICHE * STARTER

Served cold.

760 - SALADE DE CERVELAS DE LYON * ENTRÉE

Photo Saveloy salad.

SAVELOY SALAD * STARTER
Served cold with vinaigrette sauce (n° 803).

761 - SALADE DE CHÈVRES CHAUDS * ENTRÉE - FROMAGE

Photo Hot goat's cheese salad.

HOT GOAT'S CHEESE SALAD * STARTER
INGREDIENTS: green salad, breadcrumbed goat's cheeses, vinaigrette dressing.
RECIPE: the cheeses are sautéed in butter and served hot on the seasoned salad.

762 - SALADE DE PISSENLITS * ENTRÉE

Photo Dandelion salad with egg and croutons.

DANDELION SALAD * STARTER
INGREDIENTS: dandelions (bitter salad leaf), diced bacon, oil. Sauce: mustard, vinegar, garlic. Garnish: hard-boiled egg.
RECIPE: the cooked bacon is added to the salad with croutons.

763 - SALADE DE CRUDITÉS * ENTRÉE

Photo Beetroot, carrots, celery remoulade.

MIXED RAW VEGETABLE SALAD * STARTER
Served raw and cold.

764 - SALADE D'ENDIVES AUX ŒUFS DURS * ENTRÉE

Photo Chicory salad with hard-boiled egg.

CHICORY SALAD WITH HARD-BOILED EGGS
Served raw and cold with vinaigrette sauce.

765 - SALADE DE FOIES DE CANARD * ABATS

Photo Poultry liver salad.

POULTRY LIVER SALAD * OFFAL
INGREDIENTS: poultry livers. To cook: goose fat, sherry vinegar.
RECIPE: the poultry livers are cooked in the fat, the vinegar added and served hot.

766 - SALADE DE FRUITS ROUGES * DESSERT - FRUITS

Photo Strawberries, raspberries, grapes, whipped cream, mint leaves.

RED FRUIT SALAD * FRUIT DESSERT
Served cold.

767 - SALADE AUX GÉSIERS CONFITS * ABATS

Photo Gizzard salad.

PRESERVED GIZZARD SALAD * OFFAL
INGREDIENTS: gizzards preserved in duck fat, curly endive, potatoes, diced bacon, oil, vinegar.
RECIPE: the gizzards are cooked in their fat and served with the other ingredients. Served cold and hot.

768 - SALADE LANDAISE * SALADE - SPÉCIALITÉ DE GASCOGNE

Photo Foie gras and duck salad with walnuts and preserved gizzard.

FOIE GRAS AND DUCK SALAD
A SPECIALITY FROM GASCONY
INGREDIENTS: pieces of foie gras, duck gizzards and breast, croutons, pine nuts, walnuts, precooked French beans or lettuce: shallots, walnut oil, sherry vinegar, mustard.
RECIPE: the ingredients are mixed. Served cold.

769 - SALADE GOURMANDE SARLADAISE OU PÉRIGOURDINE SPÉCIALITÉ DU PÉRIGORD * SALADE

Photo Sarlat gourmet salad with duck breast, foie gras and walnuts.

SARLAT GOURMET SALAD * SALAD
INGREDIENTS: curly endive. Garnish: duck breast, cooked diced bacon, cooked potatoes, cooked in butter, cooked French beans, pine nuts, chopped chives, walnuts.
RECIPE: the cooked garnish is served hot on the salad.

770 - SALADE DE MESCLUN * SALADE DE PROVENCE

Photo Mesclun salad.

MESCLUN SALAD * SALAD
INGREDIENTS: Provence salad leaves.

771 - SALADE NIÇOISE - SPÉCIALITÉ NIÇOISE

Photo Niçoise salad.

NICOISE SALAD - A SPECIALITY SALAD FROM NICE
INGREDIENTS: lettuce and similar, green pepper, stalk of celery, cucumber, raw onion, pieces of tuna, small black olives, anchovy fillets, quartered boiled eggs, chopped tomato, olive oil, vinegar, garlic, basil.
RECIPE: the chopped vegetables are dressed with an olive oil and vinegar sauce and sprinkled with basil. Cold dish.

772 - SALADE DE POMMES DE TERRE * LÉGUMES

Photo Potato salad.

POTATO SALAD * VEGETABLES
INGREDIENTS: precooked sliced potatoes, shallots, oil, vinegar, wine, parsley.
RECIPE: the ingredients are mixed. Served cold or warm.

773 - SALADE DE POULPES * CRUSTACÉS

Photo Octoplus salad.

OCTOPUS SALAD * SHELLFISH
Served cold.

774 - SALADE DE PISSENLITS AU LARD * SALADE

Photo Dandelion salad with bacon.

DANDELION SALAD WITH BACON * VEGETABLES
INGREDIENTS: dandelion leaves, pieces of bacon, oil. Sauce: mustard, vinegar, garlic. Garnish: fried egg.
RECIPE: the fried bacon and egg are served hot on the dandelion leaves.

775 - SALADE DE TOMATES À LA MOZZARELLA * LÉGUMES SPÉCIALITÉ ITALIENNE

Photo Tomato and Mozzarella salad.

TOMATO AND MOZZARELLA SALAD - A SALAD SPECIALITY FROM ITALY
INGREDIENTS: sliced tomato and Mozzarella cheese, olive oil, balsamic vinegar, basil. Served cold.

776 - SALSIFIS * LÉGUMES

Photo Salsify.

SALSIFY * VEGETABLES
RECIPE: the salsify are cooked in boiling water, drained and gently sautéed in butter. Served hot.

SAN

777 - SANDRE EN CROÛTE DE SEL * POISSON

Photo Zander in salt crust.

ZANDER IN SALT CRUST * FISH
INGREDIENTS: zander. To coat: beaten egg white mixed with coarse salt and flour.
RECIPE: the fish is coated and cooked enclosed in foil. The salt crust is broken and the fish served hot.

778 - SANDRE RÔTI AUX HERBES * POISSON

Photo Zander roasted with herbs.

ZANDER ROASTED WITH HERBS * FISH
INGREDIENTS: zander, potatoes, garlic, vegetable stock, chervil, dill. Sauce: cream, melted butter, lemon juice and cooking juices.
RECIPE: The fish is brushed with oil, stuffed with potatoes and cooked; served hot with the sauce poured over.

SAR

779 - SARDINES À L'ESCABÈCHE * POISSON

Photo Sardines with sharp dressing.

SARDINES WITH SHARP DRESSING * FISH
INGREDIENTS: sardines, garlic, oil, wine vinegar, flour, thyme, rosemary, cumin, mild paprika.
RECIPE: the sardines are floured, browned in the oil with the ingredients and left for 24 hours. Served cold.

780 - SARDINES GRILLÉES * POISSON

Photo Grilled sardines.

GRILLED SARDINES * FISH
INGREDIENTS: sardines, olive oil, thyme, bay leaf, rosemary, savory.
RECIPE: The sardines are coated with olive oil and herbs and grilled, served hot.

SAU

781 - SAUCE AMÉRICAINE

Photo Américaine sauce.

AMERICAINE OR TOMATO AND BRANDY SAUCE
INGREDIENTS: olive oil, butter, shellfish shells, carrots, onions, shallots, brandy, white wine, tomatoes, tomato puree, garlic, bouquet garni, bunch of tarragon.
RECIPE: the flamed brandy, white wine, tarragon and garlic are cooked together with the bouquet garni, sieved and butter and flour added, stirring well.

782 - SAUCE AU BEURRE DE HOMARD, CRABE, D'ÉCREVISSES

Photo Lobster or crab butter sauce.

LOBSTER OR CRAB BUTTER SAUCE
Prepared solely from the shellfish in question.

783 - SAUCE BÉARNAISE

Photo Béarnaise sauce.

BÉARNAISE OR TARRAGON BUTTER SAUCE
INGREDIENTS AND RECIPE: mixture of shallots, egg yolks, butter, vinegar, fresh tarragon, chervil heated in a bain marie and well beaten until creamy.

784 - SAUCE BÉCHAMEL

Photo Béchamel sauce.

BECHAMEL OR WHITE SAUCE
INGREDIENTS AND RECIPE: the flour is added to melted butter over a low heat, the milk is added and stirred until the sauce is smooth.

785 - SAUCE BLANCHE

Photo White sauce.

WHITE SAUCE
INGREDIENTS AND RECIPE: the same as a Béchamel but with water rather than milk.

786 - SAUCE BORDELAISE

Photo Bordelaise wine sauce.

BORDELAISE WINE SAUCE
INGREDIENTS: onion, shallot, cep, olive oil, butter, flour, Bordeaux wine, stock.
RECIPE: the cep, onion and shallot are finely chopped and cooked in butter with the flour over a low heat; the Bordeaux wine and stock are added at the end of cooking.

787 - SAUCE BOURGUIGNONNE

Photo Burgundy wine sauce.

BURGUNDY WINE SAUCE
INGREDIENTS: butter, flour, Burgundy wine, allspice, nutmeg, onion, clove, bouquet garni.
RECIPE: the flour and butter are cooked and the other ingredients added.

788 - SAUCE CHASSEUR

Photo Chasseur or wine and mushroom.

CHASSEUR OR WINE AND MUSHROOM SAUCE
INGREDIENTS: sliced cultivated mushrooms, shallots, butter, veal stock, tomato sauce, dry white wine, brandy, tarragon, chervil.
RECIPE: the ingredients are cooked together. Served hot.

789 - SAUCE FINANCIÈRE

Photo Financiere or truffle and mushroom.

FINANCIERE OR TRUFFLE AND MUSHROOM SAUCE
INGREDIENTS: sliced cultivated mushrooms, butter, veal stock, Madeira, truffle juice.
RECIPE: the mushrooms are cooked in butter and added to the other ingredients.

790 - SAUCE GRIBICHE

Photo Gribiche sauce.

GRIBICHE SAUCE
INGREDIENTS: mashed hard-boiled eggs, chopped onion and gherkins, oil, vinegar, strong mustard, chopped herbs.
RECIPE: the ingredients are mixed.

791 - SAUCE HOLLANDAISE

Photo Salmon with hollandaise sauce.

HOLLANDAISE SAUCE
INGREDIENTS AND RECIPE: mixture of butter, egg yolk, lemon, water, beaten in a bain marie until it thickens.

792 - SAUCE MADÈRE

Photo Madeira sauce.

MADEIRA SAUCE
INGREDIENTS: butter, flour, onion, dry white wine, mushrooms, Madeira, bouquet garni.
RECIPE: a difficult sauce. The onions are cooked in butter, flour added, wine and water added, the sauce sieved and residue cooked with the mushrooms, with the Madeira added at the last moment.

792-1 - SAUCE MAYONNAISE

Photo Mayonnaise.

MAYONNAISE SAUCE
INGREDIENTS AND RECIPE: the egg yolk and mustard are continuously beaten while adding a trickle of olive oil until the sauce thickens.

793 - SAUCE MORNAY

Photo Mornay or cheese sauce.

MORNAY OR CHEESE SAUCE
INGREDIENTS AND RECIPE: a Béchamel sauce with egg yolks and grated Gruyère cheese added.

794 - SAUCE MOUSSELINE

Photo Light cream sauce.

LIGHT CREAM SAUCE
INGREDIENTS AND RECIPE: firmly whipped cream is incorporated into a Hollandaise sauce off the heat.

795 - SAUCE NANTUA

Photo Nantua sauce.

NANTUA OR CRAYFISH AND BRANDY SAUCE
INGREDIENTS AND RECIPE: crayfish butter (prepared from cooked, crushed crayfish and butter, sieved) is added to a cream sauce (N°796).

796 - SAUCE NORMANDE

Photo Cream sauce.

CREAM SAUCE
INGREDIENTS AND RECIPE: cream is added over a very low heat to a Béchamel sauce (N°784).

797 - SAUCE PIQUANTE

Photo Spicy sauce.

SPICY SAUCE
INGREDIENTS: chopped shallots and gherkins, capers, water, dry white wine, vinegar, chopped tarragon and parsley.
RECIPE: shallots cooked in wine, vinegar, filtered veal stock, gherkins, tarragon and parsley are added.

798 - SAUCE POIVRADE

Photo Black pepper sauce.

BLACK PEPPER SAUCE
INGREDIENTS: carrot, chopped onion, flour, game stock, bouquet garni, vinegar, clove, redcurrant jelly, butter, peppercorn.
RECIPE: all the ingredients are cooked in butter, sieved and the flour and redcurrant jelly added.

799 - SAUCE RAVIGOTE

Photo Ravigote sauce.

RAVIGOTE SAUCE
INGREDIENTS: shallots, chopped gherkins, capers, oil, vinegar, strong mustard, parsley, tarragon, chervil.
RECIPE: the ingredients are mixed.

800 - SAUCE ROUILLE

Photo Saffron garlic sauce.

SAFFRON GARLIC SAUCE
INGREDIENTS: egg yolk, crushed potato or soft bread, garlic, olive oil, saffron.
RECIPE: the ingredients are blended to obtain a consistent sauce.

801 - SAUCE SOUBISE

Photo Onion sauce.

ONION SAUCE
INGREDIENTS AND RECIPE: the onions are chopped, browned in butter and added to a Béchamel sauce.

802 - SAUCE SUPRÊME

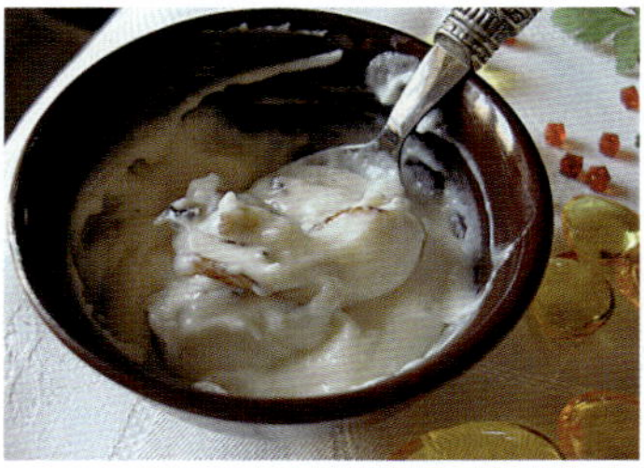

Photo Mushroom cream sauce.

MUSHROOM CREAM SAUCE
INGREDIENTS AND RECIPE: Béchamel white sauce mixed with poultry cream soup, mushrooms, cream, egg yolks - a difficult sauce to make.

803 - SAUCE VINAIGRETTE

Photo Vinaigrette sauce.

VINAIGRETTE SAUCE
INGREDIENTS AND RECIPE: mixture of vinegar, oil, garlic, shallot, herbs.

804 - SAUCE TARTARE

Photo Tartare sauce.

TARTARE SAUCE
INGREDIENTS: mayonnaise, capers, chopped gherkins and onions, chopped parsley, chervil, tarragon and chives, Cayenne pepper.
RECIPE: mixed together.

805 - SAUCE THERMIDOR

Photo Thermidor sauce.

THERMIDOR SAUCE
INGREDIENTS AND RECIPE: Béchamel sauce with mustard, egg yolks, Cayenne pepper, tarragon, chervil and white wine added.

806 - SAUCISSES AU CHOU * CHARCUTERIE

Photo Sausages with cabbage.

SAUSAGES WITH CABBAGE – COOKED MEATS AND SIMILAR
INGREDIENTS: large sausages, pork chine, cabbage, leeks, carrots, celeriac, onions, lard, meat stock, cumin, mild paprika.
RECIPE: the meat is cooked in lard and all the other ingredients added to finish cooking, served hot.

807 - SAUCISSE DE MORTEAU * CHARCUTERIE SPÉCIALITÉ DU JURA

Photo Morteau sausage.

MORTEAU SAUSAGE - A SPECIALITY FROM THE JURA * COOKED MEATS AND SIMILAR

INGREDIENTS: Morteau sausage. To cook: butter, dry white wine, poultry stock, minced onion and garlic, bouquet garni, whole potatoes.

RECIPE: the sausage is browned in butter then cooked for 30' with all the other ingredients. The cooking juices are sieved and reduced over a high heat to coat the dish. Served hot.

808 - SAUCISSE DE TOULOUSE AUX LENTILLES * CHARCUTERIE

Photo Toulouse sausages with lentils.

TOULOUSE SAUSAGES WITH LENTILS * COOKED MEATS AND SIMILAR

INGREDIENTS: Toulouse sausages, lentils, onion, garlic, clove, carrot.

RECIPE: all the ingredients are cooked together, served hot.

809 - SAUCISSON BRIOCHÉ * CHARCUTERIE

Photo Sausage in bun bread.

SAUSAGE IN BUN BREAD * COOKED MEATS AND SIMILAR

INGREDIENTS: Lyon cooking sausage. Bun dough: flour, yeast, milk, eggs, butter

RECIPE: the sausage is cooked in water and then placed in the centre of the dough to bake, served hot.

810 - SAUCISSON CHAUD À LA LYONNAISE * CHARCUTERIE

Photo Hot sausage with potatoes and shallots.

HOT SAUSAGE WITH POTATOES AND ONIONS * COOKED MEATS AND SIMILAR

INGREDIENTS: sausage, sliced potato, poultry consommé, wine vinegar, mustard, olive oil, onions, clove, sauce: minced shallots

RECIPE: the sausage is cooked in water for 45', the potatoes boiled for 15' in the poultry stock and served with the sausage (skin removed and sliced) and the sauce. Served warm.

811 - SAUMON FUMÉ À L'ANETH * POISSON

Photo Smoked salmon.

SMOKED SALMON WITH DILL * FISH
INGREDIENTS: smoked fillet of salmon, lemon, olive oil, chopped dill.
RECIPE: the salmon is marinated for 24 hours. Served cold.

812 - SAUMON GRILLÉ (DARNES DE) - SAUCE HOLLANDAISE * POISSON

Photo Salmon with hollandaise sauce.

GRILLED SALMON WITH HOLLANDAISE SAUCE * FISH
INGREDIENTS: salmon, butter, lemon juice.
RECIPE: the salmon is grilled and served hot with the sauce (see n° 791).

813 - SAUTÉ D'AGNEAU À LA NAVARRAISE * VIANDE SPÉCIALITÉ DU BÉARN

Photo Sauteef lamb with red peppers.

SAUTEED LAMB WITH RED PEPPERS
A MEAT SPECIALITY FROM BÉARN
INGREDIENTS: pieces of suckling lamb, oil, onions, garlic, vinegar, garnish: red peppers, paprika.
RECIPE: the lamb and onions are cooked quickly in oil, the vinegar, cooked peppers, garlic and paprika are added. Served hot.

814 - SAUTÉ DE VEAU * VIANDE

Photo Sauteed veal.

SAUTEED VEAL * MEAT
INGREDIENTS: shoulder of veal, lean pieces of bacon, peeled tomatoes and chopped cultivated mushrooms, garlic, butter, dry white wine, rosemary.
RECIPE: the ingredients are cooked. Served hot.

815 - SAVARIN AU RHUM * PÂTISSERIE

Photo Rum baba.

RUM BABA * CAKE
INGREDIENTS: mixture: flour, yeast, sugar, butter, eggs, cream milk. Sauce: water, rum, sugar. Garnish: whipped cream.
RECIPE: the mixture is prepared in two stages, flour and yeast to prove and the other ingredients added to bake; the baba is sprinkled with the sauce when still warm. Served cold with cream.

816 - SCAMPIS À L'AIL * CRUSTACÉS

Photo Scampi with garlic.

SCAMPI WITH GARLIC * SHELLFISH
INGREDIENTS: Scampi (Dublin Bay Prawns) boiled then fried with garlic in olive oil.
RECIPE: the ingredients are cooked. Served hot.

817 - SCAMPIS FLAMBÉS À L'ANIS * CRUSTACÉS

Photo Scampi flamed with pastis.

SCAMPI FLAMED WITH PASTIS * SHELLFISH
INGREDIENTS: boiled scampi, tomatoes, onions. Sauce: garlic, butter, Pastis, lemon, cream, aniseed, sugar.
RECIPE: the scampi are sautéed in butter, sprinkled and flamed with Pastis and coated with the sauce.

818 - SCAMPIS FRITS * CRUSTACÉS

Photo Fried scampi.

FRIED SCAMPI * SHELLFISH
INGREDIENTS: scampi, cooking oil, batter: flour, egg, oil.
RECIPE: the scampi are coated in batter and cooked in the oil. Served immediately.

SEL

819 - SELLE D'AGNEAU * VIANDE

Photo Saddle of lamb.

SADDLE OF LAMB * MEAT
Served hot.

SOL

820 - SOLE MEUNIÈRE * POISSON

Photo Sole with lemon and parsley.

SOLE WITH LEMON AND PARSLEY * FISH
INGREDIENTS: sole, lemon, oil, flour, lemon, parsley, butter.
RECIPE: the floured sole is cooked in butter and served hot with lemon juice and olive oil.

821 - SOLE GRILLÉE AU BEURRE CITRONNÉ * POISSON

Photo Grilled sole.

GRILLED SOLE WITH LEMON BUTTER * FISH
INGREDIENTS: sole, lemon, butter.
RECIPE: the sole is grilled and served with melted butter and lemon juice.

SOU

822 - SOUFFLÉ AU COMTÉ * ENTRÉE AU FROMAGE SPÉCIALITÉ DE FRANCHE-COMTÉ

Photo Cheese soufflé.

CHEESE SOUFFLE - A SPECIALITY STARTER FROM FRANCHE COMTÉ
INGREDIENTS: sauce base: flour. Butter, mixture: egg yolks, stiffly beaten egg whites, milk, Comté cheese, nutmeg.
RECIPE: the sauce base is prepared, added to the mixture and cooked for 15'. Served hot.

823 - SOUFFLÉ AU JAMBON * ENTRÉE

Photo Ham soufflé.

HAM SOUFFLE * STARTER
INGREDIENTS: mixture: chopped ham, egg yolks and stiffly beaten whites. Sauce base: butter, flour, milk.
RECIPE: the sauce base is prepared, added to the mixture and cooked for 15'. Served hot.

824 - SOUFFLÉ AU GRAND MARNIER * DESSERT

Photo Grand Marnier soufflé.

GRAND MARNIER SOUFFLE * DESSERT
INGREDIENTS: Egg yolks and whites, sugar, butter, milk, flour, Grand Marnier liqueur, grated lemon zest.
RECIPE: the lemon zests and sugar are brought to the boil with the milk, the mixture thickened with flour, the butter and yolks added with the liqueur, then the egg whites and the soufflé baked for 25'. Served sprinkled with icing sugar.

825 - SOUPE CRÉMEUSE AUX MOULES * POTAGE, MOLLUSQUES

Photo Creamy mussel soup.

CREAMY MUSSEL SOUP * SHELLFISH SOUP
INGREDIENTS: cooked mussels, shallots, butter, flour, veal stock, nutmeg, cream, lemon juice.
RECIPE: the mussel cooking juices are sieved to cook the floured, browned shallots, veal stock and nutmeg. The cream and mussels are added and the soup served hot.

826 - SOUPE DE JULIENNE DE LÉGUMES * POTAGE

Photo Vegetable soup.

VEGETABLE SOUP * SOUP
INGREDIENTS: potatoes, carrots, leeks cut into matchsticks.
RECIPE: the vegetables are cooked in water for 1 hour. Served hot.

827 - SOUPE À L'OIGNON * POTAGE - SPÉCIALITÉ D'ALSACE

Photo Onion soup.

ONION SOUP - A SPECIALITY FROM ALSACE
INGREDIENTS: chopped onions browned in butter, stock, gruyère cheese, French stick bread.
RECIPE: The onions are cooked for 30' in the stock, poured into bowls, the bread added with grated cheese to brown. Served hot.

827-1 - SOUPE DE POISSONS * POTAGE POISSON

Photo Fish soup.

FISH SOUP * FISH SOUP
INGREDIENTS: pieces of fish fillet (cod, whiting, sea bass, etc.) browned in butter, tomatoes, fennel, leek, onions, garlic, olive oil, bay leaf, thyme, saffron. Garnish: bread, grated Comté cheese. Sauce: rouille (garlic and saffron sauce).
RECIPE: the ingredients are cooked in water. Served hot with croutons.

828 - SOUPE DE POTIRON * POTAGE LÉGUMES

Photo Squash soup.

SQUASH SOUP * VEGETABLE SOUP
INGREDIENTS: squash cut in pieces, cream, onions, butter, flour.
RECIPE: the squash and onions are browned then cooked in water, blended and added to the cream, flour and butter mixture. Served hot.

829 - SOUPE AU PISTOU * POTAGE LÉGUMES SPÉCIALITÉ DE PROVENCE

Photo Pesto soup.

PESTO SOUP - A VEGETABLE SOUP SPECIALITY FROM PROVENCE
INGREDIENTS: diced carrots, courgettes, French beans, cannelini beans, red kidney beans, mashed potato, chopped tomato. For the pesto: crushed garlic and basil leaf, olive oil.
RECIPE: the beans are cooked in water and added to the vegetables with the mashed potato, olive oil and tomato. Served hot.

SOU

830 - SOUPE DE RHUBARBE ET DE FRAISES * DESSERT - FRUITS

Photo Rhubarb and strawberry soup.

RHUBARB AND STRAWBERRY SOUP
* FRUIT DESSERT
INGREDIENTS: caster sugar, fresh mint, chopped rhubarb, lemon juice, strawberry.
RECIPE: the rhubarb is cooked with the sugar and lemon juice, the strawberries added and served cold.

831 - SOURIS D'AGNEAU CONFITE * VIANDE

Photo slow-roasted lamb shank.

SLOW-ROASTED LAMB SHANK * MEAT
INGREDIENTS: lamb shank, onions, garlic, oil, butter.
RECIPE: the lamb shank is sautéed in oil and butter and cooked very slowly for 4 hours. Served hot.

SPA

832 - SPAGHETTIS À LA BOLOGNAISE * PÂTES SPÉCIALITÉ ITALIENNE

Photo Spaghetti Bolognese.

SPAGHETTI BOLOGNESE - AN ITALIAN PASTA SPECIALITY
INGREDIENTS: spaghetti (Italian pasta), minced beef, bacon, onions, olive oil, butter, tomato puree, meat stock, dry white wine, parsley.
RECIPE: the bacon is cooked for 30' with the meat and other ingredients. The spaghetti is cooked in water. Served hot together.

833 - SPAGHETTIS À LA CARBONARA * PÂTES SPÉCIALITÉ ITALIENNE

Photo Spaghetti with cream and bacon sauce.

SPAGHETTI WITH CREAM AND BACON SAUCE - AN ITALIAN PASTA SPECIALITY
INGREDIENTS: spaghetti, chopped cooked smoked bacon, grated parmesan cheese, eggs, cream, garlic, olive oil.
RECIPE: the spaghetti is cooked in water and served with the other ingredients mixed. Served hot.

834 - SPAGHETTIS À L'ENCRE * PÂTES

Photo *Squid ink spaghetti*.

SQUID INK SPAGHETTI * PASTA
INGREDIENTS: olive oil, black spaghetti (flavoured with squid ink), shallots, chopped garlic, poultry stock, saffron.
RECIPE: the cooked pasta is mixed with the ingredients browned in oil. Served hot.

STE

835 - STEAK AU POIVRE * VIANDE

Photo *Pepper steak*.

PEPPER STEAK * MEAT
INGREDIENTS: steak, onion, oil, butter, peppercorns.
RECIPE: the steak is coated with oil and peppercorns and browned for 2' with the onion. Served hot.

836 - STEAK TARTARE * VIANDE

Photo *Steak tartare*.

STEAK TARTARE * MEAT
INGREDIENTS: in order of mixing: oil, mustard, onions, gherkins, paprika, ketchup, Worcestershire sauce, capers, raw minced beef, egg yolks, chopped parsley. Served cold.

SUP

837 - SUPRÊME DE PINTADE AUX MORILLES * VOLAILLE

Photo *Breast of guinea fowl*.

BREAST OF GUINEA FOWL WITH MORELS * POULTRY
See Recipe N° 837-1. Served hot.

SUP

837-1 - SUPRÊME DE VOLAILLE AUX MORILLES * VOLAILLE

Photo Chicken breast with morels.

BREAST OF CHICKEN WITH MORELS * POULTRY

INGREDIENTS: chicken breasts browned in butter, morel mushrooms, onion, egg yolk, flour, cream, lemon juice, dry white wine.

RECIPE: the onion is cooked for 10' with the other ingredients in the chicken cooking juices. Served hot.

838 - SUPRÊME DE VOLAILLE À LA CRÈME ET AUX CHAMPIGNONS

Photo Breast of chicken with cream and mushrooms.

BREAST OF CHICKEN WITH CREAM AND MUSHROOMS

RECIPE: see Recipe N° 837-1. The morels are replaced with cultivated mushrooms. Served hot.

TAB

839 - TABLIER DE SAPEUR * ABATS - SPÉCIALITÉ DE LYON

Photo Fried tripe.

FRIED TRIPE, AN OFFAL SPECIALITY FROM LYON

INGREDIENTS: cooked tripe cut in pieces. Marinade: bouquet garni, dry white wine, lemon juice, lime, strong mustard. Garnish: eggs, breadcrumbs, cooked potato cut in pieces, olive oil, butter.

RECIPE: the cooked tripe is marinated overnight. It is then drained, sliced, egg and breadcrumbed and cooked for 3'. Served hot.

840 - TABOULÉ * ENTRÉE

Photo Tabouleh salad.

TABOULEH SALAD * STARTER

INGREDIENTS: couscous cereal, chopped mint, onions, chopped tomatoes, yellow pepper, cucumber, olive oil, lemon juice, raisins.

RECIPE: the couscous is left for 10' to absorb the hot water and then mixed with the other ingredients. Left to rest for 2 hours and served cold.

TAG

841 - TAGLIATELLES AU SAUMON * PÂTES

Photo Ribbon pasta with salmon.

SALMON RIBBON * PASTA
INGREDIENTS: fresh ribbon pasta, chopped fresh salmon, butter, garlic, cream, chervil.
RECIPE: the salmon and cream are mixed with the pasta once boiled. Served hot.

TAP

842 - TAPENADE * ENTRÉE

Photo Black olive spread.

BLACK OLIVE SPREAD * STARTER
INGREDIENTS: black olives crushed with anchovy fillets and olive oil.
RECIPE: the ingredients are mixed. Served cold.

TAR

843 - TARTARE * VIANDE

Photo Raw beef dish.

RAW BEEF DISH * MEAT
INGREDIENTS: in order of mixing: oil, mustard, onions, gherkins, paprika, ketchup, Worcestershire sauce, capers, raw minced beef, egg yolks, chopped parsley. Served cold.

843-1 - TARTARE DE SAUMON * POISSON

Photo Salmon tartare.

SALMON TARTARE - FISH
INGREDIENTS: chopped salmon, prawns, cream or mayonnaise, dill.
RECIPE: the salmon, prawns, mayonnaise or cream are mixed. Served cold.

844 - TARTE À L'ABRICOT * PÂTISSERIE

Photo Apricot tart.

APRICOT TART * PASTRY
INGREDIENTS: flaky pastry, halved apricots, butter, honey, apple jelly.
RECIPE: the apricots are sautéed in butter, glazed with apple jelly, placed on the pastry and baked for 30'. Served warm.

845 - TARTE À L'ALSACIENNE * PÂTISSERIE - SPÉCIALITÉ D'ALSACE

Photo Apple cream tart.

APPLE CREAM TART – A SPECIALITY FROM ALSACE
INGREDIENTS: shortcrust pastry: flour, water, butter. Egg yolk; filling, eggs, cream, sugar, vanilla. Garnish: sliced eating apples, lemon, sugar.
RECIPE: the sliced apple is placed on the rolled pastry and baked for 20'; the filling is added during baking. Served warm.

846 - TARTE À L'ANANAS * PÂTISSERIE

Photo Pineapple tart.

PINEAPPLE TART * PASTRY
INGREDIENTS: sweet tart pastry, pineapple, sugar, rum, custard cream: eggs, milk, sugar, flour.
RECIPE: the pastry case is precooked, the custard cream and slices of pineapple added. Served cold.

847 - TARTE AU BEAUFORT * ENTRÉE SPÉCIALITÉ AU FROMAGE DE SAVOIE

Photo Beaufort tart.

BEAUFORT TART * STARTER - A CHEESE SPECIALITY FROM SAVOY
INGREDIENTS: shortcrust pastry: flour, butter, water. Filling: chopped Beaufort cheese (n° 908), cream, milk, eggs, nutmeg.
RECIPE: the pastry is baked blind and cooked for a further 30' with the filling. Served hot.

848 - TARTE OU QUICHE AUX CHAMPIGNONS * ENTRÉE

Photo Mini quiche with mushrooms.

MUSHROOM TART OR QUICHE * STARTER
INGREDIENTS: shortcrust pastry. Filling: precooked cultivated mushrooms, cream, butter, nutmeg, eggs.
RECIPE: All the ingredients are mixed, spread over the pastry and baked together. Served hot.

849 - TARTE AU CHOCOLAT * PÂTISSERIE

Photo Chocolate tart.

CHOCOLATE TART * PASTRY
INGREDIENTS: pastry: flour, sugar, butter, whole egg, Filling: eggs, butter, cocoa, sugar.
RECIPE: the pastry case is filled and baked in the oven for 20'. Served cold.

850 - TARTE AU CITRON * PÂTISSERIE

Photo Lemon tartlet.

LEMON TART * PASTRY
INGREDIENTS: pastry: flour, butter, water. Filling: zest and juice of lemons, butter, eggs, flour, sugar.
RECIPE: the filling is mixed, put into the pastry case and baked for 20'. Served cold.

851 - TARTE AU CITRON MERINGUÉ * PÂTISSERIE

Photo Lemon meringue tart.

LEMON MERINGUE TART * PASTRY
See N° 850, the tart is topped with beaten egg whites and the meringue baked. Served cold.

852 - TARTE AUX FIGUES * PÂTISSERIE - SPÉCIALITÉ DE PROVENCE

Photo Fig Tart

FIG TART - A PASTRY SPECIALITY FROM PROVENCE
INGREDIENTS: fresh figs. Tart filling: powdered almonds, egg yolks, milk, sugar. Pastry: flour, butter.
RECIPE: the pastry is rested for 1 hour, the filling spread over the figs in the pastry case and baked for 40' in the oven. Served cold or warm.

853 - TARTE AUX FRAISES * PÂTISSERIE

Photo Strawberry tartlet.

STRAWBERRY TART * PASTRY
INGREDIENTS: sweet pastry with praline and hazelnuts. Filling: almond cream, custard cream, strawberries.
RECIPE: the sweet pastry is cooked, the filling added and cooked a further 10', the custard cream and strawberries are then added. Served cold.

854 - TARTE AUX FRAMBOISES * PÂTISSERIE

Photo Raspberry tartlet.

RASPBERRY TART * PASTRY
See N° 853 with raspberries. Served cold.

855 - TARTE À LA FRANGIPANE * PÂTISSERIE

Photo Frangipane tart.

FRANGIPANE TART - PASTRY
INGREDIENTS: pastry: sugar, flour, butter egg, almond cream: butter, sugar, eggs, ground almonds, flour, rum, vanilla.
RECIPE: the pastry case is precooked, filled with the almond cream, rested for 1 hour and baked for 15'. Served cold or warm.

856 - TARTE À LA MIRABELLE * PÂTISSERIE

Photo Mirabel plum tart.

MIRABEL PLUM TART * PASTRY
INGREDIENTS: shortcrust pastry. Cream filling: eggs, milk, sugar, ground almonds. Filling: mirabel plums browned in butter, Mirabel spirit, egg yolk.
RECIPE: the fruit is browned and flamed in the spirit. The cream and mirabels are placed on the tart to bake. Served cold.

857 - TARTE AUX MYRTILLES * PÂTISSERIE

Photo Blueberry tart.

BLUEBERRY TART * PASTRY
INGREDIENTS: sweet pastry. Custard cream: eggs, milk. Sugar; fresh blueberries, sugar, redcurrant jelly.
RECIPE: the precooked tart base is filled with the cream and blueberries spread with jelly and baked. Served cold.

858 - TARTE AUX NOIX * PÂTISSERIE

Photo Walnut tart.

WALNUT TART * PASTRY
INGREDIENTS: shortcrust pastry. Filling: egg yolks, chopped walnuts, sugar, egg white, apricot jam, whole walnuts.
RECIPE: the pastry is spread with jam and baked for 15', the filling then spread over the tart and baked further. Served cold.

859 - TARTE À L'OIGNON * ENTRÉE

Photo Onion tart.

ONION TART * STARTER
INGREDIENTS: yeast and flour mix, baker's yeast. Pastry: milk, egg, oil, filling: onions, butter, eggs, cream, parsley, cumin.
RECIPE: the prepared yeast and flour rising agent is prepared and added to the pastry, the filling added, baked for 35' and served hot.

860 - TARTE AUX POIRES BOURDALOUE * PÂTISSERIE

Photo Pear and almond tart.

PEAR AND ALMOND TART * PASTRY
INGREDIENTS: quartered pears sauteed in butter. To cook: sugar, pear spirit. Shortcrust pastry: butter, egg, sugar, flour. Almond cream: almonds, beaten eggs, sugar and cream.
RECIPE: the browned pears are caramelised, sprinkled with pear spirit, spread on the precooked pastry and cream and baked for 20'. Served warm.

861 - TARTE AUX POIRES * PÂTISSERIE

Photo Pear tart.

PEAR CREAM TART * PASTRY
INGREDIENTS: sweet pastry, soft pears cooked in lemon juice and sugar. Filling: egg yolks, cream.
RECIPE: the tart is garnished with the cooked pears and filling and baked for 20'. Served cold.

862 - TARTE AUX POIREAUX * ENTRÉE, LÉGUMES

Photo Leek tart.

LEEK TART * VEGETABLE, STARTER
INGREDIENTS: Filling: leeks, grated Emmenthal cheese, butter, oil, cream, grated nutmeg, eggs, yeast and flour mix, baker's yeast, milk, egg.
RECIPE: the yeast and flour mix is prepared and left to double in volume, the filling is spread over the tart base and baked for 35'. Served hot.

863 - TARTE AUX POMMES * PÂTISSERIE

Photo Apple tart.

APPLE TART * PASTRY
INGREDIENTS: sliced eating apples. Shortcrust pastry: butter, eggs, flour, sugar.
RECIPE: the pastry case is lined with the apples and baked for 20'. Served hot.

864 - TARTE AUX POMMES NORMANDE * PÂTISSERIE

Photo Normandy apple tart.

NORMANDY APPLE TART * PASTRY
INGREDIENTS: shortcrust pastry: flour, butter, water. Filling: apples, sugar, Calvados applejack brandy, cream.
RECIPE: The apples are browned in the sugar and Calvados then placed in the pastry case, baked and flamed with brandy and served hot.

865 - TARTE AUX PRUNEAUX * PÂTISSERIE

Photo Prune tart.

PRUNE TART * PASTRY
INGREDIENTS: pastry: flour, eggs, butter. Filling: egg yolks, flour, sugar, milk, stoned prunes.
RECIPE: the prunes and filling are spread over the precooked pastry case and baked. Served cold.

866 - TARTE À LA RHUBARBE * PÂTISSERIE

Photo Rhubarb tartlet.

RHUBARB TART * PASTRY
INGREDIENTS: shortcrust pastry: flour, butter, icing sugar, egg yolk. Filling: chopped rhubarb, cream, eggs, flour, sugar.
RECIPE: the pieces of rhubarb are put into the pastry case with the filling and baked. Served cold.

867 - TARTE TATIN AUX POMMES * PÂTISSERIE

Photo Upside down apple tart.

UPSIDE DOWN APPLE TART * PASTRY
INGREDIENTS: quartered eating apples. Pastry: butter, egg yolk, flour. Caramel: water, sugar, butter.
RECIPE: the caramel is heated in the base of the mould, the quartered apples added, then the pastry and baked for 20′ in the oven. Served hot with cream.

868 - TARTE À LA TOMATE * ENTRÉE

Photo Tomato tart.

TOMATO TART * STARTER
INGREDIENTS: flaky pasty. Filling: precooked sliced tomato, grated Gruyère cheese, butter, basil.
RECIPE: the pastry case is filled and baked in the oven. Served hot.

869 - TARTE À LA TOMME * PÂTISSERIE - SPÉCIALITÉ DU CANTAL

Photo Tomme cheese tart.

TOMME CHEESE TART, A SPECIALITY PASTRY FROM CANTAL
INGREDIENTS: for the tart: shortcrust pastry: flour and water. Filling: curds, eggs, sugar, vanilla.
RECIPE: the pastry case is filled and baked for 55'. Served cold.

870 - TARTIFLETTE * PLAT COMPLET FROMAGE SPÉCIALITÉ DE SAVOIE

Photo Tartiflette.

TARTIFLETTE, A ONE-DISH CHEESE-BASED SPECIALITY FROM SAVOY
INGREDIENTS: precooked potatoes, Reblochon cheese (n° 928), cream, diced smoked bacon, onions.
RECIPE: the potatoes, onions, cooked bacon, cream and Reblochon cheese are layered and baked in a dish. Served immediately.

870-1 - TARTINE CAMPAGNARDE * ENTRÉE

Photo Country open sandwich.

COUNTRY OPEN SANDWICH * STARTER
Served hot.

870-2 - TARTINE DE PAIN GRILLÉ AU CHÈVRE * FROMAGE

Photo Toasted open sandwich with goat's cheese.

TOASTED OPEN SANDWICH WITH GOAT'S CHEESE * CHEESE
Served hot.

TER

871 - TERRINE DE FOIE GRAS DE CANARD * ABATS

Photo Duck foie gras terrine.

DUCK FOIE GRAS TERRINE * OFFAL
INGREDIENTS: lobe of duck foie gras, Armagnac brandy, paprika.
RECIPE: the liver is prepared, refrigerated for 24 hours, placed in a terrine dish in a bain marie (or above a dish containing water), cooked for 15' and refrigerated. Served cold in slices.

872 - TERRINE DE POISSON * POISSON

Photo Fish terrine.

FISH TERRINE * FISH
INGREDIENTS: Filling: milk, butter, flour, egg yolks, cream, chopped fish, cultivated mushrooms, olive oil, chopped parsley.
RECIPE: the filling is cooked. The mushrooms and fish are browned and blended, then poured onto unbeaten egg and cream. Served cold.

873 - TERRINE AUX TROIS POISSONS * POISSON

Photo Three-fish terrine.

THREE-FISH TERRINE * FISH
See Recipe N° 872 with 3 sorts of fish: scallops, salmon, monkfish. Served cold.

TER

874 - TERRINE DE CAMPAGNE * CHARCUTERIE

Photo Country terrine.

COUNTRY TERRINE * COOKED MEATS AND SIMILAR
See Recipe N° 603. Served cold.

TET

875 - TÊTE DE VEAU SAUCE GRIBICHE * ABATS

Photo Calf's head with gribiche sauce.

CALF'S HEAD WITH GRIBICHE SAUCE * OFFAL
INGREDIENTS: Calf's head without bone. To cook: carrot, onion, garlic, vinegar, bouquet garni, flour. Gribiche sauce: hard-boiled egg, yolk mashed, white chopped, mustard, shallots, chopped gherkins, vinegar, oil, capers. RECIPE: the meat is boiled for 2 hours with the ingredients, the sauce prepared and served with the calf's head. Served hot.

876 - TÊTE DE VEAU SAUCE RAVIGOTE * ABATS

Photo Calf's head with ravigote sauce.

CALF'S HEAD WITH RAVIGOTE SAUCE * OFFAL
INGREDIENTS: same recipe as N° 875, see Ravigote sauce N° 799. Served hot.

THO

877 - THON À LA MAYONNAISE * POISSON, ENTRÉE

Photo Tuna mayonnaise.

TUNA MAYONNAISE * FISH, STARTER
Served cold.

878 - THON À LA CATALANE * POISSON

Photo *Tuna cooked with tomato and onion.*

TUNA COOKED WITH TOMATO AND ONION * FISH
INGREDIENTS: slice of tuna, olive oil, flour, sauce: tomatoes, onion, garlic, bouquet garni, olive oil. Garnish: black olives, gherkins
RECIPE: the sauce is cooked. The tuna is marinated in the sauce, then cooked in very hot oil. Served cold or hot.

TIR

879 - TIRAMISU * RECETTE DE PÂTISSERIE ITALIENNE

Photo *Tiramisu.*

TIRAMISU * AN ITALIAN DESSERT
INGREDIENTS: cream: egg yolks, whites stiffly beaten, mascarpone cheese, sponge finger biscuits. To soak: very strong black coffee, Kahlua or other coffee liqueur, vanilla sugar, cocoa, grated dark chocolate.
RECIPE: the cream and soaked biscuits are layered, finishing with the mascarpone, and refrigerated for 12 hours. Served cold sprinkled with cocoa and grated chocolate.

TOM

880 - TOMATES CONFITES * LÉGUMES

Photo *Preserved tomatoes.*

PRESERVED TOMATOES * VEGETABLES
INGREDIENTS: grilled tomatoes, olive oil, garlic, thyme.
RECIPE: the tomatoes are sprinkled with oil and thyme and cooked. Served hot.

881 - TOMATES À LA PROVENÇALE * LÉGUMES SPÉCIALITÉ DE PROVENCE

Photo *Tomatoes with breadcrumbs and garlic.*

TOMATOES WITH BREADCRUMBS AND GARLIC - A VEGETABLE SPECIALITY FROM PROVENCE
INGREDIENTS: tomatoes. Stuffing: onion, garlic, butter, parsley, chervil, tarragon. To brown: breadcrumbs, butter.
RECIPE: the tomatoes are cored, filled and baked for 10' to brown. Served hot.

882 - TOMATES FARCIES * LÉGUMES

Photo Stuffed tomatoes.

STUFFED TOMATOES * VEGETABLES
INGREDIENTS: tomatoes, olive oil. Stuffing: sausage meat, egg, chives, parsley, bread soaked in milk, onion.
RECIPE: the tomatoes are cored, stuffed and baked for 20'. Served hot.

883 - TOMATES MOZZARELLA * LÉGUMES - ENTRÉE

Photo Mozzarella cheese tomatoes.

MOZZARELLA CHEESE TOMATOES * VEGETABLES - STARTER
Served cold.

884 - TOURIN PÉRIGOURDIN * POTAGE

Photo Perigord soup.

PERIGORD SOUP * SOUP
INGREDIENTS: country bread, grated Gruyère cheese, tomatoes. To cook: onions, garlic, flour, goose fat, poultry stock and chopped tomatoes, butter, presentation sauce: egg yolks
RECIPE: The cooking ingredients are cooked for 1 hour, the egg yolks added to the soup which is put into the oven topped with bread and cheese to brown. Served immediately.

885 - TOURNEDOS BEURRE MAÎTRE D'HÔTEL * VIANDE

Photo Tournedos steak with parsley butter.

TOURNEDOS STEAK WITH PARSLEY BUTTER * MEAT
INGREDIENTS: thick tournedos. Parsley butter: chopped parsley and butter mixed.
RECIPE: the steak is grilled and served with the cold butter on top. Served hot.

886 - TOURNEDOS ROSSINI * VIANDE

Photo Tournedos steak Rossini.

TOURNEDOS STEAK ROSSINI * MEAT
INGREDIENTS: tournedos steak, soft bread, foie gras, butter, Madeira wine.
RECIPE: the bread, steak and foie gras are browned in butter and served hot.

887 - TOURNEDOS SAUCE AU BLEU * VIANDE

Photo Tournedos steak with blue cheese sauce.

TOURNEDOS STEAK WITH BLUE CHEESE SAUCE * MEAT
INGREDIENTS: tournedos steak, shallots, toasted bread, garlic, blue cheese, cream
RECIPE: the garlic and shallot are browned and the steak cooked covered with melted cheese and cream. Served hot.

888 - TOURNEDOS SAUCE AU POIVRE * VIANDE

Photo Tournedos steak with pepper sauce.

TOURNEDOS STEAK WITH PEPPER SAUCE * MEAT
INGREDIENTS: tournedos steak, pepper-corns.
RECIPE: the peppercorns and then the steak are cooked and served hot together.

889 - TOURTE À LA BRETONNE * POISSON

Photo Breton fish pie.

BRETON FISH PIE * FISH
INGREDIENTS: flaky pastry. Garnish: spinach, salmon fillet, scallops, cream, Béchamel sauce.
RECIPE: the pie is filled and baked. Served hot.

TOU

890 - TOURTE AUX BLETTES * LÉGUMES - SPÉCIALITÉ DE PROVENCE

Photo Swiss chard pie.

SWISS CHARD PIE - A VEGETABLE SPECIALITY FROM PROVENCE
INGREDIENTS: pastry: flour, melted butter, sugar, whole beaten eggs. For the filling: Swiss chard leaves, whole beaten eggs, sugar, pine nuts, grated Parmesan cheese, lemon juice, olive oil.
RECIPE: the pastry is rested for 1 hour, divided into 2, filled and baked in the oven. Served warm.

891 - TOURTEAU CUIT * CRUSTACÉS

Photo Crab mayonnaise.

COOKED CRAB * SHELLFISH
Served cold.

TRA

892 - TRANCHE DE RÔTI DE PORC FROID * VIANDE

Photo Slice of cold roast pork.

SLICE OF COLD ROAST PORK * MEAT
Served cold.

893 - TRANCHE DE GIGOT D'AGNEAU RÔTI POMMES DE TERRE À LA BRESSANE * VIANDE

Photo Slices of roast leg of lamb with Bresse baked potatoes.

SLICES OF ROAST LEG OF LAMB WITH BRESSE BAKED POTATOES * MEAT
Served hot or cold.

894 - TRILOGIE DE POISSONS / LOUP - GAMBAS - SAINT-PIERRE * POISSON - CRUSTACÉS

Photo Fish trio, sea bass, gambas prawns, John Dory.

FISH TRIO – SEA BASS, GAMBAS PRAWNS, JOHN DORY * FISH - SHELLFISH
Served hot.

895 - TRIPES À LA MODE DE CAEN * ABATS SPÉCIALITÉ DE NORMANDIE

Photo Mixed stewed tripe.

MIXED STEWED TRIPE - AN OFFAL SPECIALITY FROM NORMANDY
INGREDIENTS: pieces of tripe, ox feet, bard, sliced carrot, onions, garlic, butter, bouquet garni, cider, Calvados applejack brandy, lard, cloves, allspice.
RECIPE: all the ingredients are cooked for 8 hours and served hot.

896 - TRIPOUX D'AUVERGNE * ABATS

Photo Auvergne style lamb tripe.

AUVERGNE STYLE LAMB TRIPE * OFFAL
INGREDIENTS AND RECIPE: paunches of calf and lamb, garlic, onions, parsley, white wine. Served hot.

897 - TRUFFADE * POMMES DE TERRE - FROMAGE SPÉCIALITÉ DU CANTAL

Photo Potato cheese melt.

POTATO CHEESE MELT - A CHEESE SPECIALITY FROM CANTAL
INGREDIENTS: diced bacon, sliced potatoes, Cantal Tomme cheese, lard.
RECIPE: the cheese is placed on the other ingredients when cooked and allowed to melt gently. Served hot.

TRU

898 - TRUFFES NOIRES

Photo *Black truffles.*

Black truffles.

899 - TRUITE AUX AMANDES * POISSON

Photo *Trout with almonds.*

TROUT WITH ALMONDS * FISH
INGREDIENTS: trout, flaked almonds, lemon, butter, flour, lemon juice, parsley, salt.
RECIPE: the floured trout are cooked for 6′ in butter, the almonds added and served hot.

900 - TRUITE AU LARD * POISSON

Photo *Trout with bacon.*

TROUT WITH BACON * FISH
INGREDIENTS: trout, bacon, butter, parsley
RECIPE: the bacon is fried with the fish, served hot.

TUI

901 - TUILES AUX AMANDES * PÂTISSERIE

Photo *Almond tile biscuits.*

ALMOND TILE BISCUITS * BISCUITS
INGREDIENTS: stiffly beaten egg whites, sugar, flour, melted butter, flaked almonds.
RECIPE: the sugar is folded into the whites and other ingredients, small heaps of the mixture cooked for 4′ and as they come out of the oven, the biscuits are pressed into shape over a rolling pin.

TUR

902 - TURBOT POCHÉ AU BEURRE * POISSON

Photo Poached turbot with butter.

POACHED TURBOT WITH BUTTER * FISH
INGREDIENTS: pieces of turbot, milk, lemon. Butter sauce; butter, shallots, wine, Presentation: parsley, lemon.
RECIPE: the turbot is poached for 15' with the milk, lemon and served hot with the sauce.

903 - TURBOTIN GRILLÉ * POISSON

Photo Grilled turbot.

GRILLED TURBOT * FISH
INGREDIENTS: turbot. Sauce to garnish: shallots, butter, dry white wine.
RECIPE: the fish is grilled for 15' and served hot with the sauce

VEA

904 - VEAU MARENGO * VIANDE

Photo Veal Marengo.

VEAL MARENGO * MEAT
INGREDIENTS: stewing veal. To cook: onion, chopped shallots, parsley, cultivated mushrooms, oil, flour, stock, dry white wine, bouquet garni. At the end of cooking: tomatoes.
RECIPE: the veal and ingredients are cooked for 1 hour 30 mins. Served hot.

905 - VEAU ORLOFF * VIANDE

Photo Veal Orloff.

VEAL ORLOFF * MEAT
INGREDIENTS: cushion of veal, cultivated mushrooms. For the Béchamel sauce: butter, oil, flour, grated Emmenthal cheese, milk.
RECIPE: the veal is browned in oil and cooked for 1 hour 30 mins; the mushrooms are blended and mixed into the Béchamel sauce to finish cooking. Served hot.

VOL

906 - VOL-AU-VENT AUX MORILLES * ENTRÉE CHAMPIGNONS

Photo Vol au vent with morels.

VOL AU VENT WITH MORELS
* MUSHROOM STARTER
INGREDIENTS: morels, vol au vent cases, butter, cream, dry white wine.
RECIPE: the morels are sauteed in butter then sprinkled with wine until the liquid is reduced. The cream is added, plus seasoning; the vol au vent cases are heated in the oven, filled with the morels and served immediately.

QUELQUES FROMAGES PRÉSENTÉS PAR LES RESTAURANTS

A FEW CHEESES PRESENTED BY RESTAURANTS

ABO

907 - ABONDANCE

Photo Abondance.

ABONDANCE
From the Upper Savoy region, unpasteurised cow's milk, semi-hard, a favourite with Louis XIV.

BEA

908 - BEAUFORT

Photo Beaufort.

BEAUFORT
Pressed rind, Savoy cow's milk cheese, called the "Prince of Gruyère", matured from 6 months to 1 year, fruity flavour, nutty creamy taste, used for Savoy Fondue, existed in Roman times.

BLE

909 - BLEU D'AUVERGNE

Photo Bleu d'Auvergne.

BLEU D'AUVERGNE
A damp, fatty rind, with a slightly bitterish taste, made from Auvergne cow's milk, mixed with penicillium, at the origin of the blue vein. Photo in the foreground.

910 - BLEU DES CAUSSES

Photo Bleu des causses.

BLEU DES CAUSSES
A crumbly cheese made from cow's milk from the Rouergue and Aubrac region (Aveyron).

BRI

911 - BRIE DE MEAUX

Photo Brie de Meaux.

BRIE DE MEAUX
A soft smooth paste cheese made with unpasteurised cow's milk in the Seine et Marne region, very pale yellow when the cheese is mature. Called the "Prince of Cheeses" and "King of Desserts" by Metternich – a historical past since the Middle Ages.

CAB

912 - CABÉCOUS

Photo Cabecou.

CABECOU
A soft goat's cheese from the region of Quercy, Rouergue and Périgord, matured for 6 to 12 days, one of the best known is the Rocamadour, "Cabeçou" means "little goat" in dialect.

CAM

913 - CAMEMBERT

Photo Camembert.

CAMEMBERT
A supple paste cow's milk cheese. It takes its name from the village of Camembert in Normandy. It is the most copied cheese in the world and has existed since 1791.

CAN

914 - CANTAL

Photo Cantal, on the far right of the cheeseboard.

CANTAL D'AUVERGNE
A pressed rind uncooked cheese from the Massif Central, made from pasteurised or unpasteurised cow's milk; if matured more than 6 months is termed "vieux" (old).

CHA

915 - CHABICHOUS

Photo Chabichous.

CHABICHOUS
A soft paste cheese. The Saracens moved into Poitou in 600 with their "Chablis" or goats and made Chabichous.

916 - CHABLIS (AFFIDÉLICE AU)

Photo Chablis.

CHABLIS FROM THE BURGUNDY REGION
Made with goat's milk, has a soft paste and delicate taste that matures with time, similar to Epoisses.

COM

917 - COMTÉ

Photo Comté.

COMTE DU JURA
Creamy and fruity, made with cow's milk, the most famous cheese of the Jura mountains, also called "Comté Gruyère". Matured for 4 to 12 months.

COU

918 - COULOMMIERS

Photo Coulommiers.

COULOMMIERS
From the name of the town of that name in Seine et Marne, made with cow's milk, it has a soft paste, a larger version of Camembert and smaller version of Brie.

CRO

919 - CROTTIN DE CHAVIGNOL

Photo Crottin de Chavignol.

CROTTIN DE CHAVIGNOL
From the name in the village in the Berry region, made with full-cream goat's milk, matured for 10 days to 3 months.

EPO

920 - ÉPOISSES

Photo Epoisses.

EPOISSES
Made from unpasteurised cow's milk in Burgundy, with a distinctive taste, must be served "runny".

FOU

921 - FOURME D'AMBERT

FOURME D'AMBERT
A cow's milk cheese from Auvergne, blue-veined and the mildest blue.
Photo of Fourme d'Ambert in the middle of the cheeseboard.

Photo Fourme d'Ambert in the middle of the cheeseboard.

LAG

922 - LAGUIOLE

LAGUIOLE
From the name of the village in Aubrac, made from unpasteurised, full-cream cow's milk, a firm, uncooked pressed-rind cheese.

Photo Laguiole.

LIV

923 - LIVAROT

LIVAROT
Made from unpasteurised cow's milk in Normandy, called "the Colonel" due to the 3 bands around its orange crust.

Photo Livarot.

MAR

924 - MAROILLES

MAROILLES
Created in 962 by a monk in the Nord-Pas de Calais region, with a persistent fragrance, leaving a full-bodied flavour on the palate, a golden rind, soft and oily, with a yellowish-orange crust, used in Flamiche and Goyère dishes.

Photo Maroilles.

MUN

925 - MUNSTER

Photo Munster.

MUNSTER
From the Vosges region, a washed-rind soft paste cheese made with cow's milk, matured for 15 days; eaten with cumin, comes from a recipe entrusted to Vosges inhabitants by an Irish monk in the 9th century.

NEU

926 - NEUFCHÂTEL

Photo Neufchatel.

NEUFCHATEL
A full-fat milk cheese from Normandy, matured in 1 month; heart-shaped and said to represent the declaration of love of women peasants for English soldiers during the wars of religion.

PON

927 - PONT-L'ÉVÊQUE

Photo Pont l'évêque.

PONT L'EVEQUE
Made in Normandy from unpasteurised cow's milk, a soft paste in a brick shape.

REB

928 - REBLOCHON

Photo Reblochon.

REBLOCHON
A cheese made in the Rhône Alpes region with unpasteurised cow's milk, with an uncooked pressed rind and subtle nutty taste; matured in 8 weeks.

ROQ

929 - ROQUEFORT

Photo Roquefort.

ROQUEFORT
Dates back to the Middle Ages, made with Rouergue ewe's milk, powerful and strong, the best known cheese worldwide; Diderot called it the "King of Cheeses".

SAI

930 - SAINT-NECTAIRE

Photo Saint Nectaire.

SAINT NECTAIRE D'AUVERGNE
Made with cow's milk, matured in 8 weeks, was served at Louis XIV's table.

SAL

931 - SALERS

Photo Salers.

SALERS
An uncooked pressed rind cheese made from cow's milk in Cantal, named after the village of the same name.

NOTES

Completed to print
in april 2008
on the presses of Albédia printers
in Aurillac - France

on paper resulting from durably managed forests

Dépôt légal n° 106 2e trimestre 2008